Live
E.P.I.C.

Live
E.P.I.C.

Embracing
7 Everyday Virtues
to Increase Happiness and Personal Success

Kristin Noto

Skyhorse Publishing

Skyhorse Publishing books may be purchased in bulk at special discounts for sales promotion, corporate gifts, fundraising, or educational purposes. Special editions can also be created to specifications. For details, contact the Special Sales Department, Sports Publishing, 307 West 36th Street, 11th Floor, New York, NY 10018 or info@skyhorsepublishing.com.

Skyhorse® and Skyhorse Publishing® are registered trademarks of Skyhorse Publishing, Inc.®, a Delaware corporation.

Visit our website at www.skyhorsepublishing.com.

10 9 8 7 6 5 4 3 2 1

Library of Congress Cataloging-in-Publication Data is available on file.

Jacket design by David Ter-Avanesyan

ISBN: 978-1-5107-7337-0
Ebook ISBN: 978-1-5107-7345-5

Printed in the United States of America

CONTENTS

Introduction   vii

Part One   The E.P.I.C. Philosophy   **1**
Chapter 1   Defining E.P.I.C.   3
Chapter 2   What Is Character?   13
Chapter 3   Integrity: An Invisible Force in Our Lives   23
Chapter 4   Excellence: A Growth Mindset for Character   41
Chapter 5   E.P.I.C. 101: A Brief History of
             the Virtuous Life   55

Part Two   The E.P.I.C. Virtues   **63**
Chapter 6   Gratitude   65
Chapter 7   Faith   93
Chapter 8   Honesty   105
Chapter 9   Perseverance   117
Chapter 10   Charity   141
Chapter 11   Wisdom   157
Chapter 12   Prudence   173

**Part Three Your E.P.I.C. Mindset at
              Work in the World**   **187**
Chapter 13   Embracing the E.P.I.C. Mindset   189

Chapter 14   Virtue Contagion   199
Chapter 15   Feed Your Subconscious:
             Creating E.P.I.C. Habits   211
Chapter 16   E.P.I.C. Visualization: See It,
             Believe It, Receive It   225
Chapter 17   A New Understanding of Forgiveness   243
Chapter 18   Become the CEO of Your Life:
             E.P.I.C. Life Blueprints   261

Conclusion   283
Appendix A: E.P.I.C. Living Worksheets   285
Appendix B: An E.P.I.C. Reading List   299
Appendix C: Scientific Research   303

INTRODUCTION

THE UNEXPECTED SILVER LINING

It all began nearly thirty years ago when my then-boyfriend (now husband), Anthony, and I got engaged. Suddenly and unexpectedly, I found myself in a difficult relationship with my fiancé's mother, Roseanne. Up until this point, Roseanne and I had a heartfelt friendship going. We were both bold Italian women who shared similar personalities—a feisty, competitive side offset by a passionate side of love and family. We spent a lot of time together without Anthony. Yes, he was the common thread that brought us into our friendship, but we genuinely had a blast together. Our special bond strengthened as we spent hours cooking Italian food for pre- and post-game tailgating for Anthony's college football games. His mother's amazing, authentic Italian cooking flair always drew a crowd of players, families, and friends. She was famous for her irresistible chili that we enjoyed eating out of white Styrofoam cups, and on special occasions when she cooked chicken Parmesan and eggplant Parmesan, she really stole the show.

One of my best memories is when she invited me to fly with her to an away game. She paid for my flight, which was an incredibly generous act of love, and the entire trip we were like two giggly, amped-up teenagers going on an adventure, poking at each other on the plane, running through the airport, and miraculously making it to the game without a hitch.

As you might imagine, it was shocking for me when, within a few days of my engagement to her son, my relationship with her took a drastic and negative turn. There wasn't a specific incident, but the wedding planning process put a strain on everyone in the family, and soon sparks were flying about expectations, expenses, and preferences that quickly led to frustration and then arguments. Distrust began to circle every conversation about the wedding. No one could agree on anything in the planning process—not the number of guests, the venue, which family would contribute financially toward which line-item detail, and so on. What should have been a blending of families became the exact opposite, and I could see our two families gradually being torn apart.

I jumped into the victim role. I believed I could not possibly be at fault in all these planning decisions. For instance, I remember getting incredibly angry and upset about the guest count. We had allowed for seventy-five guests on each side, but Roseanne wanted more guests because of unique family dynamics. I refused and became so angry that I drove two hours to where Anthony lived to convince him in person that this was a horrible situation and he needed to help me hash it out. Things got so tense that at every point of contact with Roseanne, my angry, self-defensive mode kicked in, which, as you can imagine, made matters worse for everyone, not just me.

Ultimately, Anthony and I had a great wedding day, and with the stresses of the wedding planning process behind us, I assumed that our families would naturally return to those happier times I so cherished prior to the wedding. Unfortunately, this was not the case. The strife with my now mother-in-law continued past our wedding day. The entire situation was awkward and uncomfortable for all our family members.

A week after our wedding, my husband and I moved thousands of miles away so he could begin his career as a military officer. Other than phone calls a few times a month, we didn't have much contact with our families. Without resolution in these fundamental relationships, whenever there was a call or visit, I became physically sick with anxiety. I was an emotional wreck because of the festering and unresolved negative sentiment between our families.

One evening, my mother-in-law called. True to form, I immediately went into my defensive mode. Chest pressure kicked in with a "here we go again" mentality. But rather than spiral into my usual negative emotions, something different happened this time. Some part of me said, "That's it! I've had it with all this!"

The entire situation had reached a tipping point for me, and I jumped up from our sofa furious with all the nonsense that kept us from being a big happy family. At that moment, I decided I would make it my life's mission to reverse this horrible situation. I fully committed myself to doing everything I could to have the loving, peaceful family life I so desperately wanted.

The question was, how? I didn't have a clue as to how to fix the emotional wound spreading through our families, especially between Roseanne and me.

The answer came to me one day while sitting in church, praying for all the strife to end: I needed to forgive everyone, including myself, and let go of the need for control. I needed to start within myself by forgiving. I had to change first to see the change in others. I had to stop waiting around for something external to happen, and instead, I had to become a better person.

Wait a minute, what? I remember thinking. *This isn't what I came here asking for. I am not the problem! I came in search of the easy way to peace, not to be told I have to change!* The answer seemed way too hard and even unfair. Then, for some reason, I just knew that it was the right solution. My shoulders relaxed as I accepted in my heart of hearts that if I wanted resolution, I would have to take an honest look at myself and see where I needed to make changes to become a better person. I had character flaws, and that was the only thing that I had total control over. The strain in my relationship with my mother-in-law wasn't going to be resolved overnight, and it wasn't going to be resolved through a single conversation about reconciliation. We were much too far past that point. At the moment, praying in church, I decided to take it upon myself to do all I could to mend my friendship with Roseanne, and I would just have to hope it would be well received and reciprocated. But the only thing I truly had power over was myself, and that was where I would begin.

Without much to go on, I began by asking myself the simple question, *Where could I have behaved better?* Maybe if I were a better person in general, we could have avoided much of the strife. I thought about how the debate over the number of guests had spiraled unnecessarily out of control. If I had just been open to *compassionately* understanding the reason for adding a few more guests, we could have had a peaceful solution. If I had approached our conversations with *humility*, I wouldn't have felt the need to be right all the time and there would have been less arguing. If I had been more *grateful*, I would have been much less selfish and more inclusive, thus making everyone feel important.

Over time, I began to invest in myself, little by little, with small daily actions that I thought would build my character. I made these decisions intentionally and took the small actions deliberately. I soon found that these opportunities surround all of us every day and in every way—we just have to open our eyes to them. I didn't have an idea of how changing myself little by little would impact the situation. I just had faith that, as my character improved, I would be navigating from a point of goodness, and this goodness would then be contagious. Either way, I would feel right in my own skin, knowing I had done my best to avoid negatively influencing any situation. Whenever there were family events like holidays and special occasions, I re-committed to pursuing my peace mission. I learned that those uncomfortable and at times unnatural "harder right over easier wrong" decisions always paid off, and not just for myself, but for everyone around me. To my joy and relief, when I presented myself with authentic good will, that good will was received and returned.

Without my knowing it, three incredible things began unfolding. First, I was growing in integrity and character to such a degree that I was excelling not just with interpersonal relationships, but in other areas of life, such as my academic studies and my career. Life began to fall in my favor, so to speak. I got promotions at work, I got a scholarship for nursing school, and my friendships grew in number and deepened in authenticity. Second, I was restoring relationships from the ground up, and this time they were built with a foundation based on values and virtues that could weather any storm: unconditional love, unconditional commitment, and unconditional trust. Third, my personal journey became contagious. My family, friends, and coworkers were all growing in trust, humility, love for one another, and faith in our relationship.

My guiding force was that I truly and deeply believed in the process of peaceful relations and forgiveness. Once I began implementing this new mindset, never once did I regret taking action to avoid conflict or strife to pave the way for happiness. Soon, I began going out of my way to make peace. I wanted it to be the real deal. I wanted everyone to feel loved, valued, and special, the way I felt family relationships should be. I didn't expect any of those feelings in return, but as trust grew, our love began to grow and we all experienced tremendous happiness. We were all living our authentic E.P.I.C. selves and it was creating a living synergy. E.P.I.C. means Excellence Personified in Character, and it's what this book is all about.

My family and I all worked in our own unique ways over the course of many years to make this happen. We all became more trusting, more humble, more loving, more honest, and much wiser with decisions as they related to the entire family, not just to us as individuals. We became a loving family. Never in a million years would I have expected to reach our current mutual level of authentic unconditional love. Originally, I was just looking for respectful peace and love. And frankly, if peace were the only outcome, that would have been amazing.

I know my situation was not unique. The vast majority of us have experienced some form of strife in a personal relationship. Perhaps with a parent, spouse, partner, sibling, friend, or coworker. I have learned firsthand the slow unfolding of the healing process, and it has shown me that every ounce of effort that you invest in yourself and in your character development carries the added bonus of having a positive influence on those around you. When you become actively aware of the impact your character has on your life, you understand that becoming the best version of yourself will deliver amazing results in your personal and professional relationships, your career, your special interests, and your physical and mental well-being. By being aware of where you are in relationship with your virtues, you'll see where they are helping or hurting you.

In order to understand my own journey, I have studied personal character for more than twenty years. I've read dozens of books on individual virtues, moral development, and self-improvement approaches. I've read scientific research papers and philosophical manifestos from ancient and current philosophers. I've gathered as much material as possible in person and through taking courses. I've studied a range of religions. The message is loud and clear: good character delivers happiness and personal success; poor character creates negative situations and outcomes.

Our personal character is built upon virtues such as faith, charity, honesty, wisdom, and more. Unfortunately, the term "virtue" can be intimidating. Perhaps that is why we don't talk enough about virtues, yet we have an intimate relationship with them. Virtues are woven into our human nature and provide us with direction as we interact with our world, especially in the decisions we make that govern our personal lives. You use them all day, every day. I truly believe virtues were designed for our benefit. For example, when we grow in honesty and wisdom and other virtues correctly, our character will be "good" and we will experience more positive outcomes in our lives. When virtues are misused, when we lack honesty or wisdom, our character will be "poor" and there will be more negative outcomes in our lives.

It's like a number line with 0 at the center, negative numbers to the left, and positive numbers to the right. Perhaps when we're born, we're at 0. Then as we interact with our virtues, we make choices throughout each day as to what kind of person we want to be, and we move up and down on the number line. If we make good choices with our virtues, we improve our personal character, but if we make bad choices, we weaken our personal character—just as I did with my mother-in-law.

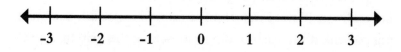

For example, someone who was regularly dishonest would be on the negative side of the scale and might consistently find themselves in negative situations. But if they shifted that virtue to the positive side, little by little every chance they got, they would most likely find their life situations improved and they would experience more positive outcomes.

The goal of E.P.I.C. living is to live in such a way that your virtues are to the right. Keep in mind that life is a journey and this is a process; allow yourself the flexibility to shift up and down the number line as you learn and grow. When we make good choices with our virtues, we experience happiness and personal fulfillment. When we make poor choices, we feel the negative effects. I trust that as you experience more happiness, you will want to continue to grow in virtue.

E.P.I.C. IN ACTION

Let's look at the virtues involved in my personal experience with my relationship with my mother-in-law.

Faith: After my epiphany moment in church, I transformed from having zero faith and hope in reconciling with my mother-in-law—a full-blown "no way" attitude—to knowing that with the strength and guidance of faith, there was hope. Throughout this personal E.P.I.C. journey, faith was my driving force. Without faith in myself and my ability to develop my personal character, none of this could have happened. And best of all? My faith became contagious.

Charity: I gradually transformed my feelings of ill will and anger to feelings of kindness, laughter, and joy, and then ultimately to unconditional love. I transformed from being selfish and wanting control of the relationship to loosening this grip by actively

engaging and sharing life experiences together and then ultimately establishing precious family moments and traditions as a
whole family.

Honesty: I gradually transformed from protecting myself with a
"don't trust anyone" mindset. I had convinced myself there was
always an element of dishonesty in every situation. To change,
I slowly allowed myself to trust others. I knew that if I didn't
begin unraveling this stronghold of distrust, there was no way to
grow. Slowly, members of both families realized the more honest
we were with ourselves, the more we trusted one another. This
created an unwavering level of trust, the most fundamental element of all healthy relationships.

Wisdom: Through reading and researching, I gradually transformed my lack of knowledge about how to resolve and restore
relations. I taught myself about positive interpersonal communication and used these new-found skills in a practical manner.
Over time, I grew in wisdom and understood that the peace I
wanted was a work in progress. It would take time and be based
on all my actions, good and bad.

Prudence: I gradually transformed from making reckless, impulsive decisions that I knew could hurt feelings to consciously
making the harder right decisions that would avoid hurt feelings
at all costs. Quite frankly, this was not comfortable in the beginning. With practice, however, my good intentions led to more
peace and happiness.

Perseverance: I gradually transformed from distancing myself
during times of conflict to diving in and seeking the peaceful solution at any personal cost. I refused to stop fighting for

my goal of a peaceful and authentic loving family relationship. Before long, we all worked toward this goal, and I learned with certainty the contagion of the E.P.I.C. journey.

Courage and Fortitude: I gradually transformed from being fearful and nonconfrontational to opening up conversations and discussions and taking action as I sought resolutions. I knew all along that this would require me to be vulnerable in ways I wasn't familiar or comfortable with. The process of being vulnerable and standing up for the greater good was the first step in the entire E.P.I.C. journey.

Gratitude: I gradually transformed from self-pity and victimhood to being appreciative for all that I had (health, family, friends, career). I realized I had the opportunity to make a positive difference in my life and in the lives of others. Without this one situation—the strife with my mother-in-law—I would not have grown into the person I am today with the amazing personal successes I've experienced along the way. I thank God for giving me the opportunity to grow so deeply by using the potential all humans share to become people of character. Perhaps even more importantly, I learned how the human soul craves goodness, peace, and happiness. Each and every one of us can grasp it as we pursue happiness.

Humility: I gradually transformed from pridefully insisting my views were the only right ones to taking a hard and honest look at myself and my behaviors. I realized that I was engaging in the same behaviors that I so quickly accused others of harming me with. I realized it was wrong to make assumptions and began apologizing as we moved toward forgiveness.

I transformed from thinking and believing I was in a hopeless situation to actually embarking on a journey of personal development. I held myself responsible for making the necessary changes to become a better person. Improving my relationship with my mother-in-law held many trials and setbacks, but over time, it transformed from that miserable low point to tolerable, fun, and ultimately amazing. Our fighting spirit that at one time created so much strife now was a key component of our successful outcome.

E.P.I.C. AS A BLUEPRINT FOR LIFE

E.P.I.C. can be used as a blueprint for life. No matter where you are or what you're doing, virtues are involved. Excellence in virtue will guide you toward what all humans seek: happiness and personal fulfillment. Consciously navigating our lives in terms of virtue applies to who you are and what you do. Ask yourself, *How can I be a better mother, father, sister, brother, neighbor? How can I be a better student, teammate, employee? How can I be a better healthcare worker, CEO, artist? How can I better handle myself in a struggling relationship, personal crisis, community crisis, global crisis?*

The opportunities to live E.P.I.C. are endless. My hope is you will achieve new levels of happiness and personal fulfillment, not just for you, but for all those around you when you embark on the journey of excellence in personal character and choose to be E.P.I.C. This book will show you how and why excellence in personal character will positively change your life, as well as the lives of those around you.

There are three main sections to this book. The first describes what E.P.I.C. is, why personal character resonates with all of us, and how—throughout the course of history and across cultures—character remains a crucial key to personal fulfillment and

Part One
The E.P.I.C. Philosophy

CHAPTER ONE
DEFINING E.P.I.C.

Epic, awesome, amazing, over the top, the best thing ever . . . The word "epic" originally meant a long piece of poetry that told the tale of heroes and their journeys. Those epic journeys transformed the heroes and their lives and the lives of the people around them, often in profound ways. It's easy to see how that original meaning has led to today's more playful slang usage of, "Whoa, that's epic!"

Your life can be epic if you'll take the focused, intentional steps to make it so—every single day. It doesn't happen in a flash. It requires deliberate action—little pieces all strung together. Small decisions and actions taken over and over again. No matter who you are or what you want to achieve, you can use my Excellence Personified in Character approach to life—the E.P.I.C. approach—and easily apply it to your life.

Think about Tom Brady, the epic quarterback who played with the New England Patriots for twenty seasons, appearing in ten Super Bowls, and getting seven Super Bowl wins. How many times has he thrown a football? Hundreds of thousands. How many quick steps has he taken with his feet? Millions.

How about Microsoft's Bill Gates? How many programming keystrokes, late nights, rewrites of code when something didn't work? Millions? Almost certainly.

Megan Rapinoe, Lindsey Horan, Alex Morgan, and all the other members of the World Cup–winning USA women's soccer team—millions of miles run, kicks taken, goals defended, drills practiced. Every action accomplished one move at a time. Every action prompted by a deliberate, intentional decision.

Tolstoy's *War and Peace*, published in 1869 tops out at close to six hundred thousand words—all of which were written by hand, one by one, strung together to make a whole.

That's how you transform your life into an epic one. You take consistent, endless, intentional small steps. Each run, each rep, each written word has a chance to be better than the one before. But they're not always better, and this is part of the process. How many missed throws, program glitches, botched kicks, or scratched-out sentences have those same epic individuals produced over the course of their outstanding lives? Countless.

The point is, they didn't stop. They stayed committed. They persevered: one step at a time, one rep at a time, one word at a time, day after day after day. Eventually, they became epic.

Obviously, most of us aren't athletic powerhouses or programming geniuses or literary legends. That doesn't really matter—you're here to become your most excellent self, not someone else's idea of what you should be. What I discovered in my own life and while raising five children is that when we focus E.P.I.C. on the virtues in our own individual, unique characters, we become happier, more connected with others, and unstoppable as we pursue our dreams.

Your character, your morals, your values all play crucial roles in the quality of your life, and they will shape the course of your life more profoundly than any material item you own or even any relationship you engage in.

So how do you improve those characteristics? How do you become excellent in your own life? You practice. There are opportunities all day, every day. You learn to recognize that every decision you make and every action you take can change you. Millions of small, seemingly inconsequential decisions and actions add up to the person you are right now. But who do you want to be a week, a month, a year, ten years from now? E.P.I.C. asks you to consider the decisions and actions you can take to become that person. Sometimes this means making the decision to do something more difficult, yet better for all involved.

I can promise you that if you commit to a pursuit of excellence, you'll experience a personal and powerful shift from the ordinary to the extraordinary. The E.P.I.C. "you" will flourish. And as you flourish, you'll notice a simultaneous transformation in the world around you. When you live as a person of excellence, amazing results show up in every aspect of your life.

WHAT IS EXCELLENCE?

The concept of excellence is simple: it's going above and beyond average. In E.P.I.C., it's consciously working toward becoming a better person. Ask yourself this: Have you or would you consider applying the concept of excellence to define the person you are, to be the best version of yourself? Can you commit to taking little steps, over and over, with the understanding that they will add up to big changes? Are you willing to explore seven core virtues (gratitude, faith, honesty, perseverance, charity, wisdom, and prudence) to see how you express them in your life, where you can improve, and, more so, with excellence?

I've undertaken this journey to improve myself by applying excellence to my virtue system, and I'll admit that it presents challenges that I fail and others that I conquer. But I've embraced this mindset as a challenge to live life as the best person I can be, as defined by the core virtues that we all share. The E.P.I.C. mindset involves giving more than just a basic effort. It requires taking personal development to the next level, and thereby implementing excellence in the classroom, on the field, in the workplace, at home, and with friends. Being aware of your moral compass is a core component of your personal growth and development as you journey through life.

All humans possess an in-born momentum of forward progression that we can call a purposeful growth. We move toward change with gaining and achieving, all in hopes of the ultimate goal of happiness. The majority of people use this forward motion as the grounds on which to improve, grow, learn, excel, and achieve.

But far too many people put off what really matters in pursuit of the things they want to achieve. Don't wait until some ideal time comes along to start this process. The ideal time is now, and you're never too young or too old to put this into action. Begin now and make E.P.I.C. a part of your life journey.

The momentum of forward growth and the application of excellence can be combined to enhance your virtues. Applying the concept of excellence to molding your personal character means that you—not society, not someone around you—will define who you truly are.

Improvement calls for small, consistent, regular steps toward becoming our best selves—rather than aiming for some grand and sudden transformation.

E.P.I.C. grew out of my deep desire to improve my personal moral character. I wanted to be a person of integrity for my children and my husband, and the rewards for stretching in this direction have been priceless. My soul is filled with a restful ease knowing that, most of the time, I challenge myself to consistently choose the harder right over the easier wrong, and I've never once regretted those hard decisions. Part of the process involves seeing which virtues are impactful in each situation and which are less so, and acting accordingly.

LET'S TALK ABOUT VIRTUES

All humans possess virtues, or character traits, which are by definition morally sound and good. These are embedded in the fabric of our human nature. The term *virtuous* describes a person who both possesses these qualities and applies them in daily life. As individuals, we vary in our level of virtuousness.

The wide range of virtues have been studied and researched throughout history. Lists of virtues vary and are often based on what any given person decides is the most important. Some of these lists contain only three items, while others are pages long. In my research and study, I have focused on seven virtues. You'll see that within the discussion of each virtue, other virtues are included, because in the end, they are all intertwined. You will connect with some virtues immediately, and with others not so much—or perhaps not at all. I encourage you to find connections even where you think there may be none, and challenge yourself to strengthen them as you develop your inner discipline of excellence, step by step, day by day, decision by decision.

And remember: This lifelong process involves awareness, learning, trial and error, and the willingness to start again, over and over, every single day. Little steps, little reps, lead to long-term transformation. Practice builds your knowledge base and an openness to growing and developing throughout your life. The goal is to keep yourself on the E.P.I.C. path. If you step off it for a moment, and we all do, just get right back on, because the path will lead you to happiness and personal fulfillment.

WATCH OUT, IT'S CONTAGIOUS!

Whether you're aware of it or not, you are an influencer. You don't have to be a social media mega star, Nobel Peace Prize winner, or CEO of the Year. Everyone in your immediate vicinity is impacted by your emotions and actions.

The social proximity effect is a phenomenon in which we begin to mirror the people around us. First semester freshman year, when my daughter came home for Thanksgiving break, she had a few new mannerisms like hand gestures, facial expressions, and body movements distinctive of her roommate. They began to dress alike, listen to the same music, and even crave the same foods. Their individual interests and viewpoints were contagious.

Psychologists have coined the term "emotional contagion" to describe the transfer of your emotions to those around you. Just as you can catch a cold or a mannerism from someone, so too can you actually catch positive and negative emotions from them. An infectious personality is a term used to describe how someone's personality can rub off on those around them. You might also call that person charismatic. They leave an impression. How many times have you been in a room when someone walked in and changed the entire atmosphere based on their mood, whether it was in a positive or negative way? The reality is that you too are impacting those around you, whether you know it or not, and whether you like it or not. You're an influencer.

With this in mind, you can now knowingly and consciously spread a positive impact to those around you, which is exactly what E.P.I.C. living will do. While you may be the primary beneficiary of E.P.I.C. living, the impact you will have on others reaches far and wide. It is what I call virtue contagion. As you elevate the caliber and quality of your life with E.P.I.C., so you will simultaneously be doing the same for those around you.

THE MARRIAGE OF EXCELLENCE TO VIRTUES IS E.P.I.C.

e.p.i.c is a *choice*. It is for each of us to embrace regardless of race, religion, socio-economic class, education, etc., and excludes no one. Arguably, the fabric of our human character is virtue-based. Embracing and growing these traits will deliver peace and happiness, in the same way that avoiding them will deliver negative outcomes. Your investment in E.P.I.C. is 100 percent up to you. Only you can create the image of excellence that applies to you, the E.P.I.C. you.

E.P.I.C. is *personal*. We all have unique, personalized visions of ourselves, of how we think we appear to the world. Visualize what E.P.I.C. looks like for you, and begin your personal journey at that point. Be honest with yourself. You will have strengths in some areas and weaknesses in others. Also understand that "success" is a personal definition. For example, I may think that getting a B+ in a challenging subject at school is excellent, and you may think getting an A+ in that same subject is excellent. Don't measure yourself against others; measure yourself against your own personal goals and visions.

E.P.I.C. is a *process*. It isn't instantaneous, nor should it be. This is a growth mindset that requires key personal attributes like self-discipline, grit, self-confidence, courage, creative approaches to challenges, and the adaptability to continually develop and grow. We learn as we go. Enjoy the process and learn to view E.P.I.C. as a lifelong journey, not a destination.

E.P.I.C. is *NOT perfection*. Excellence and perfection are completely different. Excellence is living up to your fullest potential. Perfection is flawlessness, with the notion that there is an endpoint. Excellence and character-based living is a process, and there is no specific endpoint. As we strive toward perfection, we are driven by excellence, and we enjoy happiness and personal fulfillment along the way.

The E.P.I.C. journey begins with looking at yourself and seeing where your virtues are now in your life. I don't know if virtues are embedded in our actual DNA, but it seems as if they are. Whether we're aware of it or not, we use virtues every day as a means to navigate our lives, especially as they relate to interpersonal relationships. As you refine and improve these virtues, you will see a positive and noticeable shift in all areas of your life: personal, social, professional, academic, and recreational.

I experienced this shift, and it looked something like this:

The greater my *faith*, the greater my inspiration and motivation. I grew in personal fulfillment with my relationships and myself, and I became happier.

The greater my *honesty*, the more trust I received, and the more authentic my relationships grew. I became personally fulfilled in all areas of my life, and I became happier.

The greater my *love* for myself and others, the more genuine was the love I received, and in turn, the more I gave. I reached my goal of personal fulfillment, and I became happier.

The greater my *wisdom*, the more positive impact I had on my life and those around me. I achieved success with long-term and short-term personal goals, and I became happier.

The more I practiced *prudence*, the better decisions I made that positively impacted myself and those around me. With this, I achieved much personal fulfillment and I became happier.

The more I faced my fears with *courage*, the more my anxiety and worry subsided. I increased in self-confidence and challenged myself to achieve what I once thought was impossible, and I became happier.

The more I pushed to *persevere*, for myself and for my family, the more I achieved personal goals and aspirations, the greater my success, and the happier I became.

The more I focused on being *grateful*, the more I appreciated every aspect of my life, big and small. The greater I grew in *humility*, the happier I became.

CHAPTER TWO
WHAT IS CHARACTER?

It is your character, and your character alone, that will make your life happy or unhappy.

—John McCain

From childhood on, we're taught the difference between right and wrong, good and bad. The value of these considerations stays with us as we navigate throughout life. Wise or good decisions are beneficial to you and ultimately lead to happiness. Unwise or bad decisions lead to unhappiness, as there is often a negative consequence attached to those decisions.

We are most often taught the differences between right and wrong as they relate to our personal behavior. This knowledge underlies the most fundamental understanding and goal of becoming a person of good character. It sets off a process of growth and development that starts in childhood and remains with us through adulthood. This understanding is at the core of our human nature and serves as a key in our pursuit of happiness.

Consider how we guide children to be a good friend, a person who is honest, loyal, loving, generous, and humble. We help them avoid being a bad friend who lies, doesn't keep their word, hates, cheats, and is selfish or boastful. We teach children that there may be times when it's hard to be a good friend if we've been hurt, but we should persevere and never lose our faith and belief in being a good friend. Now, let's reflect upon our own lives with this same wisdom.

Society as a whole supports the benefits of good character. Think about popular children's movies that portray the challenges of sticking to integrity, choosing to be the good guy instead of the bad guy (e.g., *Harry Potter*, with Harry versus Lord Voldemort, and *The Lion King*, with Mufasa versus Scar). Why are these blockbuster movies? It's because as humans, we connect with a soul-filled happiness to the good guy (or lion) and what they represent. We identify with their qualities of moral character. It's worth mentioning that although these movies may seem targeted to younger audiences, they in fact appeal to audiences of all ages. As I watched these movies with my children, I was thrilled with the message my children were being taught. In addition, the movies gave me the opportunity to look at my own behavior with fresh eyes.

The outer wrappings of the movies change, but the core message is always the same. If you are a person of good character, you will be able to withstand intense challenges and, in the end, live a happier, more personally fulfilling life.

TRANSPARENCY: YOUR CHARACTER STANDS OUT

Media outlets have no problem publicizing the misconduct of influential people who lack good character. We hear about business executives, such as Bernard Madoff and his $65 billion fraudulent Ponzi scheme that robbed tens of thousands of investors of their life savings and pension plans, and who ultimately landed in federal prison for 150 years. Famous athletes who continually lie about taking illegal performance-enhancing drugs, like road cyclist Lance Armstrong, who won the Tour de France seven times before being disqualified for doping. Eventually, he admitted to the allegations and was stripped of all seven titles. The list goes on, and journalists and media platforms will not let anyone forget the ripple effect of negativity that transpires as a result of the publicly exposed lack of integrity.

These accounts are offset by many positive examples of sound moral character. The Bill and Melinda Gates Foundation was created in 2000 by Microsoft cofounder Bill Gates and his then spouse, Melinda Gates, to fulfill grants and advocate for efforts to eliminate global inequalities and increase opportunities for people in need worldwide. The foundation's work to eradicate malaria has increased the quality of life for millions of people in sub-equatorial countries. Jimmy Carter (US President, 1977–1981) won the coveted Nobel Peace Prize in 2002 "for his decades of untiring effort to find peaceful solutions to international conflicts, to advance democracy and human rights, and to promote economic and social development."[1] Carter's level of influence was able to effect great change within governments. Rapid-response concerts, such as Hope for Haiti Now, The Concert for Sandy Relief, and multiple concerts after Hurricane Katrina, are performed by top musicians to raise funds for people in need after natural disasters.

In 2010, celebrity chef José Andrés founded the World Central Kitchen (WCK) after the devastating earthquake in Haiti.

---

[1] "The Nobel Peace Prize 2002," NobelPrize.org, March 28, 2002, https://wck.org/es-es/resilience, and should be cited specifically.

Andrés believes that "food can be an agent of change in distressed communities,"[2] and he tirelessly strives to prove this. Since 2010, WCK has served over fifty million meals worldwide as emergency food response for those communities in need after a natural disaster. His excellence in the virtue of charity has been contagious, and other celebrity chefs have joined the efforts of WCK, such as Rachael Ray, Guy Fieri, Marcus Samuelsson, and Tyler Florence. In 2019, Chef Andrés was nominated for the Nobel Peace Prize for his humanitarian efforts.

On the other hand, negative examples often become public spectacles. This gives us hope that people will continue to call out those who flagrantly lack good character. In the heart of our human soul, we seek happiness and goodness and will fight for justice to maintain moral standards that make our world a better place.

At the end of the day, what all of these lessons and examples teach us is relatively straightforward. Can you answer to yourself that in the future you will make the best decisions possible, even if they're the harder choices? We all slip up, but two steps forward, one step back is a great start and will get you far. Will you take responsibility for the person you are and the person you can be? Choose the path of desirable character and you can achieve an inner sense of personal fulfillment. Choose the path of less desirable character and your personal fulfillment will be compromised.

So how do we do this? We choose to grow in our moral character. We know exactly what moral character is, because it is virtue-based and we all live virtue-filled lives. The question is to what extent we value the benefits of these virtues and use them to the best of our ability. No one is perfect and we all have strengths and weaknesses, which is good because this helps us to

---

[2] www.wck.org

better understand and put into perspective the values and benefits of choosing that good path.

When it comes to our personal character, we are unique, one-of-a-kind individuals. But the building blocks of our character are the same: virtues. We use virtues all day, every day—virtues such as honesty, charity (love/giving), faith (believing in yourself, others, a higher power), knowledge (learning new skills and information) and wisdom (making better decisions), perseverance (seeing things through to the end), prudence (reasoning with skill and caution), and gratitude (being thankful and humble). Together these virtues and the ways in which you use them or ignore them shape your moral character.

THE BASICS OF CHARACTER

When people grow positively in virtues and become more honest, more humble, more loving, and wiser, they grow in moral character and live a life filled with happiness and greater success in the fulfillment of their personal goals and aspirations, whatever those may be. They find more opportunities across all areas of their lives, and their personal relationships improve, as does their physical and emotional health. And when we see these virtues being misused with dishonesty, ill will toward others, selfishness, pride, and so on, we see a lack of moral character. This brings negative consequences such as unhappiness, less personal fulfillment, and challenges with personal relationships. These differences aren't exactly as black and white as I have presented them, but this generalization makes a point. If you look at the virtues and how they are integrated into your life, you will see that you are using them all day, every day. Doesn't it make sense to grow in them positively and use them to your advantage to create a happier and more fulfilling life versus misusing them and being left at a disadvantage?

CHARACTER SHAPING; CREATING YOUR CHARACTER

I happen to be a fan of taking college courses. Any chance I get to enroll in a local college course, I try to jump right in. And what I particularly love is seeing classmates in their seventies and eighties busy taking notes, asking fascinating questions. I've had the good fortune to take a few Continuing Studies classes at Stanford University. These classes are open to anyone who chooses to enroll. One of my favorites was a Sports Nutrition class where my peers' ages ranged from young nannies to a gentleman who I believe was in his mid eighties. He attended every class and was active with class participation. The growth mindset enables us to continue to learn and take advantage of the malleable nature of our brains and embrace new knowledge. We can embrace character development with this same enthusiasm. We can continue to shape our personal belief system and moral values for the rest of our lives. Just like what we can learn in college, the opportunities to reshape our lives are nearly limitless and it's never too late to start. The key is that you have to go after it to get it.

Character is shaped by a variety of influences in your life, including life experiences, your viewpoints and perspectives, and, most importantly, those who surround you. Character is adaptable and at the end of the day, you have the final say on who you choose to be. Character is a key component of your identity. Building and evolving in character takes time, unfolds little by little, and is incredibly rewarding.

THE INFLUENCE OTHERS HAVE ON
YOUR CHARACTER . . .

Young children are taught viewpoints by their parents and guardians. They trust these adults, and when you add their naturally observant nature to this, their character takes shape. As they reach adolescence, kids spend more time with peers and have new and different viewpoints influencing the development of their identity. Peer pressure plays its role too, often challenging their moral compass, like when parents are in utter disbelief that their "perfect child" was suspended for skipping school. One of the first questions we parents ask is, "Who were you with?" We want to know the influencers.

As adults, even though we are better equipped to stand our ground to defend our character, we can still be swayed by those we spend the most time with. At times, my viewpoint is overruled by the general consensus in my family, and I find myself shifting to their viewpoint. For example, when the kids were younger, going to church was a fiasco and often met with resistance. Much to my dismay, we began skipping church occasionally. I was influenced.

COVID-19: WHEN BAD THINGS HAPPEN

Halfway through my writing this book, the first case of COVID-19 was reported in the United States. Two months later, the World Health Organization (WHO) declared COVID-19 a pandemic. Panic and fear took hold as the world shifted, country by country and state by state, into lockdown. The scope of death, skyrocketing unemployment, financial ruin, and food and basic supply shortages became incomprehensible.

Extreme crises and stress like this can bring out the best and the worst in us. Oftentimes, the situation becomes a reflection of our character. Personally, I have seen and experienced much of "the best" of our human nature during this pandemic. For all that COVID-19 has taken away from us, for many it has given us something even more powerful: the virtue of fortitude with the fierce and instinctive drive to fight for what matters most—people. COVID-19 also unleashed the virtue of charity, as we passionately fought for the well-being of one another.

Immediately, communities and families began working together to protect one another from contracting or spreading COVID-19 and to ensure basic needs were met, such as food and water, personal protective gear, shelter, and financial assistance. All over the country, individuals worked to offset unexpected shortages of essential items. Breweries and distilleries converted beer and vodka into the alcohol used for hand sanitizers. Sport helmet manufacturers re-tooled to supply medical professionals with clear face shields. People of all ages—from children to the elderly in nursing homes—worked tirelessly making homemade face masks to replenish shortages in hospitals. Gatherings of people on roadsides and in parking lots supported the emotional needs of healthcare workers, cheering them on as they traveled to and from work. These are all examples of virtues such as charity, perseverance, fortitude, gratitude, and faith in overdrive.

The ALL IN Challenge was an idea of Michael Rubin, founder and executive chairman of Fanatics. He, along with Alan Tisch and Gary Vaynerchuk, created this foundation with the goal of raising tens of millions of dollars to fight food shortages and feed those in need. Their strategy? With their many ties to people in film and music and sports, they were able to encourage these celebrities to donate some of their most prized possessions to the cause. They raised money by allowing people to enter sweepstakes for a chance to have a personal experience with the celebrity, such as going to dinner, attending movie premieres, and taking sporting lessons with the pros. The items could be bid on auction style or by entering in the sweepstake, making the challenge open to everyone. Incredible acts of the virtue of charity were displayed in the personal character of all involved.

Emily Fawcett is a registered nurse working at Lenox Hill Hospital in New York City, the first epicenter of COVID-19 in the United States. Emily and I met fourteen years ago. I had posted a "babysitter needed" ad on the job board at Darien High School. She was a junior and the only one who answered my cry for help. Emily was a godsend to us then, and she is a godsend to the many patients and coworkers at Lenox Hill during this pandemic. Emily started the "hope huddle" at the hospital to celebrate the success stories of those patients who survived COVID-19. Her goal was to spread positivity and offset the war zone–like experiences of emergency-room nurses. Soon the hope huddle grew hospital-wide. Emily drew strength for herself, her patients, and her coworkers from her personal character, and from the virtues of charity, faith, hope, perseverance, and gratitude.

Living in this era of the pandemic has revitalized the virtuous side in many of us. We've instinctively been drawn to acts of charity, faith, perseverance, courage, and gratitude to help one another survive. Our personal character is the source and the lens through which the world can see this. The added bonus is the moral support and personal strength we receive in return for our virtuous acts. Now more than ever, it has become apparent to me the incredible value of living E.P.I.C.

BENEFITS OF MORAL CHARACTER

- Moral character defines who you are. Choosing to develop an exceptional moral character will leave a positive impression, a lasting legacy of goodness.
- Moral character has a profound influence on success and happiness.

- Moral character increases opportunities and advancement in life because of qualities such as honesty, trust, perseverance, and humility.
- Moral character makes it difficult for others to criticize and challenge you.
- Moral character strengthens meaningful, positive personal and professional relationships.
- Moral character supports a growth mindset.
- Moral character will help sustain you in difficult times with a strong foundation in wisdom and faith.
- Moral character can positively influence physical and emotional well-being.

CHOOSE YOUR LEGACY

At the end of our lives, the legacy we leave behind is heavily influenced by our character. Think about people who have made a mark in history, such as Michelle Obama, Steve Jobs, and Adolf Hitler. Marks in history run the gamut from positive and transformative to the worst forms of evil. We not only remember what these people were known for, but we're left with an impression about who they were as individuals as it relates to their character, even without ever meeting them.

Think of one person in your life—a child, teacher, employer, movie star, anyone. Stop for a moment. Are you thinking more about what they are known for or how they make you feel, the person they embody? What we achieve may be remembered, but who we are will be our lasting impression.

When you choose excellence in personal character, you will experience greater happiness and personal fulfillment throughout all aspects of your life. Live your legacy. Live E.P.I.C.

CHAPTER THREE

INTEGRITY: AN INVISIBLE FORCE IN OUR LIVES

The first thing is to be honest with yourself. You can never have an impact on society if you have not changed yourself . . . Great peacemakers are all people of integrity, of honesty, but humility.[3]

—Nelson Mandela

The hallmark of a person of character can be summed up in a single word—integrity. People who possess integrity are honest, trustworthy, and reliable. Originating from the Latin adjective *integer*, integrity means wholeness. So a person of integrity doesn't just uphold the virtue of honesty, they uphold many virtues, including charity, perseverance, and prudence. These all come together to create a fully integrated, whole person of high moral character. A person of integrity will stand firm to defend

---

[3] www.miguelescotet.com/2021/a-personal-selection-of-Nelson-Mandela-best -quotes/

against negative influences to protect their integrity. You would expect this, because it is the right thing to do.

Today, we often refer to a person of integrity as being "solid." People who come to my mind fitting this description give me a sense of relief and assurance. I know I don't have to worry about dishonesty, lack of follow-through, or being led astray when I'm interacting with them. Instead, they look out for me and what's in my best interest, and I do the same for them.

Who is a person of integrity in your life? I'm lucky that I know many people who fit this picture. My friend Angie has had a tremendous impact on me. Her perspectives and actions align with her belief in doing the right thing no matter what task is at hand. When our children were younger, we would get the kids together for playdates, which really turned into play-dates for Angie and me too. We cooked new dinner recipes from our favorite celebrity chef, Rachael Ray; compared trendy arts and crafts projects for the kids; and even took family outings together, like tubing down the Connecticut River. Angie and I also experienced many moments when all heck would break loose. There would be an injured child, another walking into a dangerous situation, and another misbehaving. In a split second, without saying a word, we knew we would have to divide and conquer. Angie would always go to the child who was emotionally upset or misbehaving. She would calm them down with rational conversation, ask questions, and listen. Then she would discuss the hot topic at hand, typically related to being fair, sharing, or thinking of others' feelings and how when you do the right thing everyone is happy. As I look back now, it's clear that she was instilling integrity.

As adults, we know the importance of integrity, and we know it when we see it. Making decisions that are directed by a moral compass may not always be the most desirable, popular, or easy choice, yet we know full well there is tremendous value when we choose to do the right thing. Maybe this is why we don't talk about integrity nearly as much as we should. I find when I do talk about E.P.I.C., I get mixed responses. Some people get excited and tell me they can't wait to read this book. With other people, I get a sense of discomfort around the topic of moral values. I think sometimes people are wary of being judged by me, or assume that I'll think they don't live up to some moral standard that I've made up. Others seem to think that integrity is associated with being a goody two-shoes, or living a serious, boring life.

Whatever the reason, let's uncover the real truth about the positive power of integrity and put to rest some common mis-conceptions. As you will see, living with integrity is highly underrated and sure to overdeliver on the promise of happiness, opportunity, and personal fulfillment.

This may come to you as a surprise, but people of integrity are socially desirable. They are associated with positive charac-ter traits such as goodness, authenticity, and accountability. Their social circles are robust, and they enjoy living life to the fullest. Let's take for example a few people in the public spotlight: NFL player Drew Brees and Oprah Winfrey.

Whether or not you're a sports fan, NFL quarterback Drew Brees is an incredible example of a man of character and integ-rity on and off the field. On the field, Brees earned numerous athletic awards and accolades, including most career passing yards, most career pass completions, most career touchdown passes, and 2010 Super Bowl MVP. He was the recipient of the 2006 Walter Payton NFL Man of the Year Award (which recog-nizes excellence on and off the field); the 2010 *Sports Illustrated* Sportsman of the Year (which recognizes an athlete or team who embodies the spirit of sportsmanship and achievement); the 2011 NFLPA Alan Page Community Award (the highest honor awarded to a player who goes above and beyond in service for his community); the 2011 Athletes in Action/Bart Starr Award (which recognizes an NFL player who best "exemplifies outstanding character and leadership in the home, on the field and in the community")[4]; and the NFL 2018 Art Rooney Award (which recognizes sportsmanship, and respect both for the game and for the players of the game).

In 2016, Colin Kaepernick, an NFL quarterback, began a silent protest against police brutality and racial injustice toward black Americans by kneeling during the national anthem played before NFL games, because the country "oppresses Black people and people of color."[5] His gesture became controversial because not everyone understood the real meaning, which was about taking a stand against racial injustice in our country. Instead, many interpreted Kaepernick's kneeling as a form of disrespecting and dishonoring the American flag, and thus, the country.

Several years later, Brees made a comment during an interview with Yahoo Finance, referencing Kaepernick's kneeling during the national anthem. He said he "will never agree with anybody disrespecting the flag of the United States." His comment sparked outrage. But quickly he made a public apology on his Instagram account, saying, "In an attempt to talk about respect, unity, and solidarity centered about the American flag and the national anthem, I made comments that were insensitive and completely missed the mark on the issues we are facing right now as a country . . . and is not a reflection of my heart or my character."

---

[4] "The Bart Starr Award," Super Bowl Breakfast, https://superbowlbreakfast.com /winners/.

[5] Barry Wilner, "Kneeling with Kaepernick: a timeline of the gesture and its echoes," *Toronto Star*, June 6, 2020, https://www.thestar.com/sports/football/2020/06/06 /kneeling-with-kaepernick-a-timeline-of-the-gesture-and-its-echoes.html.

Brees then upped his game by taking this stance: "I stand with the black community in the fight against systemic racial injustice and police brutality and support the creation of a real policy change that will make a difference. . . . I am sick about the way my comments were perceived yesterday, but I will take full responsibility and accountability. I recognize that I should do less talking and more listening . . . and when the black community is talking about their pain, we all need to listen. For that, I am very sorry and I ask your forgiveness."[6]

Publicly, Brees received forgiveness. He was wholeheartedly sincere in his apology. Because he is a man of character and integrity, those who know him know that he will keep his word to make a personal change and help correct this wrong in our country. Teammate Demario Davis said in a CNN interview, "For him to come out and say 'I missed the mark, I've been insensitive but what I'm going to start doing is listening and learning from the black community and finding ways that I can help them,' I think that's a model for all of America."[7] And former teammate Saints wide receiver Joe Horn also commented on Brees's apology, making it a point to recognize all of the support Brees and his family have given the black community of New Orleans. He said, "Allow Drew a chance to think about what he said and come back and make this right. And I know he will."[8] Had Brees not been a man of such integrity and character, he would not have been able to receive forgiveness and support for his misunderstanding of the real meaning of Colin

---

[6] Justin Terranova, "Drew Brees apologizes for kneeling controversy: I'm not the 'enemy'," *New York Post*, June 4, 2020, https://nypost.com/2020/06/04/drew -brees-apologizes-for-kneeling-controversy-im-not-the-enemy/.

[7] Demario Davis, "Breaking News: Drew Brees Apologizes for 'Disrespecting the Flag,'" interview by John Berman, *CNN*, June 4, 2020.

[8] Steve Peloquin, "Former Saints Star Joe Horn Defends Drew Brees," *ESPN*, June 4, 2020, www.espn1420.com/former-saints-star-joe-horn-defends-drew-Brees/.

Kaepernick's message by kneeling during the national anthem. Because Brees is a man of his word, many are confident he will make a difference in the Black Lives Matter movement. Brees is established as a man of character, and he immediately acted upon his mistake.

What about self-made, megasuperstar Oprah Winfrey, who said, "Real integrity is doing the right thing, knowing that nobody's going to know whether you did it or not"?[9] It would seem that even with all of her wealth and success, Oprah remains humble. "Though I am grateful for the blessings of wealth, it hasn't changed who I am. My feet are still on the ground. I am just wearing better shoes."[10]

Generous in her philanthropic ventures, Oprah founded the Oprah Winfrey Leadership Academy for Girls in South Africa. Shortly after its opening, reports surfaced of sexual abuse by the headmistress. Devastated by this news, within a week Oprah flew to South Africa to meet with the girls and their families and to apologize for what had happened. Oprah said, "I promise to institute immediate changes to create a new model of excellence in social, emotional, and academic life for girls at the school."[11]

I am confident that Drew Brees and Oprah Winfrey each have fun-filled lives celebrating and socializing with many friends. Perhaps that is because of their celebrity status, but I think that can be overhyped. What I see is more than that. They appear to be calm, cool, and collected. They seem unconcerned about what others think of them or their decisions because they are

---

[9] www.goodreads.com/quotes/11106

[10] www.quotes.net/quote/19142. And Tuchy Palmieri, *Oprah, in Her Words: Our American Princess* (Booksurge Publishing, 2008), 95.

[11] "Oprah Speaks Out on School Scandal," *CBS News*, November 5, 2007, www.cbsnews.com/news/oprah-speaks-out-on-school-scandal/.

confident and at ease with who they are. They are classic examples of living with integrity. They are not constantly defending themselves. When there is a controversy, they are open and willing to hear all sides before offering their viewpoint, and if need be, they will admit to error on their part. Drew Brees and Oprah Winfrey certainly are not socially inept by any stretch of the imagination, nor are they perfect all the time.

This brings me to my next point. Choosing to live with integrity should not be associated with the concept of flawlessness or the expectation that you must be the perfect person. Not only is this unachievable, it takes away from the strength and wisdom we gain as we grow in personal character. Having flaws and making mistakes is a part of being human, a part of the journey of life. Choosing to live with integrity is about standing firm, and to the best of your ability, growing in morals and values into a person of excellent character. No one is immune to temptation, societal pressures, peer pressure, and even acts of desperation from time to time. However, we should consistently strive to take action to uphold integrity.

The E.P.I.C. journey understands this challenge, which is why it's a journey and not an endpoint. When we grow in integrity, we grow in the basic virtues that define our character. I have learned by trial and error, bit by bit, that striving to grow excellence in personal character has been the single most valuable and important part in achieving my happiness, personal fulfillment, and success.

REGRETFULLY, LESS THAN MY BEST

I have also learned that when I make decisions or take actions that lack integrity, I am left with regret. I am sure we all have moments we can reflect upon and wish we had done things differently. I am willing to bet that those changes would have been more virtue-based.

When I was a teenager and young adult, I definitely had moments when I lacked integrity. Perhaps it was a function of immaturity or not truly understanding the value of integrity, but I learned each and every time that choosing to do the wrong thing in an effort to find happiness was never the right choice.

When I was a sophomore in high school, I was on the rowing team. As part of our team training, we had to run in a town-sponsored 5K road race. The race took place on a cold, wintry Saturday morning. I wasn't feeling well, but I had to participate anyway. I ran alongside my friend Karen. We were both strong runners, equally matched in speed—sometimes she finished training runs before I did, other times, I finished before she did. In either case, we would always be top finishers in our runs. On this particular day, I knew she was going to beat me. I was fighting a cold, felt weak, and was mentally not up for this challenge. Shortly after the run began, she could tell I was pacing a bit slower than usual, so she fell back in her pace to check in with me. I told her I wasn't feeling well and wasn't sure I could even finish the race, which for me, never happened. She knew I was struggling, so instead of running her own race, she stuck by my side and ran my race. She encouraged me, saying, "Come on, you can do this," and "We're almost there! I'll stay with you," until the finish line. As much as I encouraged her to take off and capture a winning time, she wouldn't leave my side. As we approached the finish line, we both began to pick up our pace in our typical competitive fashion. However, somehow, my number registered before hers and I was awarded a trophy for third place. I was mortified. I knew that the trophy belonged to Karen, however, she humbly went on her way and didn't contest the results. I never spoke up and told officials or my coach that Karen earned the win, not me, even though I wanted her to have the trophy. Instead, I kept it. I was not proud in any way.

I felt horrible. I told her she deserved it and she just smiled. Instead of displaying the trophy as a reminder of hard work and achievement, I stored it away. It became a painful reminder of my lack of integrity and her incredible level of integrity as she compassionately encouraged me to have faith to persevere and cross the finish line.

I've held onto this experience as an inspiration to better myself. I fell short of many virtues that day. I was *dishonest* with myself, with her, and with the results of the race; I lacked *prudence* and *wisdom* by the way in which I handled the entire situation; I had little *faith* in myself and my abilities, when I was in fact able to finish the race; I lacked *compassion* and wasn't considerate about how Karen felt at the finish line when I received all of the attention and she didn't; I definitely would not have *persevered* had it not been for Karen.

I have learned that whenever I compromise my morals, I do so because of one reason: I think it's a way to ensure a happier outcome or an easy way out. Instead, it does the exact opposite. I am left unfulfilled and unhappy. I didn't win third place; I took it from Karen. Result: unhappiness and disappointment.

I am grateful, however, for learning the value of integrity and growing from this experience. I learned firsthand the enormous fact that breaking down in character, lacking in integrity, is a huge disadvantage and detrimental to myself and those around me. Instead, holding true to morals and values is an enormous advantage that will help you experience a life of personal fulfillment and happiness.

THE WORLD AROUND US

As we all know, people in all walks of life lack integrity. Sometimes these people are referred to as bad eggs. We are even warned by others to watch out or be careful when they see that we might be interacting with someone who lacks integrity. I will tell you what I've told myself and my children: their behaviors are a perfect example of what not to do.

Take a moment to think about someone you know who fits this image. Isn't there always some sort of turmoil surrounding them or associated with them? Even for those who lack integrity and seemingly get away with it, are they really happy and at ease, or are they edgy and unhappy? Do they have many friends? Do they have robust social circles? Likely not, because no one can trust them, and trust is a fundamental component of personal relationships.

What's especially damaging is when we see someone lacking integrity in positions where it is vitally important to have strong integrity. Consider, for instance, politicians, CEOs, and other public figures who are caught in scandalous affairs or in situations where they flagrantly abuse their powers. Unfortunately, the examples are endless, from the horrific acts of violence perpetrated on his young female patients by Larry Nassar, the US Gymnastics physician, to the many scandals on Wall Street involving fraud and greed, like the Enron collapse which defined accounting fraud and corporate corruption, costing shareholders $74 billion in losses.

Recently, the Varsity Blues Scandal, one of the largest college admission scandals to ever hit the US, went viral. Parents and university officials collaborated with Rick Singer, the operator of two for-profit college prep businesses, to influence undergraduate admissions at universities and colleges across the United States. The scheme involved bribery with test administrators to inflate standardized test scores and college admissions, bribery with individuals in athletic departments who claimed their applicants were student-athletes when they were not, and money laundering. The astonishing factor was not only the obvious criminal activity, but that many of the parents partaking in this scam were lawyers, doctors, and highly regarded business executives—all careers where integrity is, or at least should have been, at the forefront of character.

The common factor of this scandal was the utter lack of moral character on the part of all the participants who knowingly chose to do the wrong thing. The consequences of their actions included imprisonments, millions of dollars levied in fines, professional licenses revoked, families torn apart, students expelled from their colleges and universities, the damage done to qualified prospective students who were denied admission so that children of the cheaters could be enrolled, and the horrific emotional turmoil for all involved. This example is the epitome of the ripple effect of serious damage that can ensue when integrity is sacrificed.

How different would the lives of these families be if the parents had acted with integrity? It's the old "if only . . ." reflection of regret.

Think back to a time in your life that you wish you could have a second chance. You'd be able to do it all over again for a better outcome. This doesn't have to be as extreme as the example above; think of anything, even little events. What would that be and what would you have done differently? For me, I would have *persevered* and finished my nursing degree, instead of leaving the program three semesters shy of a BSN. I would have been *honest*, instead of lying to Fr. Bondi to get out of a $50 parking ticket when I was in college.

The common theme you will see is that there is a shift from the regret of a non-virtue-based decision that led to a poor outcome to a new virtue-based decision that would ensure a better outcome. Think about "if only" statements: if only I were *honest* and didn't cheat on the final exam, I would have my diploma; if only I'd had *faith* in my partner, I wouldn't have quit on our relationship; if only I were *prudent* instead of speeding to get to the concert on time, I wouldn't have gotten a ticket, and so on.

As you grow in integrity, these instances become fewer and further between as you experience firsthand the value of living E.P.I.C. in your pursuit of happiness and personal fulfillment.

WHY DO BAD THINGS HAPPEN TO GOOD PEOPLE?

Life isn't always fair. There are many instances where people who may not have the best character qualities seem to progress through life just fine—happy, with few trials and tribulations—while there are amazing people of good, even excellent, character who experience the exact opposite. Why is this? I don't have that answer. But what I can share is a common thread that I have seen from my personal life about when bad things happen to good people. They possess an internal source of strength to carry on that seems to be drawn from the value they have placed on living morally grounded lives.

One of my best friends from high school, Stacy, grew up in a loving family of modest means. I don't remember her father all that well; he was a bit older than her mother, was retired, and struggled with poor health related to years of smoking. Stacy's mother was an incredibly kind-hearted woman with a warm smile. She was an artist by trade and grounded in her religious faith. Stacy's only sibling, her younger sister Sara, was on the quiet side. In a short five-year period, Stacy's mother experienced horrible tragedy. Her husband passed away and then Stacy was killed in a car accident. I still can't wrap my head around the immensity of emotional devastation that she experienced. I can say that every time I saw her, she wore her warm smile, albeit with sadness, as she held true to her positive outlook on life. She leaned into the strength of her faith in God and His promises with confusion, but with trust. She also drew a tremendous amount of strength from a deep sense of fortitude to carry on for herself and Sara. It was as if she had many sources of strength from within carrying her through this time—sources that circle back to her commitment to morals, values, and living with virtue.

Another friend of mine, Nancy, lost her husband to cancer years before she and I met. After a few casual conversations on the sidelines while watching our daughters play lacrosse, Nancy shared with me that she had been widowed for many years. Since that time, she has dedicated her life to giving her children all that she could to prepare them for successful lives. It wasn't long before I realized a large part of her definition of success was to instill in her children the strength they have as a family no matter what obstacle comes their way and to always do the right thing. Nancy was driven by the principles of integrity, hard work, perseverance, and prudence—all virtues. Whether in the classroom, on a sports field, or in business, her children reflected these character traits well. Nancy didn't just receive strength from her faith in God, she received strength from a life of living with virtue. She is an amazing example of E.P.I.C.

There are many inspirational stories of people who have turned personal tragedy into a greater good—for example, parents whose child dies and who then donate their child's organs to save the life of another child. This is an incredible act of the virtue of charity to help save a life and spare others the emotional pain and suffering that comes with the loss of a loved one. In return, these parents gain strength and a sense of fulfillment that helps them in their recovery process.

Although we may not always have control over what happens to us, we can control what we choose to do in response. We can draw strength and guidance from sound morals and values. Understanding that there is emotional strength and personal fulfillment in living with the virtues of perseverance, fortitude, faith, charity, humility, honesty, and wisdom can help us through difficult times. Whether these virtues are well established or not, difficult times present an opportunity to grow in them. Embracing virtuous living offers us another and somewhat unexpected benefit that can provide us the strength and personal fulfillment we need to carry us through difficult times.

CHARACTERISTICS OF A PERSON OF INTEGRITY

People of integrity are all around us, often subtle in their presence (most likely because they are humble). The standouts are those who apply excellence to many virtues, thus creating a greater whole that defines their personal character.

Consider other key attributes as you think about what a person of integrity may look like. In addition to the aforementioned (honest, trustworthy, reliable), people of integrity are loyal, prudent, sincere, and respectful. Their actions are consistent with their words and they hold true to their commitments. They admit when they're at fault, apologize sincerely, and are quick to give others the benefit of the doubt.

If living with integrity sounds appealing to you, growing to E.P.I.C. will guide you in your journey.

FINAL THOUGHT: CONSTRUCTING STRUCTURAL INTEGRITY

As you can see, integrity is something we sculpt and build within ourselves by the way we choose to live our lives. The virtues we discuss in this book are part of our makeup. We know them intuitively and use them as we navigate our lives.

In the upcoming sections, we will discuss virtues individually so that when you put them together as a whole and apply excellence, you will grow in integrity. It's akin to the way in which structural integrity is a core consideration for civil engineers who design large structures. The term "structural integrity" refers to how effectively physical structures can withstand loads and possible outside forces. Considerations when building with structural integrity are the many components, synergistically working together, each playing an important part of the greater whole; the ability for the structure to fulfill its purpose; and the ability of the structure to withstand outside forces that would challenge the integrity of the structure. We can't see everything that goes into creating the integrity of any given structure; we simply trust that the many parts work together harmoniously to fulfill its overall purpose and that in the event of some unforeseeable issue or strain, the structure will have resiliency.

Structural integrity makes me think of the Tappan Zee Bridge in New York. For decades, I had traveled across this bridge assuming it was structurally sound. There were no physical indications that there was anything wrong and since there were no travel restrictions, why would it even occur to me there was a problem with the bridge? Then I learned plans were approved to tear down the bridge and build an entirely new Tappan Zee Bridge. I was shocked! I thought, *Wait, is there something wrong with this bridge? I travel on it all the time and it's being torn down?* Apparently, the structural parts working together to uphold the integrity of the bridge had deteriorated. Clearly, I couldn't see these parts, but I understood that they were crucial to maintaining the integrity of the bridge, making it safe for drivers.

Use this analogy to create a life of structural integrity built upon excellence in personal character. Much like the structural integrity of a bridge, we can "build" ourselves to be a person of personal integrity. We have many parts (virtues) that aren't visible. They each have their independent roles, yet they work together to support our overall character, which is where strength in integrity grows. There will be maintenance (mishaps when virtues seem to be lacking) along the way, which simply means we're growing. There will also be times when storms come though (life challenges), making it hard to carry on. If we can stay true to the definition of structural integrity, we will be able to withstand these times with an internal strength sourced in living a life of integrity, an E.P.I.C. life that will ultimately deliver on the promise of personal fulfillment and happiness.

BENEFITS OF INTEGRITY

- Integrity builds upon honesty, a cornerstone of character which leads to happiness, greater opportunities, and success in the achievement of personal goals.
- Integrity is the foundation of meaningful personal and professional relationships.
- Integrity builds personal confidence and increases the confidence others have in you.
- Integrity is positive, inspiring, and impactful.
- Integrity sets you apart in authenticity, understanding, and trust.
- Integrity provides ease and clarity in prudent decision-making.

EXCELLENCE APPLIED TO INTEGRITY

- Choose to actively grow in virtue and in moral character.
- Make honesty and trust a top priority in all that you do. These are fundamental to integrity and the foundations upon which all relationships are built.

- Be completely honest with yourself. Be courageous and do some soul-searching to uncover truths that you may or may not be comfortable with. Confront fears that have been preventing you from living life to its fullest.
- Hold true to your word even if that means going out of your way or making personal sacrifices.
- Practice what you preach. Lead by example. Actions speak louder than any words spoken.
- Share your faults or times when you've learned the hard way. Allow yourself to be human and grow in humility. Apologize more readily.
- Respect humanity. We are all created equal.
- Be aware of personal bias and strive to live unbiased.
- Stand up for what's right. Step up and step out to defend those who may not be able to defend themselves.
- Actively resolve conflict and work toward peaceful outcomes. Forgive one another.
- Be responsible for your actions, choices, and decisions.
- Respond to the outside world with integrity.
- Live E.P.I.C.!

CHAPTER FOUR

EXCELLENCE: A GROWTH MINDSET FOR CHARACTER

Excellence is never an accident. It is always the result of high intentions, sincere effort, and intelligent execution; it represents the wise choice of many alternatives—choice, not chance, determines our destiny.

—Aristotle

Vince Lombardi, legendary coach of the Green Bay Packers, nailed it: "Character is just another word for having a perfectly disciplined and educated will. A person can make his own character by blending these elements with an intense desire to achieve excellence. Everyone is different in what I will call magnitude, but the capacity to achieve character is still the same." We all have the capacity to achieve excellence and achieve character, as he put it. What varies is the magnitude of our achievement—the interest, desire, and extent to which we choose to develop excellence and our character. E.P.I.C. is about the synergy that develops when you apply excellence to your personal character.

The result is *epic*: rewarding, fulfilling, delivering on the promise of happiness and personal fulfillment.

Excellence is simply the quality of being outstanding or extremely good at something. Consider the wide range of skills and trades where people can achieve levels of excellence. These individuals are the best or most sought-after in their trade. When I was a child, my family lived near the Culinary Institute of America. Our small neighborhood consisted of about ten homes, two of which belonged to Master Chefs. One was a world-renowned Master Pastry Chef. On Halloween, Mr. Masi would open the door holding a cookie sheet loaded with dripping candy apples for us to eat on the run. I remember thinking it was the best house ever for trick or treating. If I had known the word then, I would have said it was epic.

Excellence is a mindset—one that we all have the ability to achieve. Excellence inspires, invigorates, excites, and empowers you to challenge yourself, to give it your all. It's choosing to go above and beyond, to invest in making an event, task, or even a conversation that much better. Whether you're in the midst of an enormous undertaking like planning a wedding, or something smaller like a home-cooked meal, it's not *what* you're doing that's important, it's how you are going to tackle the task at hand. This concept is linear and easy to understand. When you put forth your best effort and reach or exceed your potential, you will likely achieve success and happiness; when you do less than your best and fall short of your potential, you will have less-than-desirable results and probably be left feeling disappointed.

Knowing you have done your best is rewarding. Have you ever been told that you did something excellent? Maybe it was in elementary school when a test or homework assignment was returned to you with "Excellent" written on the top of the page in all capital letters, underlined. Perhaps it was performing a pose in a yoga class, a maneuver on a sports field, a work of art, or a speech to thousands. Whatever comes to mind, when something you do is associated with the word excellent, you become filled with feelings of happiness, self-confidence, and success. Now ask yourself what you did to reach that level of excellence. You will likely recall putting forth a lot of effort and time, using a determined mindset, and focusing on a vision. You set your sights on an outcome that exceeded mediocrity. You applied excellence to achieving the task at hand.

Consider for a moment people who have defied the odds and achieved greatness—media gurus; actors, directors, writers, and producers in the film industry; world-renowned artists; business tycoons; Nobel Prize winners; people who worked to surpass average, surpass good, surpass great until they hit the mark of excellence. Greats also abound in the people around you. Everyday heroes—your family and friends—surround you. Take a moment to think about who they may be. Who would fit the picture of great people in your life? Who has given it their best, overcome adversities, become E.P.I.C.?

When my son was playing ice hockey, the team ran countless drills to increase skating speed. One drill involved skating around cones in a figure-eight pattern for five minutes. The boys raced to finish first, but usually the same skaters took that coveted spot every time. However, those skaters who were behind the pack and never gave up, trying harder each time to get closer to the top group of skaters, were given the same high-fives as they came off the ice, but with greater enthusiasm. Why? For their excellent effort. These skaters showed that excellence isn't necessarily about winning, it's about the effort and hard work put forth.

What all of these people have in common is a mindset of excellence as they grow, going above and beyond the ordinary to the extraordinary. They, like so many others who are driven by excellence, exhibit qualities such as determination, perseverance, faith, mental and physical integrity, and patience.

EXCELLENCE AND SUCCESS

The concept of excellence is often related to success. However, if I were to ask ten people for their definition of success, I'd get ten different answers, because success means different things to different people. For some, success is measurable with quantifiable results like earning titles, awards, and accolades, or reaching financial goals. For others, success is less tangible and more subjective, and is measured by the impact they have on the world and those around them. For many of us, it's a combination.

The standard definition of success encompasses both achieving a desired outcome and attaining wealth. I think the first half of this definition is spot on. However, the second part—the attainment of wealth and other worldly markers—should be examined. Many successful people have had a profound impact on the world (think of Mahatma Gandhi, whose nonviolent campaign successfully led India in its fight for independence from British rule), yet lived modest lives. Don't measure your success against those who are wealthy financially. Measure yourself against your own goals and visions, which may change over time. Apply excellence to these, and your vision of success will surely be achieved.

Many years ago, Anthony and I were at a dinner where everyone was asked this question: What is your key to being successful? There were a variety of answers. My husband's was, "Work hard, take care of others, and do the right thing"—a mantra he lives by to this day. Others cited events that led to unique opportunities, appreciation of natural abilities, or a special someone who took them under their wing.

As the question approached me, I began to panic. I had been a stay-at-home mom for nearly a year and simply wasn't sure how to answer. I didn't see myself as successful. I even wondered if I should pass on the question. I remember thinking back to when I was in school or playing sports or in my career to spark an idea. I needed to come up with a broad answer. Then it came to me, crystal-clear, "Excellence. If I apply excellence to everything I do, I will be successful in everything I do." This is where my pursuit of personal excellence began. Putting it into words was an epiphany.

WHERE TO BEGIN?

The concept of excellence should be inspiring, not intimidating. Start gradually and ask yourself, *How can I improve this?* Begin with simple actions, such as putting forth a little more effort than you're used to, perhaps making an extra effort of some sort on a project or in a relationship. The idea is that you're trying your best, which is how you develop and grow in personal excellence.

Here are a few suggestions for how to ignite a mindset of excellence:

- Look at life around you and ask yourself how you can improve or make "X" better. In what area could you give a better effort? Is it in your eating habits? Fitness level? Do you need to reconcile with someone? Can you learn a new skill or improve a current skill? Could you say a nice word to that person you don't like very much?
- Are you meeting or exceeding expectations? When my children were in elementary school, their report cards were not the traditional number and letter grades. Instead, their academic performance fell into categories of *unsatisfactory,*

needs improvement, satisfactory, meets expectations, and *exceeds expectations.* I interpreted the *meets expectations* category to be average. There seemed to be an underlying message about effort. I remember thinking, *Okay, well, I guess I shouldn't be worried if they meet expectations.* But why not strive to jump to the next category of *exceeds expectations?* Begin thinking about exceeding.

- Are you investing in your personal relationships ("Am I a good or a great spouse, partner, friend, parent, coworker?") and in your personal growth ("Am I a good person of character or a great person of character?")? Do you take time to relax and reset, thus investing in yourself?

- Adopt an "Aim higher" mindset. Years ago we attended a children's sporting event that had many different activities. Children chose from things like running a forty-yard dash; agility courses where they ran through car tires and climbed ladders; catching and throwing a ball for completion and accuracy—it was basically a sporty kid's dream come true. One station stood out to me—the vertical jump. A skinny metal pole about eight feet tall had thin plastic tabs that extended horizontally outward, and the goal was to jump as high as you could from a standing position and tap the tabs, which served as measuring tools. My son Anthony was about eight years old. As he approached the young man conducting this test, you could see the look on Anthony's face had changed from eager to determined. We call it the game face. On his first jump, he was surprised and disappointed to fall short of his expectations. He seemed to shrug it off as he began to walk to the next activity. Then the high school–aged boy conducting the test shouted to Anthony, "Hey, where are you going? Get back here! You can jump higher." Anthony turned around with a look of confusion. I am not sure if it was that he was offered a second chance or if he questioned the concept of being able to jump higher. But he returned and gave it a second try. He did jump higher, the smile appeared, and in that same instant, before he could turn his body to walk away again, the young man holding the pole said, "Do it again. This time if you aim higher, you'll jump higher." Anthony listened to his wise advice and jumped even higher on his third attempt. To this day we use this story to remind our children that you can go further than you think. Just try harder and aim higher.

• Become more accountable. Take ownership of your responsibilities and admit when you're at fault. After all, making mistakes is part of being human. It's part of learning and growing. There was a point in time when my five children were in four different schools due to the twelve-year age difference between the oldest and youngest. This meant that there were four different websites that I had to learn and navigate, four different academic calendars for vacations and holidays, four different food programs—you catch my drift. As you can imagine, there was plenty of room for error on my part keeping up with all the details. My greatest struggle was whenever there was a change to the standard routine, like an early dismissal for a holiday performance or a late start for standardized testing. Chances were I would drop them off at their schools when they didn't need to be there, or worse, not be there for them at an early dismissal. As much as I knew I had to be on my toes, I still made mistakes and I still had to apologize to the school and my children. I had to be accountable. The more diligent I was checking and cross-checking their schedules regularly, the less likely I was to make errors. In other words, the greater the emphasis I placed on being accountable, the more success I had.

- Hard work pays off. Keep at it. Have you ever had to lose weight—not a few pounds here or there, but a large amount? It's hard. It takes a tremendous amount of time, discipline, and hard work. My mother-in-law did just this, losing more than one hundred pounds. She joined Jenny Craig, and with the help of a dedicated staff, a plan was designed just for her. She ate their smaller, low-calorie meals—a drastic difference from her normal Italian diet of pasta and sauces. She also began to exercise regularly, which she had never done before. She applied excellence in her execution, following all the details of her structured plan. She worked hard daily, and after twelve months she achieved her weight goal.

- Become more adaptable to the ever-changing world around you. Being able to adapt is both advantageous and necessary. We all live in the era of high tech and know the power of our cellular phones. Whether you're an Android or iPhone user, often you're learning a new app or relearning some aspect of your favorite app that's been updated. There are many instances where I don't have a choice but to learn a new technology as more and more services are shifting online: our medical files are all online, the DMV has shifted to online license applications and/ or renewals, and my banking is entirely online. I have no choice but to change with change. The more I embrace this, the more proficient I become, the more I grow, and the more success I experience.

- See setbacks as opportunities. Find the positive in nega-tive situations. Whether you think of the positive as the silver lining or the brighter side, find it. My eldest daughter has always had difficulty with digestion. After a series of inconclusive medical tests, her physician ordered an endoscopy and a colonoscopy to confirm their suspicions of gastritis. Not fun procedures to prepare for, but necessary. Gastritis was indeed a culprit for some of her physical issues, however, much to their surprise, they discovered a large, asymptomatic precancerous polyp. If this had not been found it would have become cancerous within a year or two. Marisa was only twenty-five years old at the time. For a healthy individual, colonoscopy screening begins at fifty, but by that time it would have been too late for her. As negative as this news was to hear, and now she will have a lifetime of close monitoring, the silver lining was that a potentially deadly event was caught early enough to save her. It was literally a matter of life and death.

- Visualization: Have you pictured something exactly the way you wanted it to appear and then it occurred just that way? Maybe it was the way you wanted to look as you dressed and prepared for a special occasion, such as a date or job interview. Perhaps it was a garden organized with specific vegetables for a hearty, robust harvest. Or maybe the image of holding your hands high celebrating after winning an election. Having a clear picture of what you want and feeling the joy of accomplishing it, even before it happens, can be powerful tools. The key here is that you need to create a specific, lasting image and think about it daily. When you do this, you will become more invested and laser-focused, and the likelihood of achieving that goal will increase.

- Adapt WIN thinking: What's Important Now. Make the best of the present moment. With five children, I have to multitask, and I don't mind at all. However, I have learned that multitasking becomes hazardous when the outcomes of those tasks at hand are sacrificed. When I would walk the dog and talk on the phone, I felt rather productive. I was actually present in the moment with my phone conversation and our dog was getting his exercise. It was win-win. When I would cook dinner and talk on the phone it was a disaster. I wasn't able to pay attention to my conversation while chopping, dicing, measuring, sautéing. I usually made mistakes with my recipe and I can assure you whomever I was speaking with at those moments must have been frustrated with me asking them to repeat themselves multiple times in a single conversation. It was lose-lose. Capture your present moment and stay focused and attentive.

As you can see, there are many ways to apply excellence to all aspects of your life. We have the capacity to be excellent and share in the far-reaching benefits of establishing a mindset of excellence.

EXCELLENCE AND PERFECTION

One caveat needs to be brought up: the concept of excellence versus the concept of perfection. People often confuse the two. Let's be very clear—excellence is *not* perfection. In fact, there is a stark contrast between the two. Excellence is about striving to be your best. It's about healthy achievement and growth in the pursuit of happiness. Perfectionism is all about the outcome and trying to reach a specific and often unattainable goal, not about the process of getting there. Perfectionism is generally considered to be a negative attribute. It's as if the best effort will never be good enough because perfection can never be attained.

Perfectionism is seen in a negative context because the perfectionist sets unrealistic standards and is often left struggling with anger, depression, low self-esteem, anxiety, and a host of other issues when those standards aren't met. In an article by Barbara Markway, PhD, in *Psychology Today*, she presents many negative issues associated with those who seek perfection. The perfectionist strives for impossible goals, values themselves by what they do, gets easily overwhelmed and gives up, can be devastated by failure, dwells on mistakes, wants to be number one, hates criticism, and has to win to keep high self-esteem.[12] Doesn't sound like much fun, does it?

In contrast, excellence is seen in a positive context. It's invigorating, energizing, and allows for human error as a means of growth and improvement toward reaching a high-set yet realistic goal. Excellence is surrounded by success and happiness.

Think about teaching a child how to make a batch of chocolate chip cookies. We review the steps necessary to bake the perfect (even though we may not say that) chocolate chip cookie. We share tips along the way of how to properly measure the flour, what firmly pressed brown sugar means versus the measurement of white sugar. We show what not to do as well. We may even share some funny failure stories we've encountered to steer clear of those paths. So when we think about those perfect chocolate chip cookies we're now attempting to bake, we are actually traveling along the path of excellence. We're remembering what we've learned from the past about what worked and what didn't.

The key is not to get caught up in actual perfection, since this is an extreme. We invest ourselves as teachers so that the students

---

[12] Barbara Markway, PhD, "Pursuing Excellence, Not Perfection," *Psychology Today*, January 14, 2013.

will find success through learning, trial and error, and additional information we add to go above and beyond the basic printed recipe. This is the fine balance between striving for excellence and perfection.

Personal excellence is choosing to apply the mindset of excellence in all that you do, whether baking, doing business, or being a good friend. Apply excellence to your friendships, family relationships, academics, career, extracurricular activities, your mental and physical wellness, etc. Step by step, begin building and investing in the concept of excellence. Set your mind for superseding good or even great. There is a tremendous sense of personal reward in knowing such outcomes will deliver success and happiness.

In his book *The Excellence Habit,* Vlad Zachary writes, "A life of excellence, therefore, is a life of paying attention and a life of deliberate, continuous change." Excellence as a process involves practice and learning and also involves adapting to changes that will improve the chances of reaching your desired goals. Have you ever cooked at high altitude? Takes longer, right? Take a lesson from an expert in a new sport and now you're gripping the golf club, tennis racket, or lacrosse stick in a new way? These are all adaptations along the way to excellence.

In the end, it's up to you. Take personal accountability by deliberately choosing to live up to your human potential and make excellence a habit.

Consider also that the application of excellence to all that you do is a tremendously powerful source of momentum that transforms ordinary living into extraordinary living. It's worth noting that if for whatever reason you don't experience the outcome you were striving for, rest assured you will walk away knowing and feeling a sense of fulfillment that you did your very best. There is nothing lost. I tell my children there is no downside to giving that extra effort because their hard work will pay off on another day, in a different way.

E.P.I.C. living is transformative. You immediately experience the rewards of excellence when you apply excellence to being the best version of YOU, specifically to the virtues that define your character. To quote Vince Lombardi, "The quality of a person's life is in direct proportion to their commitment to excellence, regardless of their chosen field of endeavor."[13] This truly captures the engine or driving force of the message of E.P.I.C. living.

---

[13] www.brainyquote.com

CHAPTER FIVE

E.P.I.C. 101: A BRIEF HISTORY OF THE VIRTUOUS LIFE

The concept of core values is common today in building an ethical culture or community in environments such as corporations, hospitals, and schools. But humanity has been exploring this very concept for thousands upon thousands of years. This is old turf we're treading. The search for what's right and wrong—on the outside, yes, but more importantly on the inside, when the lights are off and we're introspective and authentic—has haunted the greatest philosophers and religious leaders for centuries.

Many books have been written on this subject, so I'll provide highlights of some mainstream thinking throughout history. Some of these ideas will resonate with you more than others, but you will see that all have much in common with the E.P.I.C. philosophy—a philosophy you can begin bringing into your life today.

E.P.I.C. IN PHILOSOPHERS

As I was researching key points of this book's theory, I read a great deal about certain superstars of historical importance: philosophers. Not just any philosophers, but the fathers of philosophy themselves: Socrates; his student, Plato; and Plato's student, Aristotle. The origins of western moral and ethical theory can be traced back to these ancient Greek teachers.

These three great minds all searched for the answer to the question, "Where and how do we find happiness?" In fact, their answers were found in the context of virtues. Sound familiar? I assure you this will not veer off into a history lesson, but I did find it extremely interesting. They lived and taught nearly 2,500 years ago, but their interest in ethics, investigation into the human self, and exploration of what "the good life" truly is coincides neatly with mine, and it revolves around happiness. They focused on building an improved ethical structure, which delivered true happiness, as opposed to striving for worldly goals of wealth, educational status, career success, and other external markers of validation.

Socrates lived from 469 to 399 BCE, and his main teachings centered around how to live a virtuous life. Socrates believed that all people desire happiness and that happiness could be obtained through human effort. In other words, happiness is available for all of us with some effort. And a person's true happiness is achieved by doing what's right.

Plato felt that human virtue is whatever enables human beings to live a good life and that we choose those actions to reach that good life. A "good life" can be defined generally as the quality of a person's life in the context of well-being, optimal functioning, life satisfaction, purpose in life, and overall happiness. Plato discussed specific virtues that were attached to happiness. For example, wisdom is the use of our mind and intellect to understand morals and apply them to our lives. Courage is how we face adversity and stand up for what we believe in. Temperance (moderation) is the ability to govern ourselves with self-control; when we do not use temperance but listen to our desires in a negative way, we compromise our character. Finally, justice: "The just person has a healthy soul, in which reason rules the appetites and our desires for honor. The just person is fulfilled, at peace and truly happy."[14]

Aristotle's influential *Nicomachean Ethics* describes the ways in which we can achieve humanity's highest goal: happiness. He believed that happiness in and of itself is the central purpose of human life. Aristotle felt that the highest impact factor in achieving happiness was to live a virtuous life and have a good moral character. The goal of happiness comprised a person's entire life and required making the right choices along the journey of life. "Happiness depends on acquiring a moral character, where one displays the virtues of courage, generosity, justice, friendship and citizenship in one's life."[15]

Aristotle challenges us to not only look at our lives and who we are, but to make a plan for the "right ultimate end"—again, happiness. He introduces the concept of creating a habit of making the right choices in order to achieve happiness. Virtuous choices are habits, and constant practice of a habit leads us to excellence.

As we can see, these great philosophers shared a common interest, a deep desire to discuss and analyze one another's thoughts and perspectives on the moral character of human beings. Moral character was a much more prevalent and

---

[14] Michael W. Austin, PhD, "Achieving Happiness: Advice from Plato," *Psychology Today*, August 11, 2010, https://www.psychologytoday.com/ca/blog/ethics-everyone/201008/achieving-happiness-advice-plato.

[15] "Aristotle & Happiness," Pursuit of Happiness, www.pursuit-of-happiness.org/history-of-happiness/Aristotle.

frequently discussed topic thousands of years ago than it is today. There was a profound interest in trying to understand and grasp the moral character of people, what goodness actually meant, and how it related to the ultimate goal of happiness.

It's simply amazing how closely aligned these great philosophers were with the development of excellent character (developing virtues) as the means to the ultimate end we as humans aspire to reach: happiness and personal fulfillment. They knew that this was a process and a choice. This is exactly what I am bringing to light in E.P.I.C. living. We need to stop and realize that the same virtues that existed thousands of years ago exist in us today. We use these virtues every day. When we apply excellence to these virtues, we too will live happy, meaningful, and successful lives.

E.P.I.C. IN CIVILIZATIONS

Throughout history, the concept of virtues and the importance of moral character have been embedded as a foundational part of all cultures, not just in ancient Greece.

Ancient Egyptians used the term *Ma'at,* which was a concept of truth, balance, order, law, morality, and justice. Ma'at also personified a goodness regulating the stars, seasons, and actions of both mortals and deities. Many sources such as autobiographies and ancient texts, known as wisdom literature, revealed which behaviors were acceptable and which were not in the ancient Egyptian culture. Ideals such as justice, honesty, fairness, mercy, kindness, and generosity were especially desirable.[16]

In medieval Europe, the Code of Chivalry was introduced as a moral code for the knights of the courtly system. Different accounts describe what those virtuous behaviors included.

---

[16] Jimmy Dunn, "The Ethics and Morality of the Ancient Egyptians," Tour Egypt, http://www.touregypt.net/featurestories/ethics.htm.

For example, the fourteenth-century Duke of Burgundy listed chivalric virtues such as faith, charity, justice, sagacity, prudence, temperance, resolution, truth, liberty, diligence, hope, and valor.[17]

In medieval Japan, Samurai warriors held to the Bushido code, also known as "The Samurai Code of Chivalry" consisting of eight guiding virtues to live by for a balanced life. These virtues were Gi—justice or rectitude; Yu—courage; Jim—mercy or benevolence; Rei—respect or politeness; Makoto—honesty and trust; Meiyo—honor; Chuugi—loyalty; and Kanji—character and self control.[18]

E.P.I.C. IN RELIGION

Nearly all religions have foundational core virtues and moral beliefs which are meant to be upheld and practiced for the greater good of peace and happiness. Most religions also emphasize the consequences of failing to follow these moral beliefs. The strife that transpires to oneself and others leads to unhappiness and unrest.

Christianity holds to seven Christian virtues, which are divided into two separate categories, the theological virtues and the cardinal virtues. The theological virtues are faith, hope, and charity. The four cardinal virtues are prudence, justice, temperance, and courage. The Ten Commandments are the standard by which Christians are expected to live.

Chinese Taoism, or Daoism, is based on "te," which translates to "power; virtue," "heart," and "inherent character, personal character; inner power inner strength; integrity."[19] The word Tao (or Dao), which generally means "the way," is the belief of how humans should behave ethically and morally.

Hinduism holds to the concept of Dharma (path of righteousness), which is how humans should strive to uphold

---

[17] Medieval Life and Times, https://www.medieval-life-and-times.info/.

[18] www.kwunion.com/interesting/Bushido-code-the-8-virtues-of-the-samurai/

[19] www.nationsonline.org/oneworld/Chinese_Customs/taoism.htm

positive order and thus be liberated from the cycle of karma. Hindus believe that without Dharma, there is no happiness at all. "The very definition of Dharma is that which brings happiness. Any tiny happiness that we experience today comes directly from having acted virtuously in the past, and that act was Dharma, whether it was generosity or kindness, patience or right understanding. And all the happiness we will experience in the future is entirely dependent on our creating only virtuous actions from now on, and that is Dharma as well."[20]

In Islam, the Qur'an is believed to be the literal word of God, the definitive description of morality (virtue) and guidance for humanity. The Qur'an is filled with teachings that promise a benefit for oneself or for humanity as a whole. These teachings include charity, contentment, courtesy, courage, dignity, discipline, firmness, forgiveness, frankness, frugality, generousity, gratitude, honesty, hope, humility, justice, kindness, loyalty, mercy, patience, perseverance, prudence, sincerity, spirituality, unity and wisdom to name only a few. [21] Muslims are expected not only to live a virtuous life, but to enjoy doing so.

In Judaism, the Ten Commandments included in the Torah (a part of 613 commandments revealing ethical guidance) are central to Jewish views on virtue. Morality is a central component of Judaism. The key moral virtues include justice, righteousness, kindness, and compassion. Hillel the Elder (110 BC–10 CE) said, "What is hateful to yourself do not do to your fellow man," a teaching that is widely known as the Golden Rule.[22]

---

[20] Kyabje Lama Zopa Rinpoche, "The Perfect Human Rebirth," Lama Yeshe Wisdom Archive, https://www.lamayeshe.com/article/chapter/chapter-1-what-dharma.

[21] www.islam.ru/en/content/story/36-Islamic-everyday-virtues

[22] The Editors of the Encyclopedia of Judaism, "Jewish Ethics: Some Basic Concepts and Ideas," My Jewish Learning, https://https://www.myjewishlearning.com/article/jewish-ethics-some-basic-concepts-and-ideas/.

How interesting is it that so many religions around the world were founded upon basic principles involving virtues? The virtues differ, but are nonetheless the guiding principles of each religion—ones that when followed, will lead to a better life, a life of happiness for not just the individual, but also for those in their community. E.P.I.C. living is well established in history, religion, and culture as a path toward happiness and personal fulfillment.

E.P.I.C. IN STORIES

The majority of us don't stop to contemplate the views of the great philosophers as they relate to morals and values. However, we can relate to a different historical delivery of moral messages that have stood the test of time—fables and parables. These stories date back thousands and thousands of years as a means to deliver a moral message. Stories speak to all of us. They touch a common thread in all humans that we can relate to in one way or another. These clever, creative stories were typically short, simple, and used to teach life lessons that had deeply meaningful results. Everyone in the audience, even young children, could take away the message of moral goodness (the virtue) as well as the not-so-moral message (the vice). These stories used common, relatable knowledge to impart a meaningful message about morals and values and the use of wisdom to make decisions and choices based on these morals.

Aesop, a Greek slave who lived 620–564 BCE, was one of the most profound and prolific storytellers of fables. His mark on history is astonishing. His fables literally traveled around the world thousands of years ago in different countries and in different languages, delivering the messages of moral goodness. Examples might be "The Shepherd Boy and the Wolf," which teaches that no one believes a liar, even when they start telling the truth. "The Hare and the Tortoise" teaches that you can be successful by doing things slowly and steadily, rather than carelessly and quickly. And "Mercury and the Woodman" teaches that honesty is the best policy. Even today, as we see in William Bennett's "The Book of Virtues," the human soul embraces the connection to our moral goodness that connects us to one another—a goodness that simply warms our hearts and inspires us to want to be better versions of ourselves.

Parables have also been incredibly impactful in teaching moral wisdom. In the Christian Bible, Jesus traveled from town to town teaching in parables. In addition, the Book of Proverbs is a compact, concise collection that directs the reader toward moral-based living. Similarly, in the Jewish religion, the Talmud has hundreds of parables used to deliver a moral message on how to live with character.

Both fables and parables are powerful in that they touch the moral side of all of us. They present a moral situation where the virtues and vices are clear, and then communicate the value/reward for living by high moral standards. They often state the negative outcome that will come if you choose otherwise. Our human nature continues to connect to virtues and the desire for goodness and happiness.

For thousands of years, religions, cultures, and societies have been built upon morals and ethical behavior designed for the betterment of humankind. Happiness and success are achieved when these guidelines are followed. When they aren't, societies crumble, religions weaken, and cultures fall by the wayside.

Each of us has the tools (virtues) built into the fabric of our human souls to live a better quality of life with peace, happiness, and personal fulfillment. By applying excellence to your virtues, you will experience happiness and an increased quality of life. As you make these self-improvements and drive yourself toward happiness, you will in turn positively impact those around you, and they too will soon be living E.P.I.C.

Part Two
The E.P.I.C.
Virtues

CHAPTER SIX

GRATITUDE

As we express our gratitude, we must never forget that the highest appreciation is not to utter words but to live by them.

—John F. Kennedy

On the most basic level, when we think of gratitude, we often think of a common synonym: thankfulness. The words "thank you" are usually spoken with open gestures, warm smiles, and even hugs. This simple phrase tells others you value them and their actions and that you're grateful. Although brief in nature, a "thank you" can create happiness between people, both for the person expressing his or her appreciation, and for the person receiving the acknowledgment. It is joy shared.

Now consider the virtue of gratitude on a deeper level. Ask yourself, *What am I grateful for in my life?* Literally count a few things out on your fingers or jot them down. Many things will come to mind for which you are grateful. I'm willing to bet that while you were thinking of those things, you instantly felt a sense of happiness, appreciation, and perhaps even relief.

As I did this exercise, asking myself, "What in my life am I grateful for?," I noticed that my answers were at first very broad—my family, health, friends. However, when I challenged myself to be more specific, my gratitude grew as my mind captured deeper emotional connections. My answers became positive, heartwarming, and genuine. My depth of gratitude became more meaningful, making me even happier.

For example, I'm grateful to be blessed with five healthy children, a loving and dedicated husband, and my parents. Yes, these were very general and generic until I thought about everyone individually. Marisa, our eldest, was my sidekick. She helped keep the peace tending to her younger siblings with bottles, reading stories, or simply keeping them out of trouble. They adored her so much they would run to her bedroom, not mine, when they had nightmares. Gabriella took on the sporty, physical tasks like teaching the younger kids how to dive and how to ride their bikes. She was my immediate go-to helper when I needed speedy assistance if one of the twins took off in a crowd or ran toward a dangerous situation. Ellie's even keel and easygoing personality brought much peace into our lives. She was also the first to lead joyous celebrations using her natural talent of dance. Whether it was a night of laughter and dance in our kitchen or kickstarting a party at a wedding or tailgate, Ellie was our lead. As I mentioned earlier, Avery was the "happiest kid ever." She made everyone smile with her contagious smile. As the baby, she kept all of us entertained and on our toes, especially with her sneakiness like placing her chewing gum under the coffee table or stealing sugar packets from restaurant tables that we would later find under her bed. As the only boy, Anthony was the focus of a lot of attention. His compassionate nature led him to take care of Avery, his twin. We often watched him on the baby monitor as he jumped out of his crib to retrieve Avery's beloved baby blanket or pacifier after she had purposely thrown them out of her crib onto the floor. When they were toddlers, he helped her fall asleep by getting her all of her favorite stuffed animals and books.

My husband is incredibly patient, loving, and committed, even when I am not so e.p.i..c, especially when I may need forgiveness.

Gratitude can be felt at all levels of our lives. When we moved to California, we all struggled saying goodbye to our close friends. Gabriella, who was a very social rising junior in high school, had an especially hard time. She was seventeen, independent, and fully capable of traveling alone, so we told her that if we could swing it, we would work with her to plan a trip or two back to Connecticut to see her friends. She eventually made the trip, and my dear friend Michelle stepped up and stepped in for me as a mother figure. When Gabriella was in town, she went out of her way to care for her, inviting her for home-cooked meals, making sure she had rides here and there, even taking her in for a few overnights when she needed the comfort of feeling "at home." My heart was overwhelmed with gratitude for these gestures and even more so for the reason behind the gestures. By taking care of Gabriella, Michelle was taking care of me.

Gratitude begins the moment you recognize that you've received a benefit of sorts from someone or something. We can learn to be more grateful and actively incorporate a grateful mindset, or an "attitude of gratitude," throughout each day in a meaningful and beneficial way.

When you reflect back on your life to a moment when you felt a tremendous amount of gratitude, did you also feel relief? More specifically, was your memory a positive outcome from a crisis of sorts? I've certainly experienced countless of these grateful moments. If you were to ask my children a phrase that they heard me say a million times in their childhood, chances are it would be, "Thank you, Lord Jesus, that . . ." which is a genuine acknowledgement of gratitude. Most of the time, this phrase was in response to something related to safety. With five children, the number of brushes with danger is astonishing.

When Gabriella was two and a half years old, she went missing for fifteen minutes (which felt like an hour) at our YMCA, sending me and everyone around me into a widespread panic and search. I was in the locker room with Marisa after swim team practice and Gabriella was sitting on the bench next to us. In the mere five minutes I took to help Marisa change out of her wet bathing suit and into warm clothing, Gabriella was gone. Marisa and I searched the entire locker room, calling her name, asking everyone around if they had seen her. Then we searched the pool deck, the gym, the racquetball courts, even the childcare center on the other side of the building, thinking perhaps she had wandered there in search of toys. Again, she was nowhere to be found. Enough time had passed for me to call in the big guns and ask the management to lock the doors of the facility. While they were beginning this process, I ran back to the locker room, hoping she had returned. It was totally empty. Then I heard a noise that sounded like something hitting the metal lockers. I walked in the direction of the sound. No one was there. I heard the sound again, louder this time. I realized I was in the same section where we had lost Gabriella. Then I heard a voice tentatively say, "Hello?" I quickly opened the locker door and in a split second Gabriella jumped out into my arms. I will never forget how grateful I was to find her. You may think I would have been mad or frustrated, but no. I had thought the worst—she had been harmed or abducted. I thanked God endlessly that she was safe and sound—and, might I add, having fun—in that locker.

Then there was the time when Avery was a toddler and, as I leaned over her crib rail one evening to give her a final goodnight kiss, I noticed something colorful around her wrist. Curious, I pulled up her pajama sleeve and found about twenty elastic hair bands bound so tightly around her wrist they were cutting off her circulation. Her tiny hand had begun to turn blue. I think she must have seen her older, middle-school-aged sisters putting their extra elastic hair bands around their wrists for safekeeping.

The scenarios are endless. I am so grateful for all the tragic events that didn't happen.

When we begin to consider gratitude as a part of everyday life, it helps to broaden our perspective and consider the many different areas where we can be grateful. In doing so, we will be able to seek more opportunities to grow the virtue of gratitude. So, where do we begin?

It's become apparent to me that there are some general categories to consider when embracing the virtue of gratitude. First, we can be grateful for people. Not just your favorites, or those immediately close to you, but the people who have impacted you in some way along the course of your life. Perhaps someone who taught you words of wisdom or an inspirational quote that you hold dear to your heart. Is there someone who taught you a skill?

My parents are E.P.I.C. role models. As I reflect back on my own childhood, I smile with joy and happiness as a result of the gratitude I feel. I'm forever grateful for one lesson in gratitude, in particular, that my father taught me during the summer between my freshman and sophomore years in college. I was living at home and working full-time as a water safety instructor and lifeguard at a popular fitness club about thirty minutes away. This was a logistical challenge, because I shared a car with my mother. One day I left work early to take a CPR class, the last step in my lifeguard certification process. I needed the certification to continue working. As I drove down the ramp to merge onto the highway, I rolled into and through a stop sign. Two minutes later, I heard a siren and saw red lights flashing in my rear-view mirror. When the police officer asked me what I had done, I told him that I "thought" I may have failed to make a complete stop at the stop sign before entering the highway. He confirmed this and asked me why. I told him I was late for my CPR class. The officer didn't issue me a ticket because he felt that I was providing a valuable service for our community. Yes, I was very lucky and very happy. Within about ten minutes, I was back on the road and arrived at class just in the nick of time. I left with my CPR certification in hand.

Later that day, my father walked into the kitchen where I was eating dinner and asked me how my day was. I answered, "Great." He seemed a bit surprised and asked me, "So why did you get pulled over today?" My eyes popped wide open and my heart sank in shock. How on earth did he know? After all, it had happened twenty miles away from our home. I was embarrassed for a split second, then rather proudly I said, "Oh, I got pulled over for going through a stop sign. But don't worry, I got off because the officer thought I was doing a good thing by getting my CPR certification." I thought for sure my father would be happy for me. He was not. He made it clear that this was nothing to be happy or proud about. He said, "I know the exact stop sign you're talking about and it's a very dangerous spot. You could have gotten into a serious accident, killing yourself or someone else." I'd never thought of it this way. I was just grateful that I hadn't gotten a ticket. My father made sure I understood that what I should be grateful for was avoiding a serious accident that could have cost lives.

A few days later, my dad pulled into the driveway with a white Pontiac Sunbird—a car he'd purchased so that my mom and I didn't have to juggle our schedules to share a car any longer. I ran out, eager to jump behind the wheel and take it for a spin. Dad had a different plan. He asked me to get out the hose, a bucket, his special car wash soap, brushes, and rags. For the next two hours, he taught me how to properly care for the car. Together, we washed and dried the exterior surfaces. We scrubbed the wheels and sprayed them with a special product that made the rubber shine. Then we moved to the interior where we vacuumed the fabric seats and floor, wiped down the hard surfaces, scrubbed the rubber mats, and cleaned the windows inside and out.

Just when I thought we were finished, Dad said, "Get the container of Turtle car wax in the cabinet." I was a bit tired but didn't dare challenge his request. He gave me a brief lesson on how to properly wax a car, then we waxed the entire car from top to bottom. Other than the engine, we cleaned every square inch of that car.

Looking back, what I thought was a lesson on how to properly care for the car was actually much more. My father wanted me to respect the privilege he and my mother had given me with this car. He led by an example of hard work. He taught me how to be prudent by working in a stepwise fashion to avoid extra work, and he taught me to persevere working until the car looked brand new. I learned firsthand about gratitude and humility.

What he may not have realized was that this was a special bonding moment for me that I still hold near and dear to my heart. We never once talked about my mishap with the stop sign. Instead, we enjoyed our time together. I knew he had faith and trust in me. I felt his unconditional love.

Let's talk now about being grateful for our health—emotional and physical. Based on your life experiences, I'm sure you can relate good times and bad with an understanding of why emotional and physical health are so valuable. Living with physical diseases such as cancer, Lyme disease, or heart disease, or emotional diseases such as depression, anxiety, or bipolar disorder can turn your life upside down.

Many years ago, I suffered a miscarriage at the beginning of my second trimester. I had made it past the vulnerable first trimester and hit the milestone when women typically share the good news of their pregnancy with family and friends. I had eagerly awaited this moment. Then in an instant, life came tumbling down. I had lost the baby. I will always remember the simultaneous physical and emotional pain. I remember immediately wanting Marisa and Gabriella physically close to me. Whether it was snuggling on the sofa, cooking, or doing an art project, their presence made me feel blessed. This loss rekindled my deep appreciation for them in my life. Looking back now, I realize that my healing was centered around the virtue of gratitude. I was so grateful that I had children and I cherished every moment we were together. Gratitude gave me true happiness and emotional respite in my time of grief. In addition, gratitude helped heal my emotional pain as my physical body recovered.

Events are another area of our lives where we can find gratitude. You can be grateful for events you might participate in, such as a graphic design contest where your design was chosen to be the logo of a major corporation, or a robotics tournament where you won an academic scholarship. Perhaps the event was more along the lines of an experience like skydiving where you conquered your fear of heights, or when someone did something for you. How about volunteer events where you feel gratitude afterward for the experience? We also commonly see gratefulness for opportunities—being offered a new position within your company, which allows you the chance to show more of your personal strengths or perhaps increase your salary. Maybe you've been offered a role in a play that was so successful that you, your cast, and crew earned a coveted spot performing on Broadway.

Finally, we can be grateful for the natural world we live in— fresh air, clean water, a snowstorm for a snow day off from school or a fresh powdery path for skiing and sledding. The material world includes those life essentials—your home, warm clothing, and food.

Gratitude can sometimes take you by surprise. Not long ago, I attended the Challenged Athletes Foundation (CAF) Gala in San Francisco. The CAF provides opportunities and support (prosthetics and programs to support mental and physical wellness) to physically challenged people so they can continue to play sports and live an active lifestyle. This was my first time attending the event, and I didn't know what it was all about. The program began with an inspiring video followed by CAF recipients sharing their personal stories. Much to my surprise, the recipients did not talk much about themselves and how far they had come. Instead, they profusely thanked CAF for giving them the necessary equipment and opportunities to dramatically improve the quality of their lives. Some thanked CAF for giving them the will to live life boldly with their challenges. Others were grateful for the ability to keep the still-functioning parts of their bodies healthy with the proper equipment to support movement and strength, something I never even consider in the course of my day-to-day life. A young boy, perhaps ten years old, couldn't stop thanking CAF for his basketball wheelchair, without which he would not be able to play his favorite game. The normal health that so many of us take for granted was considered a privilege by the recipients and they expressed immense gratitude.

I had expected the evening to be about educating members of the audience on the mission of CAF, which is "to provide opportunities and support to people with physical challenges, so they can pursue active lifestyles through physical fitness and competitive athletics."[23] Yet, my takeaway was entirely about the immense gratitude shown by its recipients. It was this deep, heartfelt appreciation that ignited the guests with an energy of love and emotional connection more profound than could be expressed with words. Gratitude, once again, delivered a positive human impact.

THE SCIENCE OF GRATITUDE

Dr. Robert Emmons of the University of California, Davis, is considered one of the world's leading scientific experts on gratitude. He has written and edited several books and conducted extensive studies and scientific research on gratitude.

Dr. Emmons defines gratitude as having two aspects. First, "it's an affirmation of goodness. We affirm that there are good things in the world, gifts and benefits we've received." This doesn't mean that life is perfect; it doesn't ignore complaints, burdens, and hassles. But when we look at life as a whole, gratitude encourages us to identify some amount of goodness in our lives. Second, "we recognize the sources of this goodness as being outside of ourselves. . . . We acknowledge that other people— or even higher powers, if you're of a spiritual mindset—gave us many gifts, big and small, to help achieve the goodness in our lives."[24] Gratitude doesn't stem from anything we have done ourselves. Rather, it is a positive response to someone or something that has benefited us.

---

[23] Challenged Athletes Foundation, https://www.challengedathletes.org/mission-and -history/.

[24] "What Is Gratitude?," Greater Good Magazine, https://greatergood.berkeley.edu /topic/gratitude/definition.

In 2003, Dr. Emmons, along with Dr. Michael E. McCullough of the University of Miami, released the results of their research, *Counting blessings versus burdens: An experimental investigation of gratitude and subjective well-being in daily life,* which was designed to compare "the effect of a grateful outlook on psychological and physical well-being" (this quote is from the published study). Three studies were contained within this research. The first study looked at weekly journaling over a ten-week period from three different participant groups; one group journaled five things they were grateful for, the second group journaled five "hassles" in their lives, and the third group was a neutral group that recorded events and circumstances in their lives without making a negative or positive association with them. The second study had a similar design; however, journaling was daily (versus weekly) and the study was conducted over a three-week span, rather than ten weeks. In the third study, the participants (adults with neuromuscular diseases) were divided into two groups—the gratitude group and a control group— both tracking daily experiences. The results, which compared well-being before and after the studies, revealed similar outcomes across all three studies. Those participants who were a part of the grateful groups showed consistently and considerably more satisfaction with their lives, more optimism, more joy, and better physical health than the control and hassle groups.

What does this mean for you and me? Simply put, benefits. Dr. Emmons discusses gratitude as having the power to heal, to energize, and to change lives (taken from the YouTube video "The Power of Gratitude"). The benefits of gratitude far exceed the instantaneous burst of happiness and lasting joy. There are many other benefits you may be surprised to discover, all of which are supported by science-based evidence.[25]

---

[25] "31 Benefits of Gratitude: The Ultimate Science-Backed Guide," Happier Human, August 1, 2020, https://www.happierhuman.com/benefits-of-gratitude/.

PSYCHOLOGICAL BENEFITS OF GRATITUDE

- Happiness
- Reduced anxiety and stress
- Happier memories
- Less envy
- More self-esteem
- More spirituality

PHYSICAL BENEFITS OF GRATITUDE

- Increased sleep time
- Lower blood pressure
- Boosted immunity
- Increased energy
- Increase in time spent exercising

INTERPERSONAL RELATIONSHIPS AND BENEFITS OF GRATITUDE

- Increased social capital—people will like you more
- Increased friendliness
- Deeper relationships
- Enhanced careers—better networking and decision-making capabilities, increased productivity

Dr. Emmons is actively involved in the field of positive psychology and serves as the founding editor-in-chief of *The Journal of Positive Psychology*. The founder of positive psychology is generally acknowledged to be Dr. Martin Seligman. In 1998, Dr. Seligman formally introduced this concept to the American Psychological Association. He used systematic and scientific techniques to uncover why people were unhappy and pessimistic. He found that people had the ability to find and create their happiness. Positive psychology was created with the aim to "begin to catalyze a change in the focus of psychology from preoccupation only with repairing the worst things in life to also building positive qualities."[26]

Over the past twenty years, the evolution of positive psychology has gained tremendous momentum with its emphasis on pursuing a good life—a life directed with purpose, meaning, and positivity, and in which an individual is thriving. Positive psychology teaches that the things that give your life meaning and purpose are what keep you on your path to happiness. This is a shift from the more traditional abnormal psychology, where the psychotherapy approach is to uncover the cause of unhappiness and work to resolve that situation, with the belief that happiness will return as this process evolves. Today, we see these different approaches used separately and in tandem.

What's the connection? Gratitude and the field of positive psychology both focus on an overall meaningful, positive outlook on life. There is a long-term, lasting effect of joy, optimism, and satisfaction with and throughout life common to both. Many of the benefits of gratitude overlap with those of positive psychology and the overarching goal—the pursuit of happiness, much like choosing to be E.P.I.C.

Positive psychology appears to support my theory of E.P.I.C. living. The field of positive psychology "at the individual level . . . is about positive traits: the capacity for love and vocation, courage, interpersonal skill, aesthetic sensibility, perseverance, forgiveness, originality, future mindedness, spirituality,

---

[26] Martin E. P Seligman and Mihaly Csikszentmihalyi, "Positive Psychology: An Introduction," *American Psychological Association*.

high talent, and wisdom. At the group level, it is about civic virtues and the institutions that move individuals toward better citizenship: responsibility, nurturance, altruism, civility, moderation, and work ethic."[27] Positive psychology encourages you to shift from living an ordinary life to living an extraordinary life, a more fulfilling life with increased happiness. Dr. Seligman coauthored a book with Christopher Peterson, *Character Strengths and Virtues: A Handbook and Classification,* because "good character was so consistently and strongly linked to lasting happiness."[28]

Integrate the virtue of gratitude in your daily life. Actively reflect on what you are grateful for. Keep a daily, weekly, or even a monthly journal. Make it a topic of dinner conversation more often than once a year at Thanksgiving. When you begin to take notice of the opportunities that surround you to be grateful, you will see your life in a brighter light. Developing an attitude of gratitude will definitely increase your happiness and success and will have a positive impact on those around you.

GRATITUDE IN A PANDEMIC

As I write this book, we are in the midst of the horrific COVID-19 pandemic, a time of uncertainty, fear, and loss. How could it be that I am feeling deeply grateful? Because when life seemingly couldn't get worse, I am finding comfort and strength by focusing on what I have to be grateful for, instead of on what I don't. This is gratitude.

Today, we are all experiencing the emotional pains of grief and loss. We've lost loved ones, jobs, income, health. Lifelong

---

[27] Martin E. P. Seligman and Mihaly Csikszentmihalyi, "Positive Psychology: An Introduction," *American Psychological Association* 55, no. 1 (2000): 5–14, https://doi.org/10.1037/0003-066X.55.1.5.

[28] "Martin Seligman & Positive Psychology," Pursuit of Happiness, https://www.pursuit-of-happiness.org/history-of-happiness/martin-seligman-psychology/.

careers have been forever changed, weddings and graduations have been postponed or modified; the list feels endless. Gratitude is one of many ways to cope with this stressful time.

I find myself constantly changing gears, strategizing to find solutions to adapt to loss. Through it all, I have a new definition of what's essential in my life. I've placed a much higher value on many things I had previously taken for granted.

For example, let's start with the "little" things. Who knew butter, yeast, and yes, toilet paper, would ever be such valued items? And bleach? I was so grateful when I received a case of three jugs of bleach I had ordered on Amazon that I christened them "liquid gold." I opened the boxes like it was Christmas morning. As my supply began to run low, I rationed and was even more grateful for the little that remained.

What has become most impactful are the big things in life I have taken for granted. My habitual, quick goodnight kiss for my children became a kiss followed by a hug with a meaningful pause, a deep sense of gratitude. I realize how fortunate I am to be able to share resources and help others, ranging from making home-made hand sanitizer and face masks to financial support. I've used the virtue of gratitude to draw strength during this pandemic.

A useful way to practice gratitude is to make lists. Here are a few things on my COVID-19 gratitude list today. I am:

- Grateful for my family and friends: I feel better immediately upon hearing their voices, reading their texts, and in some cases seeing their smiling faces on a drive-by visit. I am even grateful for the painful two-hour phone conversation I had with a relative of my husband's whose sister had been hospitalized with COVID-19. I feel comfort that she and I could connect and support one another. I began creating friend groups on social media platforms with the intention to check in from time to time to see that everyone was okay. Much to my surprise, this quickly turned into support sessions sharing survival tips. We've been introduced to a new family game, Codenames; a new no-fail homemade bread recipe from the *New York Times* cooking app; and using spray bottles designed for cooking oils as spray bottles for our hand sanitizer.

- Grateful for the people on the frontlines: I feel fortunate and a bit guilty to be on the receiving end of their dedication and hard work. Emily and Katherine, dear family friends, are nurses in hospitals in New York and Connecticut. At one point, Emily's job was to sit at the bedside of patients and comfort them as they were dying of COVID-19. This task is completely unfathomable to me. Katherine works in the ER, the first point of contact for COVID-19 patients. I'm also grateful for the men and women working through the night to stock the shelves of grocery stores, pharmacies, and other essential businesses. What about the thousands of FedEx, UPS, and USPS personnel whose physical workload increased so much with all of the e-commerce deliveries?

- Grateful for "virtual" life: We've lost in-person human connection during quarantine, and we've seen faces via Zoom, FaceTime, Skype, and other platforms. I hold very near and dear to my heart the image of seeing my parents huddled close to one another sitting on their leather sofa so their faces could fit together on their FaceTime screen. They were wearing brave, optimistic smiles on the outside, letting me know they were healthy, but I could see the concern they held on the inside. Let's not forget the incredible value these platforms have given us in our "remote" lives, keeping students learning, businesses open, and people able to connect with their healthcare providers.

Although this is a short list of what I am grateful for during these unprecedented times, I do immediately feel happier after writing it down. Gratitude has helped me fend off some of the empty feelings of loss and the overarching sadness and stress during this pandemic.

BENEFITS OF GRATITUDE

- Gratitude increases overall happiness, optimism, and positivity.
- Gratitude makes you humbler and more appreciative, approachable, and compassionate.
- Gratitude embraces generosity and reduces materialism.
- Gratitude is good for your physical health and has been shown to improve sleep, strengthen our immune system, decrease blood pressure, and increase energy levels.

EVERYDAY EXCELLENCE IN GRATITUDE

- Speak it!
  - Add key "gratitude phrases" in your daily life. Shoot for a goal of using phrases like the ones below three times a day.
    - "I am so appreciative you helped me with. . . ."
    - "Thankfully I . . . "
    - "How fortunate is it that. . . ."
  - Mealtime conversation. The spirit of the Thanksgiving holiday should be celebrated all year long. At meals, or while relaxing outside near the fire pit, go around the

group and share the "highs and lows" of everyone's day. Be sure to find the silver lining of the "lows" to help cultivate a grateful mindset.

- Write it!
  - ◆ Gratitude journal:
    - → Keep a journal on your nightstand and jot a few notes before you turn out the lights. Begin with general categories like people, places, things, and events, then try to narrow these down with specific instances: from friends and family to strangers that have lent you a hand, from spaces where you relax and unwind to places you've visited for the first time that have left you in awe, from everyday items that you may take for granted to unique gifts, from activities that have become daily routine to that special event you've been planning for all year long. Write one thing in each category every night. Research shows writing in a gratitude journal before going to bed makes for a better night's sleep.
    - → "Thank you" technology. With the accessibility of texting and email, you can easily send a quick, heartfelt thank-you. When someone sends you a gift, take a selfie with the gift and text this with your "thank you." Or maybe a send a picture wearing the new ski hat your friend gave you a few months back with a caption "thinking of you, thank you again for my warm hat."
- Letters as gifts. Instead of buying gifts, consider writing a meaningful note or letter expressing how grateful you are to have that someone special in your life. Begin with "thank you for being YOU" and describe how they make you feel, how they have helped you, and what makes them so special.

- Find the silver lining. Cultivate this concept in your everyday life. Put a Post-it note on your refrigerator with the phrase "Find the Silver Lining" as a daily reminder to keep an optimistic outlook on life.
- Extend appreciation. Be sure to recognize those who played a role in helping you with your achievements. Whether it was your best friend's parent who gave you a ride home from school every day so you could go to work to earn money to buy a car, or maybe it was a friend who submitted your résumé giving you the opportunity to land the job of a lifetime. It's never too late to send a note recognizing them for their efforts. Consider the concept "had it not been for you ..." Give a public recognition to someone you're grateful for, like a "shoutout" or a high-five the next time you're at a large gathering to the person who gave you that hot stock tip that doubled your investment. If you have social media accounts, consider posting a picture to publicly thank the person(s) who helped make a dream a reality, like a selfie of you celebrating the purchase of your first car with a caption #WithYourHelp (name).

HUMILITY

There is a universal respect and even admiration for those who are humble and simple by nature, and who have absolute confidence in all human beings irrespective of their social status.

—Nelson Mandela

All too often, the term "humble" has been associated with being meek or lowly. As a result, the virtue of humility has fallen by the wayside. After all, how many of us want to be meek or lowly? I sure don't. I want to have impact.

In this way, humility is misunderstood and underused. It's time to demystify the assumption that humility is a liability and to see humility for what it truly is: an enormous asset. There are many ways in which humility is powerful, not pitiful, not the least of which is how it elevates the level of excellence in your character.

So what exactly is humility? C.S. Lewis said, "Humility is not thinking less of yourself, it's thinking of yourself less." The humble person is modest in their self-importance (not to be confused with self-worth, or how we value ourselves) and quick to be interested in others and their perspectives. Humble people are true to who they are, their strengths, and their weaknesses. Humility enables you to be more emotionally grounded in the world. Writing in *Psychology Today*, Dr. Karl Albrecht references humility as being about *emotional neutrality.* "It involves an experience of growth in which you no longer need to put yourself above others, but you don't put yourself below them either. Everyone is your peer—from the most 'important' person to the least. You're just as valuable as every other human being on the planet, no more and no less."[29]

Humility keeps us open to learning and lets us embrace the understanding that we will experience failure or frustration, which will only help us grow. It encompasses an appreciation of lessons learned.

I experienced tremendous humility when we moved our family to California from the east coast. When we arrived, I confidently hit the ground running, registering the children in schools, on sports teams, in clubs, and with many different

---

[29] Karl Albrecht, PhD, "The Paradoxical Power of Humility," *Psychology Today*, January 8, 2018.

medical practices, such as pediatricians, primary care physicians, dentists, and so on. I quickly realized that the learning curve to recreate my family's support system was astronomical.

Looking back, I hadn't realized that my knowledge base was built over twenty years from living in the same town. Back home, I was a guru on children's activities, sporting teams, doctors, schools, restaurants, and so on. Let's say I was very comfortable doing the talking, and rarely did the asking. When we moved to California, I didn't even consider for a moment that I would be clueless. I just assumed it would be easy to mainstream my children into their new lives. Wrong! I had to ask strangers for help all day, every day, for months, while simultaneously making endless mistakes. Simple things I took for granted were now ordeals and disasters that derailed me daily. So where does humility come in? It rescued me. I needed to let go of being a know-it-all about the intricacies of managing the lives of children. I recognized that the lack of knowledge, the mistakes, and the failures were all on me. Without even being aware of it, I had moved to California with a lot of pride.

For example, when we lived in Connecticut, I rarely needed to use my car's GPS. I could drive to a destination, arrive, and completely forget the trip there because it was just second nature. In California, I used my GPS constantly for years. I would get lost going to the grocery store, taking the kids to their new schools, finding banks—everywhere. One night I had to drive to the nearby ER with my daughter, and yet again, I took a wrong turn and made the trip much longer than it needed to be. To make matters worse, I found myself consistently late for appointments and events. And for someone like me who is early for everything, this was a tough one. Eventually, it seemed like I began every email and every conversation with, "I am sorry, I just moved here. Can you . . .?" I even coined the phrase, "I am mistaking my way through." All of this sounds rather pessimistic, but I didn't mean it that way. I wasn't afraid to make mistakes—I learned, and I pressed on. I was finding success along a different path. It was refreshing, invigorating, and yes, very humbling. It was a great personal growth experience that I now cherish.

During this time, I learned that pride can be seen in two opposing lights, positively or negatively. It's positive when we respect or honor someone. The phrase "I am proud of you" builds someone up by making them feel worthy, capable, and loved. It's okay to be proud if you just won the NYC marathon; you worked hard to earn that coveted spot. It's not okay if you brag, boast, and think you're better than everyone else because of this win. That would be pride as a negative—acting arrogant and conceited. In order to avoid pride in a negative context, we act with humility.

Humility is giving of yourself and serving others for their benefit, not yours. Sometimes it means putting the needs of others before your own. A great example of humility can be seen in the heroic acts of service when tragedy strikes. We see this in our families, communities, and in acts of public service. Celebrities and other notable people in the public eye have set excellent examples of humility. After Hurricane Harvey struck Houston in August of 2017, NFL superstar and Houston native JJ Watt immediately began working to help his fellow Houstonians. He led relief efforts on the ground, distributed supplies, and created a fund that raised $41.6 million (the largest crowd-sourced fundraiser in history). Diana, Princess of Wales, frequently visited people suffering in hospitals, third-world countries, and organizations that supported relief efforts. She genuinely connected with the common person by reflecting and embracing the virtue of humility. Mother Teresa dedicated her life to service for the poor and destitute around the world. She, too, was a living example of the virtue of humility. But you don't need to be a world-class athlete or a princess to help others with humility. You can begin with everyday acts of kindness.

Charity organizations are excellence applied to the virtue of humility. I have been forever humbled by the work of Scott Harrison in the creation of Charity: Water, an organization based out of New York City whose mission is to solve the world's unclean water crisis. While spending two years on a hospital ship off the coast of Liberia, Scott witnessed firsthand the extreme physical and emotional suffering directly related to unclean water. Since 2006, Harrison and Charity: Water have supplied clean water to more than ten million people. His passion and drive to help the underserved made me take a hard look at my life and ask myself where I was making a difference for humanity.

Humility is also being able to admit you're human and make mistakes. Sometimes you need to say you're sorry; sometimes you must take responsibility for your mistakes. This is not a sign of weakness, but a reflection of strength and courage.

We've all had to apologize for something at some time in our lives. I encourage you to continue to do so. It's humbling and healthy for both the sender and the receiver. Apologies show your imperfections, show that you care, and offer a pathway for the ultimate goal of happiness.

Taking responsibility is an act of bravery and humility. Alcoholics Anonymous is an international fellowship of people who struggle with addiction to alcohol. The premise on the road to recovery begins with an individual admitting they have a problem with alcohol and, by doing so, taking responsibility for their problem. Meetings are held in a group setting where individuals openly admit and accept their problem with alcohol as they share their personal journey of ups and downs. The member support system in Alcoholics Anonymous is a crucial component on the road to recovery. The humbling first step of admission is the beginning of a journey toward happiness and personal fulfillment.

It takes humility to be able to receive honest, and perhaps unwanted, feedback. The best example is constructive criticism. Although I am working on this skill, I still have to take a deep breath when someone points out something that I have done wrong. I typically take offense at such feedback and feel the need to defend myself. I have to consciously ask myself if there is truth in what someone else is pointing out about my behavior, my perspective, or my actions. In other words, how am I at fault or wrong? I can attest from a variety of life experiences where I have been faced with the discomfort of constructive criticism, it's always benefited me to ask myself these questions. The feelings of happiness and success are often delayed, but in the end, growing in humility has allowed me to be open to the change that I need to grow into a better person. I've even embraced a more positive phrase: constructive advice.

LEADERSHIP AND THE VIRTUE OF HUMILITY

What does it take to be a successful leader? This question has been widely studied and researched in history, in business, and in pursuit of personal advancement. You could argue that humility would never be a character trait of a leader; however, that's not true. An enormous amount of information supports the importance of humility in being an excellent leader.

Humility carries with it qualities of trust and respect, which are crucial in a leadership role. In coordinating and working with people, the nature of leadership itself is enhanced by humility because of the value placed on others' viewpoints and opinions.

Humble leaders look to their peers for new ideas and fresh perspectives. Humility also allows leaders to gain merit without feeling a sense of superiority.

In *Humility: The Secret Ingredient of Success*, Pat Williams and Jim Denney discuss traits of a humble leader: they learn (listen to ideas of coworkers and don't assume they have all of the answers); they are servants (they care for their people); they respect the individual (help people reach their goals); they surround themselves with smart people; they surrender control (empower their subordinates to make decisions); they demonstrate genuine empathy and caring for subordinates; and they treat their customers like royalty.[30]

In the world of corporate business, we see the benefits a humble CEO can have on their company. One study investigating market performance of 122 companies with humble CEOs found that these firms performed better because financial analysts tended to set lower market expectations, increasing the probability they would outperform those expectations. And they do.[31]

Another study of 105 firms in the computer and software industry found that humble CEOs built integrative top management teams that had better collaboration, made more decisions jointly, and had a greater shared vision. There was also a lower pay disparity between the CEO and their top management team, which further enhances top management team integration. Finally, humble CEOs contribute indirectly to the pursuit of operational *ambidextrous strategies*, which is when an organization

---

[30] Pat Williams and Jim Denney, *Humility: The Secret Ingredient of Success* (Barbour Publishing, 2016).

[31] Oleg V. Petrenko, Federico Aime, Tessa Recendes, and Jeffrey A. Chandler, "The case for humble expectations: CEO humility and market performance," Wiley Online Library, July 22, 2019, https://onlinelibrary.wiley.com/doi/abs/10.1002/smj.3071.

efficiently manages day-to-day business and simultaneously has the adaptability to handle tomorrow's business demands.[32]

Leadership is embedded in the fabric of military establishments. The importance of excellent leadership is crucial to the success of military operations. *8 Leadership Lessons from the Military,* published in *Forbes,* lists effective leadership skills contributed by eight different military leaders, which I paraphrase here. Effective leaders embrace change by asking questions with an open mind; they lead with empathy; they are connectors; they don't take purpose for granted; they believe that inclusiveness is key to solving complex problems; they focus not just on results but on how you get those results; they believe that a strong culture requires a servant's heart, good bedside manner, and the Socratic method; and they believe that building a team requires trust and communication. At least six of these are characteristics of humility![33]

Legendary businessman and billionaire, Warren Buffett, who with all of his wealth has lived in a modest home for nearly fifty years, still drives his own car. Not only has Mr. Buffett given away a great portion of his wealth for philanthropic purposes, he is passionate about being charitable. Three of his best pieces of advice for entrepreneurs are to develop excellent character and habits, stay out of debt, and be *humble.*[34] How remarkable is this!

---

[32] Amy Y Ou, David A. Waldman, and Suzanne J. Peterson, "Do Humble CEOs Matter? An Examination of CEO Humility and Firm Outcomes," *Journal of Management,* https://createvalue.org/wp-content/uploads/Do-Humble-CEOs-Matter.pdf.

[33] Sanyin Siang, "8 Leadership Lessons from the Military," Forbes, March 31, 2019, https://www.forbes.com/sites/sanyinsiang/2019/03/31/8-leadership-lessons-from-the-military/?sh=2e2f788e2210.

[34] Matt Wilson, "What is Warren Buffett's Best Advice for Young Professionals?," Under 30 CEO, September 26, 2013, https://www.under30ceo.com/what-is-warren-buffetts-best-advice-for-young-professionals/.

As we have seen, there is much more to humility than meets the eye. There is no denying the impact that humility can deliver on the E.P.I.C. promise of happiness and success.

BENEFITS OF HUMILITY

- Humility is a powerful attribute, especially for those in leadership roles (parent, teacher, coach, CEO, physician, etc.).
- Humility reduces insecurities arising from comparing yourself with others and prejudices toward others.
- Humility improves personal relationships with increased compassion and the intentions to resolve conflicts with others.

EVERYDAY EXCELLENCE IN HUMILITY

- Grow in humility.
  - Get to really know others when meeting for the first time. Ask questions to learn about them and refrain from talking too much about yourself. Think of the acronym "LIFE" and ask questions to learn where they live "L" (which town, or which street they live on if you're from the same town); their interests "I" (extracurricular activities, clubs, or hobbies); their family "F" (do they have children or siblings, where did they grow up); and their employment "E" (what do they do for a living).
  - Roll up your sleeves and help out. The next time you go to a friend's house for dinner, take the initiative to thoroughly clean up the dinner dishes and the kitchen, or an overused powder room you pass by on the way to taking out the garbage. Being a guest doesn't mean all of the work should be left for the host.

- Don't be pride-filled.
  - ♦ Accept correction with poise. We know it's not easy to hear correction from others, but learning to do so without feeling the need to defend ourselves will help us grow in humility. It allows us to take a moment to think about what is really being said. My children are old enough to correct my faults, one of which is being too loud. The first time they told me I immediately said, or shall I say yelled, "No I'm not." After a few repeat instances, I grew to accept what they were saying as truth and now, I thank them for letting me know whenever I am doing this. Think constructive advice, not constructive criticism.
  - ♦ Admit your mistakes and ask for forgiveness. We all know no one is perfect and no one knows everything. The next time you're late for an important event like a wedding rehearsal (or worse, the actual wedding), be humble and apologize for your tardiness and ask for forgiveness. It's as simple as, "Please forgive my tardiness, I am so sorry."
- Ask for feedback and seek critique. There is always room for improvement. Before you submit a proposal to win a bid on landing your next client, or résumé for a new job, ask someone to proofread your work. You will surely feel relief when a fresh set of eyes spots silly grammatical errors.

CHAPTER SEVEN

FAITH

Faith is taking the first step even when you don't see the whole staircase.

—Martin Luther King, Jr.

FAITH is *believing* in the right thing. It is a confidently held belief, a trust in someone or something that you cannot see, but which you are hoping for. Faith is a driving force in our human nature that allows us and empowers us to believe in ourselves, others, and the world as we choose to see it.

Two key components of faith help us gain a better understanding of how it impacts our lives: hope and conviction. In the Old Testament book of Hebrews, 11:1, we find an excellent description of faith that hits on hope and conviction. "Now faith is confidence in what we hope for and assurance about what we do not see."[35] In other words, faith is a deep-seated knowing in your heart of hearts, that what you believe is real and can be trusted as you cast your sights into the future. Faith

---

[35] NIV 11:1

is believing without seeing, so that maybe someday we will see what we were believing in. Faith is also perseverance through the hardships of life and its journey. I have faith that as you work through this book, you will gain an understanding of the impact character plays in your life and on the lives of those around you. While I may never know for sure, I truly believe e.p.i.c will deliver much happiness and personal fulfillment in your life.

The term "conviction" locks in the commitment that faith is built upon. You have to be truly convicted in what you're believing. This is important. There's no second-guessing; it's pure belief. There is an underlying, unwavering strength. It's not simply a certainty, it's a stronghold. For example, "There is no doubt in my mind that what I am sharing with you will positively impact your life and I am fully convinced that there is no downside."

Joel Osteen, pastor and author, said, "I wouldn't ever say if you're having tough times, there must be something wrong with you or your attitude. Life's a fight. It's a good fight of faith." He is not only discussing faith, but the *conviction* you have in your faith. It's easy to have faith and feel confident when times are good, but when times aren't so good, true faith is the driving force that helps you when you need it most. This is when the phrase "a test of faith" comes into play—when you need to hold on tight in the face of obstacles that come your way.

I have said "Dig deep!" many times to myself, my children, and my friends. This phrase reminds me that I have both the ability to persevere and the faith that I can do so. In these moments, the virtues of faith and perseverance converge. Faith, however, comes first, and it's believing that "I can" that allows me to persevere.

At the end of every spring semester in college, my daughters find themselves running on fumes as they approach final exams.

They experience burnout on a variety of issues, from academics, to time away from home, to the stress of getting ready for upcoming internships. We openly talk about "digging deep" to cross the finish line and complete another academic semester and that when they do, they will experience no regrets and all reward. They need to be reminded that they will make it through, just as they have every other year. They just need to hear it to believe it. And when they *believe* it, it'll happen.

Take a moment and think back to a time when someone believed in you when you were having a hard time or found an obstacle in your way. It may have been a teacher, coach, family member, friend, even perhaps a stranger who encouraged you and believed in you when you needed it the most. Perhaps it was the first time you rode a bike, or swam independently, or excelled in a hard class—someone guided you because they had faith in you.

My husband often talks about Sister Patricia, a Catholic nun who saw something special in a misbehaving young boy with poor grades. She realized that he was very bright, but not all that interested in school. So, Sister Patricia came up with an incentive plan (candy!) for a competitive boy. She set academic goals and clever challenges that engaged Anthony by making learning more fun and showing him he really was an "A" student. To this day, he credits Sister Patricia as one of his influencers. She *believed* he could achieve academic success, and her belief helped him believe in himself.

A similar theme is found in *The Little Engine That Could* by Watty Piper, which is a family favorite of ours. This children's book tells the tale of a little steam engine facing what seem to be insurmountable obstacles. She convinces herself that if she perseveres, gives it her all, and doesn't give up, she can defy the odds and complete her journey up and over the mountain and down the other side. The story has become famous for the phrase "I think I can, I think I can"—a friendly reminder of two things: first, listen to what you're telling yourself and second, believe in yourself. Not many readers are aware of the sequel to Piper's book, *I Knew You Could* by Craig Dorfman. It's full of wisdom about what to expect on your journey through life, and is written from the experiences of the little engine. It reflects the faith we need to carry us through our lives.

The story begins by drawing from the little engine's successful experience in *believing* and persevering to get up and over the mountain. It then teaches readers about the different tracks in life and choosing one that's right for you, the reality of planned and unplanned stops, the importance of being steady during dark, scary tunnels until you travel through them into the light again, and all the people you meet along the way. The final page wraps up with this advice: "Because figuring things out on your own helps you grow. Just trust in yourself!"[36]

TYPES OF FAITH: RELIGION-BASED AND NON-RELIGION-BASED

When the majority of us hear the term "faith," we make an association with religion or spirituality. This is understandable, as faith is the foundation upon which most religions are built. In fact, approximately 84 percent of the world population associates itself with religious faith.[37]

Religion-based faith fills our human soul on a spiritual level. It is also a point of connection for groups of people who may

---

[36] Craig Dorfman, *I Knew You Could: A Book for All the Stops in Your Life* (Platt and Munk, 2015).

[37] "The Global Religious Landscape," Pew Research Center, December 18, 2012, https://www.pewforum.org/2012/12/18/global-religious-landscape-exec/.

or may not know one another, yet unite under one common set of beliefs. I am a Christian and, no matter where I travel, when I find a church for Mass, I am in the presence of people who share my core beliefs. This is empowering. Even with the variety of religions across the globe, the fundamental concept of faith connects everyone. The difference is found in the variation of what different religions define as their core beliefs.

Faith isn't always about religion. Non-religion-based faith is the basic trust or wholehearted believing in someone or something. We see this faith in terms of personal productivity (goals and achievements) and interpersonal relationships (support, inspiration, and love) in our day-to-day lives. In this context, we use faith all day, every day.

From as far back as I can remember, my mother has been an incredible person of faith, both religiously and secularly. She approaches life this way because it works. As a devout Catholic, my mother has used her religious faith to navigate all aspects of her life. She created an atmosphere in our home, perhaps without even knowing it, that relied on faith. Every night as she tucked me into bed, she sat on the edge of the mattress and recited prayers with me until I memorized them. She was kind with my frequent word slip-ups, smiling warmly with patience and understanding. And just before we would wrap up our prayer practice, we would express our thankfulness for everyone in our lives. She was instilling gratitude.

My mother had a few sayings that ring through my childhood memories. "God give me strength," "And this too shall pass," and "I'll pray"—all faith-based, all with the intention to get through a challenging time. To this day, whenever one of our children is going through a tough time, she will lean toward them and say, "I'll pray for you." Now they ask her to pray for them when they're feeling a bit weak in faith.

Her secular faith is strong as well. As a nurse, she values the importance of physical and mental well-being. Because she saw firsthand the negative effects that poor decisions can have on health, she truly believes in the importance of proactively taking excellent care of herself. She has always kept up with the latest health-related information, with her favorites being the Harvard Health Letter and the Mayo Clinic Health Letter. Now in her late seventies, she hasn't skipped a beat with her belief and faith in prioritizing her wellness. She is physically active with routine walks and several rounds of golf per week. She keeps mentally acute by participating in a mahjong club and reading historical novels, and exercises her spiritual muscles by belonging to a bible study group and volunteering in her church community.

The virtue of faith, of truly believing, can be seen in our relationships with spouses, partners, family, and friends. Faith is the powerful force that binds and connects us to one another much like love. A faith-filled relationship works in synergy and continues to grow over time.

One of the purest examples of faith is that which a young child has in their parent or guardian. The term "childlike faith" embodies the pure and innocent view a child has of the world, where they have no worries or concerns because they truly *believe* they are taken care of. Children are filled with trust, innocence, wonder, forgiveness, and openness. Most children also tend to see the good in others and are surprised to learn that there are people in this world who will actively hurt others (bullies, thieves, etc.). Children are believers and are comforted in the happiness that their faith returns to them.

Another great example is seen in the exchange of marriage vows. These vows are built upon both religious and secular faith in the present moment that extends through a future shared life. The future always has uncertainties, yet they become manageable when bound with the security found in faith. It is interesting to note that the majority of religious vows spanning a broad base of religions include the commitment to stand strong during difficult times. This acknowledges not only the future unknown, but the reality that life can and will bring trials. The power of faith will pull you through these difficult times.

Just a short time ago, my brother-in-law passed away at the young age of forty-seven. It was sudden and an absolute shock to our entire family. Tom was the fun uncle who always goofed around, laughing and giggling. He would stop everything to play with his nieces and nephews, doing silly things kids can't always get away with when their parents are around. He had a mischievous side that the kids eagerly sought out every time they were together.

At the time of Tom's death, our kids were at an age where they questioned death and wondered what happened afterward. I have always held a personal and very strong *belief* in Heaven and the pure peace and happiness that defines heavenly life. I talked to them and described this, but it seemed like they just heard my words, nodding their head in agreement while not really buying into what I was saying.

At this point, I decided to share with them my experience seeing Tom after he had passed. I told them how I arrived at his hospital room about two hours after he had died. I had to walk around the foot of his bed of his bed to see his face. In that moment I saw the most beautiful, peaceful smile permanently on his face—the same smile that put so many smiles on our faces. There was no doubt in my mind this was his first and lasting experience with Heaven. He was at peace and he was definitely happy.

No one can predict the future, but my faith and *belief* keep me continuously driving forward. I plant the seed of faith in myself and in others. When you truly *believe* in someone, they can feel your power of faith. The emotional contagion is immediate. Faith in others encourages them to *believe* in themselves when they otherwise might not be able to do so. It's a connection that keeps them inspired and empowered to move forward in whatever they are striving for.

Consider, for instance, a family member or friend who has just received a cancer diagnosis. This person is most likely experiencing a heavy dose of anxiety and fear. You have the ability to lessen the fear and anxiety for both of you by purposely embracing the faith, whether religious or secular, needed to *believe* this disease can be defeated. You can absolutely step in and step up, fueling them with the faith necessary to strive for health and wellness. In this way, you join them emotionally in their physical fight.

Faith reflects an enduring personal commitment regardless of circumstances. Faith is resilient and helps you withstand life's challenges. Can you call to mind a time when you or someone you know lost faith or stopped believing in a situation or person? That loss of faith certainly didn't help cheer anyone up and might have made the situation worse. Having faith in someone gives them strength, while removing your faith weakens them.

My husband will always stand out in my life as "that" person whose radical faith and *belief* in me during a time when I had little, if any, faith in myself, profoundly changed the course of my life.

Before we began to officially date, we were great, longtime friends. We met in middle school and shared many of the same classes and friend groups all the way through high school. Then we each set off to college, keeping in touch with an occasional letter. He went to an amazing school where he grew and flourished, receiving accolades in academics and athletics. I was in awe of his success. I knew how hard he worked for his achievements in high school and he carried that drive over to college.

I, on the other hand, had a challenging time with the transition to college academically, socially, and emotionally. I transferred colleges not once, but twice. Although I finally found a school that I loved and a major I was passionate about, when I looked at myself, I saw failure. Worse, I felt it. I was afraid to fail again, so I hovered around the safe zone of mediocrity. I lacked confidence, accepted my embarrassing college journey, and focused on simply keeping afloat and staying on track.

By the end of the summer going into our senior year of college, we had been dating for a few months and our conversations had become more meaningful. One night, we were sitting at the kitchenette table in my studio apartment having a heart-to-heart about life. Then, for whatever reason, I gathered up the nerve to open up about the struggles I had during my first few years in college. I was afraid he would think I was a loser and a failure. I distinctly recall immense fear that he might not want to continue to date if I said something that he found unappealing. But he sat there fully attentive, listening to every word, without a flinch. My heart sank. I thought for sure it was over because he seemed emotionless. Instead, he looked me straight in the eye, nodding his head with complete unconditional understanding. Suddenly, I could see and feel in his body language that he didn't judge me. He was accepting me fully.

He told me not to let my college experience define me and to leave it in the past. He told me I was crazy for thinking I was anything less than the person I had been in high school—confident, capable, happy, and successful. He lit a spark in me that allowed me to think differently.

His belief in me was so unexpected and so unwavering that he was able to emotionally change my mindset. I immediately felt an agreement with his viewpoint. He accepted me for being me. He planted the seed of faith in me that I hadn't had for years. To this day, I will always be humbled and grateful for the gift of faith he gave me that night in the kitchenette of my apartment. "If it's to be, it's up to me" is one of the most impactful quotes he lives by and I am a living testimony of being the recipient of his emotional contagion.

Take a moment and think about how faith is part of your life. Can you have a greater amount of faith in yourself, in your goals and aspirations, or in others? Now consider applying excellence to faith in your life. When others see your passionate *belief* in someone or something, they will find your energy and enthusiasm contagious and empowering.

I like to say, "If you believe it, you will receive it." When you apply excellence to what you believe in, you will shape your faith with additional power and precision. Remember that faith can be religion-based but also can be without a religious underpinning. It's all faith.

BENEFITS OF FAITH

- Faith and belief provide a driving force that carry you through life in good times and in bad.
- Faith is believing in and expecting the best. It's a source of optimism, positivity, and confidence.
- Nonreligious faith embraces the positive power of truly believing.
- Religious faith fills and soothes our spiritual soul with vitality, peace, and happiness.
- Belief and faith give us meaning and purpose in our lives.

EXCELLENCE APPLIED TO FAITH

- Persistently optimistic: Develop a positive mindset. Make it a daily practice to believe in yourself, your abilities, your strengths with a "can do" attitude and positive affirmations. Every time a negative thought comes to mind, offset it with three positive thoughts. The next time you begin a new job search, shoot for the stars. Do not begin with "I am not qualified" or "I don't have enough experience"; instead *believe* in yourself with positive affirmations like "this may be a stretch, but I know I can do this" or "when I land this job, I will exceed expectations." For an added punch, practice speaking positive affirmations like these out loud in the mirror or while driving around town.

- Speak it!
  - ♦ What you say to yourself is very impactful. Engage a buddy who will help you to eliminate negative self-talk. Every time this person hears you use the phrase, "There is no way I can ...," "I can't....," or "They will never ..." you owe this person a dollar! Then reframe each of these thoughts based on belief. There is an app called "I am" that contains positive affirmations that you can customize based on categories like personal growth, new beginnings, and self-love, to name a few. Then create settings to send push notifications as a reminder to believe in yourself.
  - ♦ Encourage others. Take the time to encourage others by helping them through challenges. Believing in others not only helps them to believe in themselves, but also helps the power of faith to grow in you. Phrases like "I believe in you" and "you always finish what you start" or "you have what it takes" are surprisingly empowering for others to hear, and it promotes an attitude of self-belief that is contagious.
  - ♦ Be determined. Remind yourself of this simple proverb, "where there is a will, there is a way." If you really

want to begin living e.p.i.c, you will get creative and take measures into your own hands to make it happen. Maybe you will take notes and annotate this book, or create a new "e.p.i.c" journal to jot down and celebrate your e.p.i.c moments. Perhaps you will use Post-it notes with quotes and fresh ideas as friendly reminders to live E.P.I.C. For those who *will* live E.P.I.C., there are endless *ways*.

- Spiritual growth: For those who are looking to grow their lives more spiritually, find a strategy that will work best for this kind of personal growth. Perhaps that is joining a weekly or monthly bible study, or maybe there is a local house of worship where you can volunteer once a month teaching in the youth program about your beliefs and customs. Search through the app store on your phone to find daily devotional apps that you can download so you can wake up every morning with an inspirational notification to start your day. Perhaps you want to broaden your understanding of religion in general. Check out "The Story of God with Morgan Freeman" on Netflix for an overview of the beliefs in various religions throughout the world.

Having faith and believing in yourself and your abilities is a crucial component of the value of the virtue of faith. Fueling the virtue of faith with excellence can and will have a positive impact on your life and the lives of those around you. Faith allows you to believe that the virtues that exist in all of us are for our good and the good of others. Faith provides the backbone to all virtues in this book. Faith is the foundation in *believing* in E.P.I.C.

CHAPTER EIGHT

HONESTY

No legacy is as rich as honesty.

—William Shakespeare

Benjamin Franklin said it best: "Honesty is the best policy." If you're nodding your head in agreement, then you understand the value of the virtue of honesty. You may appreciate the positive impact truthfulness can have on your life. Or perhaps you're agreeing because you're thinking of a time when dishonesty caused a lot of chaos. Maybe at some point you distorted some facts just a teensy-weensy bit to give you an edge, such as exaggerating an illness or omitting a detail that would have helped a competitor. Maybe instead of saying "no" outright to someone, you came up with excuse after excuse to wiggle out of some request. We've all experienced situations in which our levels of honesty were compromised. And yet almost everyone can agree that the virtue of honesty is truly valuable.

Honesty demands that we be truthful, genuine, and free of falseness, deception, and fraud. Honesty is arguably the most important factor in establishing authentic, deep, and meaningful relationships. We feel a sense of comfort when trust is established as the foundation of any relationship. Consider the most basic instinct of a newborn baby and the bond of attachment with an adult. This bond is built on the infant's innate trust that an adult will fulfill their most basic needs of love and nourishment.

Honesty is also considered to be one of the most admired character traits of any successful, responsible person, because their success is achieved authentically. As a result, we are happy for these individuals because there is a sense that they earned their success. The positive and trusting feelings associated with their identity are rock-solid, and this combination of success and integrity leaves a positive legacy.

Let's consider a clear-cut example of the difference between the legacy left behind by an honest person versus a dishonest person. Arguably, one of the most powerful positions of authority and leadership in the world is the presidency of the United States of America. It's a position where the spotlight shines and the depth of this individual's actions is felt around the globe.

Abraham Lincoln ("Honest Abe") and Richard Nixon ("Tricky Dick") have nicknames that speak for themselves. Lincoln was universally known and respected, even by his adversaries, as a lawyer and politician who possessed integrity and honesty. There are numerous historical accounts of Lincoln's character. One of the most noteworthy is in his work, *Notes for a Law Lecture,* where he writes, "Resolve to be honest at all events; and if in your own judgment you cannot be an honest lawyer, resolve to be honest without being a lawyer."[38]

Richard Nixon, on the other hand, was connected with countless dishonest acts, most notorious of which was his

---

[38] "Did Lincoln deserve the nickname, Honest Abe?," House Divided, https://www .abrahamlincolnonline.org/lincoln/speeches/lawlect.htm.

involvement in the Watergate scandal that rocked the nation. Watergate was the attempted burglary and illegal wiretapping of the Democratic National Committee's offices by President Nixon's staff, an event that happened shortly after Nixon's reelection in 1972. Interestingly, President Nixon had many noteworthy accomplishments as president, including successful diplomatic relationships with the People's Republic of China, the then-USSR, Egypt, and Israel, and the agreement to end the Vietnam War. However, these are usually overshadowed by his involvement in the Watergate scandal and, therefore, President Nixon's name will forever be synonymous with cheating and dishonesty. As you can see, not only can the devastation and destruction left by dishonesty overshadow the good that you can accomplish, it can become your legacy.

Moral standards in society are upheld by businesses with ethical work practices and core values, in schools with an honor system, by religious institutions, by the legal system, and even in public spaces as codes of conduct. While most of us have an obvious issue with flagrant crimes, cheating, lying, and stealing, we must be more conscious of those less flagrant acts—the day-to-day instances where you may compromise your level of honesty, either by lying or by using half-truths to avoid outright lies.

For example, think about lying by omission. This is when important information is purposefully omitted in order to hide the truth from others or when knowingly inaccurate information is left intact. My husband and I have been fortunate enough to financially help other people on several occasions. A while back, I was helping a close friend work through some financial difficulties. It was clear that student loans, bank loans, and credit card debt were big stressors. We came up with a plan of attack that included several action items, like reducing living expenses, looking for higher-paying career opportunities, and finding different ways to begin paying down the debt. The overall situation was tough, and our relationship grew with this struggle as we brainstormed a productive and positive game plan to get him back on track financially. We were in close contact each week, celebrating their success and the feelings of empowerment as financial goals began to coalesce.

Part of the plan included financial assistance by my husband and me. We offered to help pay down some debt to relieve their burden and reestablish their credit rating. Every month we sent money to apply to their credit card bills and student loan payments. After about four months, I asked them to resend the spreadsheet so I could see how our plan of attack was working. Much to my surprise, the credit card balances hadn't budged. They were the exact same amount, to the penny, as they had been four months prior. The money we had sent every month was going elsewhere; they'd hidden from me what it was actually being used for. I asked for an explanation, and they said they needed the money for basic living expenses, like food and gas. But in our original plan, we'd already allocated funds for those expenses. The extra money we sent had been specifically earmarked for reducing debt. After all that we'd tried to help them with, it was hurtful to discover they were lying to us. I was left reeling, knowing I'd been taken advantage of and betrayed.

What about white lies? These little lies are used to *please* another person or to avoid hurting them, and are often considered innocent in nature. Classic examples are the little lies necessary when planning a surprise party or even encouraging children to believe in Santa Claus. There is no harm in these, and the intention is for a greater good.

The problems arise when the term "white lies" is stretched to become synonymous with "little lies"—meaning you can justify the lie because you have deemed it harmless, but the intention is not to help someone. An example of this would be if I asked my children if they finished their homework and they said yes, when in fact they hadn't. Homework completion—or lack thereof—isn't harmful to me as a parent and they may think that if they said yes, that would make me happy. But, as we all know, little lies can lead to bigger problems. What would happen if at school the next day, the teacher threw a pop quiz on the homework material? There would likely be a terrible grade on this assessment, which would open up an inquiry on my end as to why this was the case. Or what if this situation led to a sudden "stomachache" in order to escape to the nurse's office and miss the quiz altogether (new set of lies)? Even worse, what about the temptation to cheat and glance at another student's answers? You can see how one little lie can lead to a landslide of other problems. Consider how much you bend the truth and the possible ramifications.

Several years ago, I decided that I wanted to be an emergency medical technician (EMT). The town I lived in had a unique medical emergency response system wherein the majority of the EMTs were high school students. Certification classes were held each year, and due to high demand and limited slots, it was difficult to enroll. I tried for a full year to get into this class. I then decided to try the class in a neighboring town, thinking perhaps their numbers would be lower. On my first attempt to register, the class was at capacity. As I became more frustrated, I also became more determined to find myself a spot in the EMT program. I asked when the class would be offered again, and I was told that classes were offered based on the need for EMTs in the field, which meant there were no scheduled upcoming courses.

A few months later, I saw that a new class would be offered the next spring. I immediately called to register. The woman who conducted the enrollment process asked me outright what my intentions were—specifically, was I looking to be a full-time EMT? She made it clear that they didn't have the space for students who wanted the certification but didn't intend to become active, full-time members of their EMT team. That statement made me stop and think. I knew I wanted to be certified as a volunteer EMT, but I also knew I couldn't handle a binding schedule. With four of my five children still at home and my husband's hectic travel schedule, I could not make a full-time commitment. I told her I wasn't sure if I could commit to becoming a full-time EMT but assured her I would do my best. Basically, I knowingly glossed over the truth to get into this class and felt horrible for doing so. I knew I wasn't being honest, and I was possibly taking the spot of someone who could have gone on to be a full-time team member. She must have been able to see though my intentions because she kindly said, "You are now placed on the 'B' list of the waitlist." In other words, I wasn't just on the waitlist—I was on the second-tier waitlist! About two weeks before the session was to begin, I received a phone call saying I had made it into the class.

Clearly, I am still growing as I make mistakes, but the important point here is that, although I had not told the full truth, which I regret and take responsibility for, thankfully the woman was able to place me where I properly belonged in the rank order of the applicants. When I did get the call offering me a spot in the class, I felt it was honest and authentic. I grew from this E.P.I.C. instance. It showed me that I am not perfect, that I am still working toward being E.P.I.C., and that, in the end, it pays off. I was successful and happy. If I'd been placed on the A waiting list and then admitted into the class from that position, I would have always felt that I had lied my way into the class.

HONESTY WITH SELF

Honesty is more than simply telling the truth to others. It begins with being honest with yourself. I call this "being true to you." It's respecting yourself enough to see and accept your strengths and weaknesses, likes and dislikes, and everything in between. It's allowing yourself to be human. Self-honesty sparks a willingness to take a critical look at the qualities that you love about yourself and those you may not love.

Being honest with yourself is personal. It's between you and you, and can be an incredibly powerful tool for self-improvement. You are likely already doing this when you identify an aspect of your life that you want to change. Take, for example, a New Year's resolution. You're evaluating a part of your life that you want to change for the better. Maybe it's getting physically fit, or striving for a certain career, or being the best version of yourself you can be—living E.P.I.C.

An example of me being honest with myself is writing this book. As my children began entering their college years, I realized that they may never come back home. I wanted to leave my children with words of wisdom to add to their own repertoire to help them achieve happiness and success. The only viable option, in my mind, was to write a book. My challenge was that my greatest weakness has always been reading and writing. There was no denying it. I was honest with myself, knowing it would take me a long time and a good amount of struggle to write an entire book. So, I set reasonable goals, sought support, and grew in faith that I could reach the ultimate achievement. I knew I needed to change for the better to accomplish this, and it took honesty with myself to make it happen.

Someone who is honest with themself radiates a sense of authenticity. Other people sense this authenticity. On the other hand, some people are fine with possessing less-than-desirable character traits, and in their own way, are also being honest with themselves. Self-honesty liberates you to feel content with how the world sees you and how you see yourself. There is no mental turmoil over hiding behind secrets or skirting around insecurities.

Embracing the concept of self-honesty can be a bit scary. No one is perfect, and that surely is *not* the goal here. Rather, it's more of a moment to check in with yourself, accept you are human, and decide to make honesty a priority, if it isn't already. Be ready and willing to see some truths about yourself, good and bad.

You may be asking yourself, *Okay, how do I do this? Where do I begin?* The best way to approach this is to undergo a self-assessment with thought-provoking questions. This process can uncover some realizations that may be difficult to accept, while others may be personally empowering. Allow yourself to be open to the truths you reveal. The purpose of this exercise is not so much about the question, but the process of seeking honest answers.

- If you could change anything about yourself, what would it be and why?
- What are your specific strengths and weaknesses?
- What are you passionate about?
- If you could have anything in the world, what would that be?
- What are your biggest fears?
- What's holding you back from your dreams, aspirations, and desires?

As Maya Angelou says, "There is no agony like bearing the untold story inside you."

HONESTY WITH OTHERS

To paraphrase William J. Bennett, it's been said that honesty is a yardstick used to measure whether or not you'll associate with someone.[39] Think about how true this is. I am much more comfortable with someone whom I feel I can trust than with someone who is dishonest. I am actually physically uncomfortable around dishonest people. Personal relationships, whether intimate or social, that are built upon honesty are more valued, more authentic, and more enduring than those built on lies and half-truths.

I have purposely avoided discussing vices in this book because I want to focus on the power of positivity and the value of the virtues. But as you can see, honesty can be best comprehended by understanding what it is not. Many of us would even define honesty as "telling the truth and not lying." Let's briefly examine why people lie so we can better understand and avoid this trap.

People lie for three major reasons. First is the fear of not meeting another's approval, so lying becomes a tool to get that approval (protecting oneself) and avoid rejection. Second is the fear of hurting others' feelings (protecting others). Many people justify lying in this scenario because they feel it is for a greater good. Finally, lying can be used as a tool for personal gain (greed).

To add to this, sometimes we're taught to lie by the very people who should be teaching us to tell the truth: our parents or guardians. Your childhood has an enormous impact on the way you see honesty. For some parents, lying is a part of everyday life, a way to leverage themselves in crisis situations, almost like a survival skill. Some parents lie and cheat on simple things like an innocent game of Monopoly, or in more extreme situations like

---

[39] William J. Bennett, *The Book of Virtues for Young People* (Simon & Schuster, 1993) 245.

committing infidelity or tax evasion. What children see around them is what they will consider to be an acceptable standard.

Children often use lying as a survival skill to avoid punishment by parents, teachers, and other authority figures because, in those moments, the belief that honesty is the best policy just doesn't seem to be real. And that leaves the only other opinion: dishonesty.

Now, ask yourself if you use or have used these reasons to justify dishonesty. When you really examine your motives, can you still support your decision to be dishonest?

Honesty is a hallmark virtue in choosing to be E.P.I.C. Although this may be easier for some than for others, growth in honesty can begin today in subtle ways. Just begin by saying the phrase, "To be honest . . ." and then follow up with an honest statement, whether you're talking to yourself or to someone else. Set your sights on the prize of inner peace and the successful outcomes that honesty will deliver.

BENEFITS OF HONESTY

- Honesty builds strong, meaningful relationships and positive connections.
- Honesty develops trust, credibility, and respect while creating new opportunities for personal growth and success.
- Honesty reduces stress and anxiety associated with dishonesty.
- Honesty is the cornerstone of integrity.

EVERYDAY EXCELLENCE IN HONESTY

- Begin owning up. Start by being more truth-filled and honest. Raise the bar for yourself by growing more honest in your everyday life. Admit to shortcomings, like when your weekly finances fall short of what is expected. It's better to speak the truth, "I spent more money than what we agreed upon for dad's birthday gift," than to conjure up a lie. It's more admirable to admit to mistakes than to try to be "flawless" in the eyes of others. If you are pulled over for speeding, we know chances are you were indeed speeding. Ask the officer how fast you were going before claiming you were not speeding.

- Take responsibility and be accountable. This will require getting comfortable with being uncomfortable for the sake of honesty. If you're late for lunch because you added an extra errand or business call that threw you off schedule, don't conjure up an "excuse" like you were tending to a sick child or your assistant overscheduled your calendar to try to maintain a tarnish-free image in front of your friends. Be honest and say something like, "I tried to squeeze too much in my morning, I am sorry for being late."
- Respect rules/regulations/laws:
  - ♦ Stop trying to beat the system—making cash transactions to avoid paying taxes, recycling used tickets to events or movies to get more friends in or save a buck, sending multiple family members into the grocery store for individual transactions when there is a promotion "buy one get one free" limited to one per customer.
  - ♦ Recognize that there are reasons for seemingly arbitrary rules and protocols like the TSA screening process, or age verification for drivers' licenses or boating licenses. They exist for our protection and the protection of others. Recommit to honoring these rules and protocols.

- Don't compromise your integrity and lie for others. This seems very straightforward and rather obvious. Have you ever been put in a situation where someone asks you to lie and say "tell them I am sick," "tell them I had a doctor's appointment," or "tell them my phone is dead"? Awkward, isn't it?

CHAPTER NINE

PERSEVERANCE

Character cannot be developed in ease and quiet. Only through experience of trial and suffering can the soul be strengthened, ambition inspired, and success achieved.

—Helen Keller

The virtue of perseverance is about being persistent and sticking to a wise course of action, especially in the face of challenges and adversity on the path to pursuing your goals. It's finishing what you've set out to achieve, ultimately with a reward that will deliver happiness. Perseverance is an essential life skill and we are all capable of developing and using this skill. It's just the degree to which we choose to use this virtue that varies from person to person. You don't have to have special talents, natural abilities, wealth, or even know people in high places. If you persevere, you can reach your goals.

Perseverance overlaps with the virtues of fortitude and courage. The virtue of fortitude is subtly different from perseverance in that fortitude often includes emotional motivation driving you toward your goal and is powered by mental stamina and courage in the face of adversity. Courage is a necessary component of both perseverance and fortitude, because courage helps us to overcome fears and stay brave through discomfort on the path to achieving our goals.

In this chapter, I'll discuss perseverance, fortitude, and courage in detail. Let's start with a look at the virtue of perseverance and the important role it plays in the E.P.I.C. journey.

ALLISON

Many years ago, my sister, Allison, went through an extremely difficult breakup with her then-boyfriend. They had been together for more than ten years, and they basically went through a divorce (division of residences, finances, household goods, etc.) minus the legalities. The emotional toll as she battled heartbreak, extreme loneliness, and loss was devastating. I don't know how she managed, but she picked herself up and began channeling her negative energy into positive energy by setting a lofty goal for herself: competing in an Ironman Triathlon. She had run the NYC marathon twice, but an Ironman race is arguably *the* most physically challenging competition. Not only does it include running an entire marathon, but participants also swim 2.4 miles and bicycle 112 miles. Her second marathon had resulted in a right tibia stress fracture from overuse, and clearly, another endurance event—especially one of this magnitude—could pose a huge problem. But she'd made up her mind, and the Ironman was her goal.

Phase one began with joining a triathlon club. She needed to learn new skills and techniques for competitive biking and swimming, and she had to establish a regimented training schedule designed to meet her goals.

Phase two was competing in smaller triathlons so she could make the necessary qualifying times to be eligible to participate in the Ironman. All along, she did everything in her power to keep her body healthy and avoid any potential overuse injuries—sports massages, active release treatments, chiropractor visits, ice baths—you name it. She eventually earned her Ironman slot.

Phase three was to compete and complete the Lake Placid Ironman. During this final phase of training, about six weeks before race day, she began to feel that same pain in her right tibia that she had felt when she was diagnosed with a stress fracture a few years earlier. She was terrified at what the X-rays would reveal. Her orthopedist confirmed her suspicion—she had another stress fracture. To make matters worse, the fracture was in the upper portion of her tibia, so there was additional concern that the tip of the tibia could break off completely. Her physician was cautiously optimistic that she could heal in time for the Ironman to compete in the swim and bike, but not the run. But missing out on running was not an option for Allison. She had her mind set to complete the full race.

Her determination and perseverance went into overdrive. For the next six weeks, she maintained her original training regimen for the swimming and biking segments of the race. Instead of running, she trained on an elliptical machine, which meant she had to work harder and for longer periods of time to maintain her stamina. After five grueling weeks, she returned to her physician in hopes of getting the green light to fully participate. She did! However, she had to run the marathon in an air cast, something she had never done before. She didn't even wince at this latest obstacle because she was beyond elated. Then, thirty-six hours before race day, she developed a horrific migraine. She was in bed for twenty-four hours, unable to eat an ounce of food due to the nausea that comes with migraines. She was depleting her energy reserves and becoming dehydrated. Somehow, she managed to eat half of a peanut butter and jelly sandwich the morning of the race.

On that bright sunny day in July, Allison crossed the finish line with the most radiant smile ever, one that spoke loud and clear, "I did it and I defied my obstacles." When she reflects back on this experience, she says, "I truly believe I willed myself to the start!" I continue to look at her in awe because of the way in which she persevered and fought through obstacles to make her dream come true. She was living E.P.I.C. and was rewarded with extreme happiness and personal fulfillment, feelings that she continues to experience to this day.

GRIT

Today, the trendy term "grit" is sometimes used when talking about perseverance. There is, however, a subtle difference. Grit has the added element of passion as a source of motivation. Angela Lee Duckworth is a guru on this topic. Her interest began while teaching seventh-grade mathematics. She realized that IQ was not the differentiating factor between her best and worst students. Instead, she noticed that some students were great performers, yet were not so bright; conversely, some bright students didn't perform so well.

Ms. Duckworth left teaching to pursue a PhD in Psychology where she was able to study and research her passion in the field of performance full-time. She soon realized that a key predictor of success was grit. She defines grit as "passion and perseverance for very long-term goals. Grit is having stamina. Grit is sticking with your future, day in, day out, not just for the week, the month, but for years, and working very hard to make that a reality. Grit is living life like it is a marathon and not a sprint."[40]

---

[40] Angela Lee Duckworth, "Grit: The Power of Passion and Perseverance," TED Talks Education, April 2013, video, https://www.ted.com/talks/angela_lee_duckworth _grit_the_power_of_passion_and_perseverance?language=en.

Both grit and perseverance embrace a never-quit mentality. Perhaps one of the reasons quitting isn't an option for those who persevere is because they already understand, and often knowingly accept, there will be obstacles along the way that they will struggle with to get to their final goal. These obstacles and struggles are not seen as excuses or reasons to quit, but as an expected part of the process. For those who lack perseverance or grit, obstacles and struggles are reasons to give up. Quitting can have a negative impact, creating feelings of being unsuccessful and unhappy versus the feelings of happiness and completion felt by those who persevere.

In *Choose the Life You Want,* Tal Ben-Shahar, PhD, states, "When we hear about extremely successful people, we mostly hear about their great accomplishments—not about the many mistakes they made and the failures they experienced along the way. In fact, most successful people throughout history are also those who have had the most failures. That is no coincidence. People who achieve great feats, no matter what field, understand that failure is not a stumbling block but a stepping-stone on the road to success. There is no success without risk and failure."[41]

Perhaps this can best be summed up in Denzel Washington's 2011 Commencement speech at the University of Pennsylvania, in which he said, "Fall forward. This is what I mean: Reggie Jackson struck out 2,600 times in his career, the most in the history of baseball. But you don't hear about the strikeouts. People remember the home runs. Fall forward. Thomas Edison conducted a thousand failed experiments. Did you know that? I didn't know that, because the 1,001st was the light bulb. Fall forward. Every failed experiment is one step

---

[41] Tal Ben-Shahar, PhD, *Choose the Life You Want* (Experiment Publishing, 2014).

closer to success."[42] Have you ever thought about perseverance this way? About all of the failures that can be stepping-stones and lessons learned on the path to success?

Obstacles, adversity, and failures are part of the process in reaching goals, and frankly, a part of life. That makes it all the more important that we recognize and embrace this virtue. We need to be able to persevere on our journey of life.

BRING IT ON!

I had grit as a young girl. I loved any form of challenge and had a "bring it on" mindset. When I was about eight years old, my family hosted our annual backyard July 4th barbecue. One of our traditional appetizers was raw clams and oysters. My uncle would labor away shucking the clams, while I watched and kept his work area tidy. One year, he bet me $5 that I would never be able to pry open an oyster shell. I thought for a moment and realized he gave me a harder task (shucking the oyster versus the clam) than what he was doing. I distinctly remember thinking, *Yes I can.* I tried for about twenty minutes as my frustration grew. I had a difficult time holding the oyster because it was slippery and larger than my small hand. I used a variety of knives and tools. I tried different locations along the perimeter of the shell. I even thought about the perfect angle to wedge the knife between the top and bottom shell. Finally, I was able to open the shell. I knew I would open that oyster; the question was just how I was going to do it. In other words, I needed to find the process. It never occurred to me to quit or give up. My success was earned, and I was happy.

---

[42] Denzel Washington, "Fall Forward," May 16, 2011 University of Pennsylvania Commencement, https://singjupost.com/denzel-washingtons-famous-fall-forward-speech-full-transcript/.

For some reason, as I grew older, I began to succumb to the concept of an easy way out. There were times when giving up became an option and perseverance became more difficult to sustain. As an adolescent and young adult, my responsibilities and goals became more challenging. Whether it was struggling with academics or fighting for a spot on a sports team, I wasn't always able to tap into my childhood gritty self with that "bring it on" mindset and persevere. Sadly, there were many times when I slacked off and fell into the trap of quitting. Each time this happened, I was left feeling disappointed, like I had failed myself. I learned the hard way that quitting came with a hefty price—regret, lost opportunity, and frustration.

My biggest regret was not finishing my nursing degree. At the time, my husband, our one-year-old daughter, and I lived in Georgia. We decided to take advantage of a great career opportunity for my husband and moved to Chicago. I was three semesters away from earning another bachelor's degree at the school I was attending in Georgia. I did my due diligence. I could transfer to a number of amazing schools in the Chicago area and complete my nursing degree. We moved in February, and I missed the deadlines to apply for the upcoming fall semester. I was now faced with a year off before returning to school. In that year, I slowly convinced myself to quit. I used excuse after excuse, from the responsibility of having a young child, to not having enough time to invest in studies, to needing to work to make ends meet. These were the exact same obstacles that I had when we lived in Georgia, yet I was able to persevere through them there. Why couldn't I do it in Chicago? Because I decided to quit on myself and my dream.

This experience taught me the immense benefits of perseverance. When I quit, I was so close to earning a BS in nursing. I had completed all the classroom work, and the last stretch was clinical experience in a hospital setting. The regret I have from quitting has left me with a lingering sense of failure, which has translated to a lifetime of unhappiness every time I think about that decision. Compared to the personal fulfillment and happiness I feel to this day having completed my degree in psychology, it's shocking. If I could do it all over again, I would never have quit. Perseverance adds tremendous value to our lives. We have to be wise and look at the long-term benefits when we choose to persevere and live E.P.I.C.

Since perseverance is a part of our daily lives, embracing this virtue and enhancing it will help bring on our mindset of excellence. Just think about all the obstacles you pressed through in the past week. Now imagine adding an enhanced inner strength, poise, and determination to press through them. You will be left feeling personally empowered, successful, and happy.

Perseverance allows us to become wiser with our mistakes and braver in our battles. Even when we feel we have given it our all, there are times when some things are out of our control and the outcome isn't what we set out to achieve. We need to believe that someday, and in some way, we will reap the benefits of our hard work, determination, and steadfastness. The virtue of perseverance defines what it takes to embrace and pursue the E.P.I.C. journey.

BENEFITS OF PERSEVERANCE

- Perseverance develops a tenacious, never-give-up attitude that helps you achieve your goals and aspirations.
- Perseverance gives you a tremendous sense of accomplishment and self-confidence. It builds resilience, motivation, and faith in yourself.
- Perseverance develops humility, compassion, and empathy.

- Perseverance allows you to experience the feeling of accomplishment when you see something through to completion.

EVERYDAY EXCELLENCE IN PERSEVERANCE

- Create a plan that is clear and achievable to reach that goal you have visualized. Make a list of goals and share them with a trusted person in your life who will hold you accountable for following through with these goals. Then set achievable milestones and create a timeline to periodically check in with your "accountability partner." If you want to exercise three times a week, take a selfie after your workout and send it to you partner, or if you've set out to read more books for pleasure this year, join a book group to serve as an "accountability partner" to help you to stay on track and achieve your goal.
- See obstacles as "detours." When things don't go as planned, think of it as a detour, not an excuse to quit. Understand there is often more than one path to achieve your goals and this will allow you to continue to persevere. When presented with a detour, ask yourself, *What are my options? How am I going to get to my goal?* If you've pledged $5/mile on a fifty-mile bike tour to raise money for a charity and halfway through you pop a flat tire, see this as a "detour." Think of options to stay on course and complete the race. See if there is a spare bike that you can use, see if someone can help change your flat tire, maybe you will need to walk your bike across the finish line.
- Finish what you started. #Completion: This may seem cliché, but take a look at all of the ideas, goals, activities

you've begun and left incomplete. Ask yourself, *How many books have I started and haven't finished? How many exercise programs have I begun that I didn't complete? How many unfinished craft projects are there left in my closet?* For some, the concept of completion may be easy, but for many, finishing what you started is a perfect opportunity to practice perseverance.

- Take a fresh approach to "failure." When you see failure as a way to learn and as a means to gather important information, you will be at an advantage. Take a moment to understand the "why" behind a mishap and ask yourself, *What did I learn here?* Suppose you failed your road test for your driver's license because you hit a curb pulling out of the parking lot at the DMV. I can assure you, the next time, you will make a wider turn to avoid this error and greatly increase the chances of passing your exam. Many "failures" can and do lead to success.

FORTITUDE

The ultimate measure of a man is not where he stands in moments of comfort and convenience, but where he stands at times of challenge and controversy.

—Martin Luther King

In this chapter, I've combined two virtues—courage and fortitude—both interwoven with the virtue of perseverance. Fortitude is much like perseverance in that there is a determined, never-give-up mindset. However, fortitude has the added component of mental strength and courage to endure adversity while pressing through to achieve a desired outcome. Perseverance, on the other hand, is more about pressing through and being persistent about reaching your goals whether or not you encounter adversity.

We see the virtue of fortitude when the goal or outcome is for a greater good for yourself or someone else. Whether you're an Army Ranger on a critical and dangerous mission to save the lives of fellow soldiers, Mother Teresa facing challenges in missionary work to relieve the suffering of others, or a person helping to carry another's emotional burden in times of distress, the virtue of fortitude carries you through because you are emotionally invested.

No one is immune to trials and tribulations throughout life. We all have times when we need to dig deep emotionally and persevere through extreme challenges. If I were to ask you, "What was one of the toughest periods in your life?" I am sure you would come up with a time when you were emotionally connected in the face of adversity—a time when you didn't think you could make it another day, but you did. Somehow, you found a way.

My epic Week

For some reason, well before I even thought about writing this book, I had a week in my life that I refer to as my "epic" week. It was mentally and physically challenging but also personally rewarding, and the only reason I made it through was because of the virtue of fortitude.

Shortly after the twins were born, my husband was called out of town on a work assignment, our sitter was on vacation, and our backup help had a family emergency. I was home alone with Marisa, twelve years old; Gabriella, eight years old; Ellie two years old, and the twins, a mere three weeks old. I was confident I could hold down the fort and frankly eager to take on this "solo" challenge.

My goal was twofold. First, I wanted to do my best to preserve "normal" life for the older girls as it related to their school schedule, after-school activities, and especially a restful night's sleep. The only real challenge was when it came time to leave the house. Because they were so young, all five children had to travel with me everywhere I went, and I had to be sure to plan appropriately. This didn't mean I had to simply load up the car with the twins in their infant seats and Ellie in her toddler seat; it meant I began planning an hour prior to be sure they were well fed with dry diapers. Thankfully, the older girls could lend a hand with these transitions and it all worked out.

My second goal seemed like the simple one: meeting basic needs, such as making sure everyone was fed and bathed, but it wasn't. Newborns' needs tend to trump almost everyone else's needs. Based on the recommendations from twin experts, if we could get them on the same sleep and feeding schedules, life for everyone would be more manageable. Up until this point, I had been close to making this happen with extra help. But after a few days alone, I realized this was now definitely not going to happen. After all, how on earth was I going to feed two babies at the same time? I wanted—I needed—happy babies, so instead of manufacturing a synchronized schedule, I let nature take its course. I fed them when they cried that they were hungry, and I let them sleep whenever they wanted to. Interestingly, the babies seemed to alternate who ate every two to three hours. It took about thirty minutes to feed a single bottle. This cycle ran through each twenty-four-hour period without a break. I felt like I was constantly feeding them, but it worked. I was never overwhelmed, just continuously busy.

Then it happened. One night, or shall I say early one morning, for some reason, the twins cried hysterically for bottles at the same time. My stress level spiked. I had to figure this one out.

I tried to feed one and keep the other happy with a pacifier, no luck. I rocked one while I fed the other, no luck either. Nothing I tried worked. They had to be fed at the same time. It just so happened that we had bean bag chairs in our family room. I sat on the floor in between two bean bag chairs and placed a baby in each one. I held a bottle in my left hand for the baby in the left bean bag chair and one in my right hand for the baby in the right bean bag chair. At first, I was afraid they wouldn't take the bottles without the comfort of human touch, without being held, but thankfully they did. I thought to myself, *Phew, this works!* Then after only a few minutes, I realized my arms were getting tired because of the angle I had to hold the bottles at to be sure air didn't get in while the babies were drinking. I thought, *How am I going to hold this position for twenty more minutes?* Without interrupting the babies, I managed to contort myself to reach some pillows on the sofa to prop under my elbows. It worked, and soon I had happy, well-fed babies.

Looking back, I'm not sure I could tell you how I managed every single incident that week, but the overriding factor amongst all the on-the-fly solutions was fortitude: that innate drive I have as a mother taking care of her children.

Ellie living E.P.I.C.

As a young child, my daughter Ellie was always bright-eyed and bushy-tailed, very observant of her surroundings. Although she was rather quiet, there was no doubt she took in what was happening all around her at any given moment. Shortly after she began preschool, we noticed that she wasn't able to grasp some basic phonics while learning to read. It was subtle, not alarming, so we kept watch over her progress but didn't intervene. When she entered kindergarten, it became apparent she was falling behind her peers academically. We began the investigative process to determine why she was having such difficulty. After six months of testing, ranging from hearing and vision testing to a battery of psycho-educational testing to diagnose learning differences, it was determined that Ellie had an audio processing disorder. She experienced a delay between when she heard a sound and the ability to make sense of that sound, which explains why as a young child she was very alert, yet very quiet. She was trying to piece together what was happening in her immediate surroundings. Learning, especially reading and writing, was a huge challenge for her because the basics of reading and writing depend so heavily on recognizing spoken sounds and translating those sounds into words and sentences.

With the help of her school and outside tutoring, we created a specialized learning plan for Ellie. She needed to work twice as hard and twice as long compared to her peers. Not only did she struggle with this challenge academically, she also felt awkward socially because of all the accommodations in place to help her. Ellie desperately wanted to be like her classmates who didn't have all the extra work, and she was determined and courageous as she forged her way through her challenges. She had fortitude. Never once did Ellie complain, resist, or challenge the process. At every parent/teacher conference, the message was clear and consistent. It was Ellie's determination, drive, and work ethic, all examples of mental toughness, that gave her the ability to press through her challenges. This continued for the next four years.

Finally, in fifth grade, when we felt Ellie had overcome this hurdle, we decided to have her retested. While our hunch was right—she no longer had an audio processing disorder—we were surprised to learn that she now had a reading disorder. So, although she was able to process information more efficiently and effectively, she still needed help reading. Thankfully, Ellie had been working on her reading for years and she already knew that it wasn't her strong suit. The good news was that Ellie had indeed mastered the skills necessary to navigate learning with her audio processing disorder and was an A student working side by side with her classmates.

Fast forward to tenth grade. The state of California requires a new set of psycho-educational testing for those students who have learning differences and continue to seek academic accommodations once they have turned sixteen. Since these accommodations had been a crucial component of Ellie's academic success, she was tested. Yet again, after the testing process, we were surprised. This time, we found out Ellie was dyslexic. After ten years of fighting her way through school, Ellie now had a new diagnosis. Was this going to be a new learning obstacle? Not really. She was extremely attuned to the learning style she had mastered, and she handled this news rather well. Ellie's determination to apply excellence to fortitude has enabled her to consistently achieve academic success and deliver on the promise of personal fulfillment and tremendous happiness. This is a lesson she will carry throughout the rest of her life, and one which she is proud to share.

Let's better prepare for life's battles with the power of fortitude. When you develop and grow this virtue, using it daily and knowingly embracing the power fortitude offers, you will be much better equipped to handle various challenging situations when they present themselves. With the application of excellence to fortitude, you will have a new-found inner strength and ownership to help yourself and others. Forge forward with fortitude and experience success and happiness.

BENEFITS OF FORTITUDE

- Fortitude enables you to stand firm and fight for what you believe in, for a greater good, in the midst of adversity.
- Fortitude develops emotional and physical strength, stamina, resiliency, and self-confidence.
- Fortitude uses the power of courage to face challenges and obstacles that interfere with you reaching your goals and aspirations.

EVERYDAY EXCELLENCE IN FORTITUDE

- Think resiliency. Use resiliency as armor to forge through setbacks. Use positive self-talk to inspire you. Phrases like "I got this . . ." and "I am going to have to dig deep, but I can do this" provide a sense of ownership coupled with ability. Get inspired by motivational music. There are many playlists online and on various music apps like Spotify and iTunes that you can use to keep you inspired.
- Courageously press through personal discomfort and difficulties for the greater good of others. Whether you or someone you are close with is faced with a physical or emotional burden, we know how important it is to have someone supporting you along the way. Be that "someone" for others and commit to helping them through recovery. Whether that's driving to chemotherapy appointments, or providing dinner every night for a month to a new, single mom—stick it out and make a positive difference in their lives.
- Mental wellness and mental strength: We know the immeasurable value of these. Take the time to nurture

and grow in these areas. Work with a counselor or support groups, and read books to build this foundation in your life.

COURAGE

I learned that courage was not the absence of fear, but the triumph over it. The brave man is not he who does not feel afraid, but he who conquered that fear.

—Nelson Mandela

Let's examine the well-known story of David and Goliath, the classic biblical story of courage in which a young Israelite, David, faces a nine-foot-tall Philistine giant, Goliath, in a single battle. The winner takes claim of the land for their people. All of the Israelite men cowered in fear at the thought of head-to-head combat with Goliath. Seeing that no one would take on this daunting task, young David stepped up and courageously volunteered. On the day of the battle, instead of wearing heavy armor for protection, David chose to defend himself with stones from a nearby stream. When the battle began, David ran up to Goliath and with a slingshot sank a stone into Goliath's forehead. The giant fell facedown on the ground, and while he was in this vulnerable position, David killed him. David had faith that God would protect him, but it was the virtue of courage that gave him the ability to face the unfavorable odds of battling Goliath. David's success was shared by all Israelites—an *epic* ending to a classic story.

Courage is most commonly associated with overcoming fear. It's mustering up the mental strength to open ourselves up to be vulnerable and to bravely press through an uncomfortable situation or obstacle for a desired goal. Courage is about confronting. At times this confrontation is difficult, like in the case of extreme fear; there are also times when confrontation is bold, like when taking a stand to right a wrong. When we act with courage, we break free of the negative emotion associated with fear and replace it with the positive emotions of confidence and self-esteem.

Courage is used in many different circumstances. We are courageous when we stand up for ourselves, for others, for justice and fairness. We also use courage when we make decisions or take actions with an unknown outcome and when we bravely face emotional setbacks knowing we will need to persevere not just for ourselves, but sometimes for those around us (after the death of loved ones, or during divorce or financial distress, for instance). In all these scenarios, courage gives us the ability to take action.

In his book *Back to Virtue*,[43] Peter Kreeft describes courage as "The willingness to freely go beyond the call of duty, to make sacrifices, to choose the difficult thing, to take chances. Courage. Not just folly, recklessness, not just physical strength, not even physical courage, the ability to endure pain, but moral courage, the willingness to act on your own convictions even if it costs you something, such as convenience or social acceptance." Here, Kreeft mentions moral courage, which is the courage to stand up for your beliefs against overwhelming opposition.

It's staggering to think of the magnitude of moral courage men and women have employed to challenge human injustices and permanently change the course of history: Rosa Parks, known as the "first lady of civil rights" in the 1950s when she refused to give up her seat in the colored section of a city bus when the white section was full; Martin Luther King Jr.,

---

[43] Kreeft, Peter. *Back to Virtue* Ignatius Press. San Francisco: 1992. p. 62.

perhaps the most recognizable leader in the civil rights movement; Gloria Steinem, who in the 1960s became a leader of the American feminist movement; Barbara Gittings, the head of the 1950s civil rights movement for the LGBTQ community. What incredible and profound impacts these individuals have had on the world—they created truly *epic* outcomes from E.P.I.C. living.

Everyday life gives us the opportunity to act courageously, often in the form of standing up for others. Many of us have acted in defense of a friend or family member who has been treated unfairly. Whether it's coming to the aid of a child being bullied on a school playground, stopping cyber-bullying, helping the elderly who may not be able to stand up for themselves, or assisting people who endure unfair workplace environments, we can all exercise courage on behalf of others, even if it causes us discomfort or awkwardness. Courage gives us the ability to take these actions.

The One Love Foundation was established in 2006 after a young University of Virginia women's lacrosse player was murdered by her boyfriend. Yeardley Love was trapped in an abusive relationship, and it is believed that this crime could have been prevented if there had been more awareness and support about the dangers of such relationships. The One Love Foundation has two missions. First, to teach young adults about the difference between unhealthy and healthy relationships, specifically those behaviors that are acceptable and unacceptable. Second, to know how to be courageous and stand up for yourself and/or your friends who are in abusive relationships. This involves drumming up the courage to take a stand, which can be very frightening, yet is crucial for healthy living.

Joyce Meyer, a Christian pastor, has a phrase that sums up the "how" to act with courage. She says, "Just do it afraid." I love this because we will always have a certain level of fear when we decide to do something that is outside our comfort zone or our societal norms. We will always feel uncertainty about the ramifications of our actions. We also may not be confident that what we're doing will result in what we hope for. So, when we think ". . . do it afraid," courage is there to help us take the leap of faith to take action.

Not long ago, my youngest daughter, who was in seventh grade at the time, slowly became withdrawn and appeared to be very sad. Of all my children, Avery has always been the most bubbly, happy, and exuberant, all day, every day. She never carried a worry or sorrow and was known to all of us as "the happiest kid ever." As adolescence came rolling in, like most teenagers, she hung out in her room for hours on end. Avery, however, seemed different. She liked to be in her room with her lights off. She never wanted to come out, even on the weekends. Her shift from childhood interests to adolescent interests were extreme and definitely concerning. There seemed to be a heaviness weighing her down and she seemed depressed. I knew something outside of the ordinary was bothering her, and before I had the chance to sit with her for a more in-depth talk about the changes I had seen in her both at home and at school, she asked to see a therapist. I met with her therapist as well; our conversations were general due to patient confidentiality, so nothing specific was shared with me as to why she seemed so depressed other than the typical "girl trouble" that is sadly so common in middle school. Several months later, Avery and I went to a local basketball game for a mom-daughter night. On our hour-long drive home, I could see out of the corner of my eye that she was just staring blankly through the windshield as if she were in a trance. She was silent and still. I asked, "What are you thinking about?"

She paused for several moments and replied seriously, "Do you really want to know?"

"Of course." At this point, I sensed we were both nervous.

Avery then took a deep breath, clearly in an effort to calm her nerves, and said, "I am pansexual." She glanced at me to see my response.

I replied, "That's awesome, Avery, that's awesome. Tell me all about being pansexual, because I'm actually a bit outdated and don't fully understand what you mean." Within a split second, she was giggling, happy, surprised, physically and emotionally relieved—all things I hadn't seen from her for months. She then proceeded to delightfully and quite thoroughly educate me on the evolution of her sexuality and the complexities of being pansexual.

Avery had the courage to face her fear of what people would think, a fear that had her emotionally and physically sick for six months. From that moment on, her rate of emotional healing rapidly accelerated and soon she returned to her happy, cheerful self. The vice of fear crippled her, and the virtue of courage freed her. Courage gave her happiness with the relief of knowing that, no matter what, the love our family had for her was unconditional. Avery also had the added bonus of successfully overcoming a personal obstacle. She applied excellence to the virtue of courage. She had an E.P.I.C. moment.

I believe we all have experienced something in our lives that has held us back. Perhaps you acted courageously and battled that fear, or perhaps now is the time. Maybe it is the fear of trying something new or the fear of being vulnerable. Opportunities exist all around us to apply excellence to courage and positively impact your life and the lives of others. The benefits of acting with courage, regardless of whether it's on a large or small scale, mean that you will become more self-confident and empowered, all while setting a positive example for others. This is living E.P.I.C.

It takes a lot of courage to apply the E.P.I.C. principle in your life. I assure you that there is no downside to purposely deciding to live E.P.I.C. Be courageous and boldly take the actions that will define you as a person of excellent character.

BENEFITS OF COURAGE

- Courage confronts fears that create emotional turmoil and hold you back from personal growth.
- Courage empowers you to take a stand against a wide array of injustices in our world.
- Courage builds confidence and faith in yourself that you can use to help others grow in courage.

EVERYDAY EXCELLENCE APPLIED TO COURAGE

- Cultivate confidence:
  - Celebrate your successes and accomplishments. Whether that's a six-week "no sugar" challenge or earning "Salesman of the Year," it's healthy to share your success and feel good about your hard work. Your confidence will be contagious and will likely inspire those around you to take on new challenges in their lives.
  - Set boundaries. Saying "no" when you feel uncomfortable with a situation will build confidence. Every year, my New Year's resolution is to "say no" more often. I am perpetually overcommitted volunteering

for school events, extracurricular activities for the kids like sports and music lessons, hosting luncheons and dinners, and it's because I have a hard time saying "no." Why? Because I lack confidence in doing so. For some reason, I feel like I will let others down if I don't say "yes." I have been working to grow in confidence by setting boundaries and simply saying, "I would love to, but I am spread too thin right now with commitments and it wouldn't be fair to you to give less than my best. Let's circle back in a few months."

- Face your fears. Think about how fears may be holding you back from living a full life. Is the fear of flying keeping you from attending the annual family reunion? Is the fear of snakes keeping you from joining your friends in their weekly hike? Perhaps you have a fear of hospitals that is keeping you from scheduling important routine health screenings like mammograms or colonoscopies. Don't let fear be a deterrent and begin stepping out of your comfort zone.

CHAPTER TEN
CHARITY

Love is not patronizing, and charity isn't about pity, it is about love. Charity and love are the same—with charity you give love, so don't just give money but reach out with your hand instead.

—Mother Teresa

Love is arguably the most powerful and important of all the virtues. Love resides at the core of our human existence. The depth and breadth of the role love plays in human nature is hard to fathom. Just consider how deeply it is sunk into our very nature: We crave love from the moment we are born. Newborns are immediately comforted with love by being warmly cradled close to another human body. They also possess the ability to instinctually read love on the faces around them. We know that the foundation of a loving environment and being loved from such a young age is crucial for the development of healthy emotional relationships throughout life. Our human nature continues to crave the fulfillment of being loved and giving love as we journey through life.

That being said, the most important form of love is self-love. This is not prideful love, but rather loving and accepting yourself, being kind to yourself, encouraging and taking care of yourself. This also means you need to eliminate being self-critical and negative.

When you apply excellence to the virtue of self-love, you release positivity, radiance, and a purposeful style of living that you may not even be aware of, yet which positively impacts all aspects of your life. The level of personal peace and happiness you experience will enable you to thrive, which will in turn impact all those around you.

The more traditional context of the virtue of love (the giving and receiving of affection) can be seen in a variety of settings. There's romantic love, friendship love, familial love (parents, children, siblings, etc.), universal love for others, nature and/or God, playful or uncommitted love (flirting, seducing), practical love out of duty and long-term interests, and self-love.[44] You can see how our lives are filled with love throughout the day, every day, even though we may not traditionally recognize love in this way.

Gary Chapman wrote an excellent book titled *The 5 Love Languages*. During his thirty years as a marriage counselor, Chapman observed that couples ran into difficulties when they had differing definitions of what it felt like to be loved and appreciated. Based on his experiences, he categorized five distinct "love languages." Chapman concluded that everyone has a primary love language, and the best way to keep a relationship's emotional connection robust is to understand your love language and that of your partner. Chapman's five love languages are words of

---

[44] Neel Burton, MD, *Psychology Today*, June 25, 2016. www.psychologytoday.com /us/blog/hide-and-seek/201606/these-are-the-7-types-love

affirmation (using words to build up another person), receiving gifts, acts of service, quality time, and physical touch. The impact Chapman has made is not just in trying to figure out your love language, but also that of others. We should recognize what other people need to feel loved and appreciated. Chapman writes of a primary love language, but we can also relate and find value in other love languages. The awareness of different languages of love allows us to focus on the need to nurture love in relationships instead of just allowing nature to take its course.

Even though Chapman's work originated in marriage counseling, he identified the languages of love that are common to all our relationships. If you can identify the love language in all of your relationships, not just the romantic ones, you will have better-quality relationships.

After reading Chapman's book, I was immediately able to identify my love language and my husband's, and then I realized I could apply this valuable concept to my children and learn their unique love languages. (*The 5 Love Languages of Children* by Gary Chapman, PhD and Ross Campbell, MD goes into detail about applying love languages to children.)

My twins, Anthony and Avery, are a perfect example of how a primary love language can appeal to one individual and not another. Avery loves gifts of all types. She has the same bubbling joy whether I give her a strawberry-shaped eraser or a new bike. She also has this same level of excitement for others as they open their gifts, regardless of what that gift may be. Anthony, on the other hand, isn't as motivated by gifts. One Christmas morning, he literally opened two gifts and left the remaining unopened for hours. I had to tell him to go back and open the rest! Both, however, share the love language of physical touch, which has been an endearing quality to see between them. Overall, the one love language all my children share is quality time. Perhaps it is because with a large family this is hard to come by, and now that they're older, they make sure to ask for "our family time" during the holidays or vacations. When we do manage to make this happen, even if it is only a day or two, they always reflect on how special it is for them and for our family to be together as a whole.

The process of determining someone's love language applies excellence to love. It enhances relationships, because when you're able to give love in a way so that someone else feels most loved, you're truly fulfilling their basic human need to be loved.

Unconditional love is one of the most beautiful forms of love we can experience, both as a giver and as a receiver. It is best described in the verse from Corinthians 13-4 which outlines love's breadth and depth. "Love is patient, love is kind. It does not envy, it does not boast, it is not proud. It does not dishonor others, it is not self-seeking, it is not easily angered, it keeps no record of wrongs. Love does not delight in evil, but rejoices with the truth. It always protects, always trusts, always hopes, always perseveres."[45]

I have experienced the unconditional love a parent has for their child. In its highest form, this love means loving in such a way that no matter what happens (argument, difference of opinion, consequences of a bad decision, etc.), the love is enduring and unchanging. It has little to do with the type of relationship (e.g., romance or friendship), but rather with the immense love for others without expecting anything in return.

BENEFITS OF LOVE

- Love creates immense joy and happiness and reduces ill-will, judgment, and even hatred toward others.

---

[45] 1 Cor. 14:2, *Life Application Study Bible, 2525.*

- Love improves the quality of all personal relationships.
- Love increases your sense of purpose and fuels passion.

EVERYDAY EXCELLENCE APPLIED TO LOVE

- Self-love: Be kind to yourself with a positive self-image—both inside and out. Shift thinking like "I'm too short" to "I want to feel a little taller today so I am going to wear a pair of heels," or "I am not smart enough to take that class" to "This may be a hard class, but if I make sure I have extra time in my day to dedicate to my studies and add some tutoring if I need it, I will be just fine." Think of it this way, would you say these things to your friend? No? Well then why would you say these things to yourself? Make a list of the qualities you're most proud of and those that you may want to improve upon. Be accepting of your humanness and in doing so, you will be growing in self-compassion.
- Other-love:
  - Follow the Golden Rule that says we should treat others the way we want to be treated. Here are a few ideas to spark the spirit of following the Golden Rule. If you have a point of conflict with a friend or spouse, speak to them in private instead of exposing this in the company of others; refrain from gossiping about your friends and family to your friends and family; speak calmly and respectfully in heated conversations; don't accuse others of actions that you assume they have taken. Ask them to clarify what they may or may not have done; freely give others the benefit of the doubt and second chances; and compliment others instead of criticizing them.

- ♦ Spread kindness. The next time you're greeted by someone walking into a theatre, hotel, or perhaps the greeter at Walmart, take a moment to stop instead of walking past them, wish them a good day, and thank them for "spreading a positive vibe."

- Look at the positive qualities in others instead of the negative. Instead of seeing someone as nosy, see them as curious; instead of seeing someone as bossy, see them as confident or a go-getter, someone who gets things done. Give the benefit of the doubt. Perhaps that person who is edgy and short with you may not even realize they are behaving this way because they are struggling with chronic physical pain or an extremely difficult situation at home. They could very well use some "other love," a simple recognition that the work they are doing is making a difference or maybe a compliment on the new sneakers they're wearing. This is a great time to practice not being judgmental.

COMPASSION

The worst sin toward our fellow creature is not to hate them, but to be indifferent to them: that's the essence of inhumanity.
—George Bernard Shaw

Compassion is the ability to gain a unique understanding of another person's challenging situation by mentally or physically putting yourself in their place. It's often associated with kindness and sympathy, but the impact is the deep meaning that is shared during compassionate moments. This virtue positively affects those around you, those you are helping, and you. There is absolutely no downside or even the possibility of a less-than-positive impact. Sometimes we think that being compassionate is a sign of being soft or weak, but that's not true. Caring for the welfare of others is both courageous and bold.

The virtue of compassion drives us to help others when we see they're in distress, pain, or suffering. We can all think of situations we were involved in that still pull at our heartstrings—situations where you took action to help others or those where you wish you had taken action.

The importance and benefits of compassion are powerful, well established, and incredibly noteworthy. Stanford University's School of Medicine offers an eight-week course called *Compassion Cultivation Training*, "designed to help you improve your resilience and feel more connected to others—ultimately providing an overall sense of well-being."[46]

The action taken when sparked by compassion shows the application of excellence to this virtue. When you take action to assist a suffering person, you not only see the immediate results in your work toward others—the relief of their mental or physical pain—but also feel the happiness and love you extended returning to you.

Charity and Compassion Story

We've all experienced a time or two when someone was nice to our face, and then not so nice behind our backs. In all honesty, we have probably all been the not-nice, gossiping person on occasion. Don't take it lightly if you're tempted to get others to think poorly of someone else. Depending on the topic and severity of impact on that person, your best and most compassionate choice is usually to be silent. If a situation requires

---

[46] "About Compassion Training," The Center for Compassion and Altruism Research and Education, ccare.stanford.edu/education/about-compassion-training/.

discussion, simply present the facts as you know them in a fair and unbiased manner and let others decide.

Not long ago I was having a conversation with my eldest daughter about the concept of charity in terms of giving not money, but more of yourself. We were talking about sharing skills, networking/mentoring, volunteering time, etc. Suddenly, our conversation shifted as she became frustrated and upset about a recent situation that occurred on the packed NYC subway one morning on her way to work. The subway had been packed with people from all walks of life: business people, professionals in hospital scrubs, young school-aged children, the elderly, and so on.

At one point, a man without any legs hopped off the seat and struggled his way across the floor by putting his hands forward on the floor, then swinging his torso toward them. She was shocked by the way bystanders treated him. Those closest to him physically turned their bodies so their backs were toward him, and not a single passenger made eye contact. At the same time, she noticed other passengers looking straight at one another as if concerned with what the legless man was going to do. The poor guy was treated like an absolute outcast, all because he appeared to have extreme needs. There was no doubt in her mind that he felt the negativity of every gesture. Why do we so commonly look the other way when we are around people who are clearly in need of help?

So when we think about compassion, let's heighten our awareness of the hearts of others. Consider a basic smile, a simple conversation. You never know the struggles and burdens others carry. You may be that ray of sunshine they so desperately need to make it through the day. In the case above, a friendly smile might have touched his heart and it would have made you feel better. That's excellence applied to compassion.

Little Anthony with a Big Heart

In seventh grade, my son and the players on his Pop Warner football team experienced something both unforeseeable and unfathomable. One of their teammates' older brothers committed suicide. The coach sent a message early in the day to the parents with this news. We were all shocked and speechless. In the message, the coach explained that there would be a meeting for both players and parents immediately following practice with this announcement for the boys.

Although I knew many of the players on this team, I didn't know the player who had lost his brother, and oddly, I couldn't seem to figure it out during the meeting. When the meeting ended, the parents and children gathered in groups embracing one another with tears of grief, sadness, and disbelief. My son happened to be on the other side of this gathering. I knew it would take me a few moments before I could make my way to him, but I wasn't concerned because I assumed he would be finding his way to me, and we would meet somewhere in the middle. Soon, I realized my son wasn't rushing to me at all. I actually couldn't find him. I wasn't worried, but as his mother I wanted to nurture him in this difficult moment. Before long, the players and families began to leave. Still, no Anthony. By this time, I was awkwardly standing alone. I started to ask around to see if anyone knew where Anthony was. No one knew.

I decided to walk with the parents and players toward the parking lot, thinking perhaps he was there. As the crowd thinned out, off in the distance I saw a boy walking with his arm around the shoulders of another boy, who was leaning in to him as if he was telling him something. It was endearing. I felt the simultaneous warming of my heart with love and the breaking of my heart with knowing the heaviness behind what led to this kind gesture. I wondered who these players were and instantly realized it was Anthony with his arm around the player. Their conversation went on for about five minutes and ended with a brotherly smack on the back as they parted ways. I just waited. The car ride home was silent. When I tucked him in that evening, my son was still quiet, but we briefly talked about his friend and the circumstances. As I was leaving his room, I leaned back in and asked him who was the player that he had his arm around after the meeting; it was the boy who had lost his brother.

When you explore your inner virtues, consider examining how they are expressed in children, especially honesty, trust, charity, and compassion. It's remarkable, refreshing, and pure.

BENEFITS OF COMPASSION

- Compassion teaches us to be somewhat vulnerable and less afraid of suffering as we grow in empathy.
- Compassion gives the receiver the experience of unconditional love, which is especially meaningful and appreciated during times of need.
- Compassion enables you to gain a better understanding of others' lives and their unique set of needs that you may not have otherwise known.
- Compassion increases inner peace and joy, elevating your mood instantaneously when you actively help others.

EVERYDAY EXCELLENCE APPLIED TO COMPASSION

- Empathy cultivates compassion. Being empathetic is important, it can be learned and practiced every day. Make it a point to put yourself in others' shoes and see life through their eyes. When someone comes to you with a problem, hear it out and before you give advice or try to come up with a solution. Ask, "So how does that make you feel?" And then follow up with, "Why do you feel that way?" You will be surprised with the depth of perspective from *their* viewpoint that you would not have known had you not asked. If you're going to volunteer at the local Boys & Girls Club, try to find out about the lives of the students at home and at school. You may be surprised to learn that the reason James comes dashing into group study ten minutes late every session is because he needs to take three different busses to get to the clubhouse. Connect with James outside of study group. Ask him if he wants to grab a smoothie and get to know him. Break the ice with the "favorites" game. You can begin with any topic, like your favorite musical artists or movie, and simply go on from there. Growing a friendship may help you get a better understanding of what it is like to walk in his shoes and thus grow in empathy.

• Be vulnerable. Allowing yourself to connect emotionally to those who are suffering is an act of compassion, but often requires you to be vulnerable. Many of us avoid this type of connection for fear that the pain and suffering of others could stir up similar pain and suffering in us. Break through this barrier. If a friend has just shared with you that she is getting a divorce, try to meet her where she is emotionally comfortable. Be open to the chance that she may share some potentially painful emotions that could be upsetting for you to hear, but if you believe you are up for it, perhaps you can be her ear to listen or shoulder to cry on. Opening yourself up to this vulnerability is being compassionate.

CHARITY

The virtue of charity (giving) is important for all of us, and a personal one for me. I have always said and felt that the greatest gift I can give is the gift of myself. This may seem boastful or prideful, but it is quite the contrary. I am passionate about helping others. All through high school and college, when someone would ask me, "What do you want to do with your life?" I would shrug my shoulders and say, "I don't know, I just want to help others." Clearly that leaves a wide range of options. In following my heart to help others, I studied psychology to help with people's emotional needs, then returned to school to study nursing, taking on the challenge of assisting in the physical needs of others.

I originally chose to study psychology because of the tremendous impact it had in my life. During my freshman year in college, I lost touch with my true self. I had a difficult time with the transition to college, attended a school that wasn't a great fit for me, and for the first time in six years, I did not have my beloved sport of rowing to participate in. After trying to navigate a roller coaster of emotion, I sought the help of a therapist. She had such a profound impact on my life that I wanted to do the same for others.

Shortly after I got married, I realized that as a military wife who would be relocating often, establishing myself as a therapist would be challenging. I found a nursing program at a local college in our community that would allow me to still deliver relief from pain, but this time physical pain. Due to changing life circumstances, I never practiced as a therapist or a nurse, but through the virtue of charity, I have been able to fulfill my passion to help others as a career mom and by being an active volunteer helping others in a variety of settings including hospitals, schools, churches, and community organizations.

There are infinite opportunities to give of yourself, whether it's your time, your money, your ability to help people, your skills, etc. There is absolutely no reason why you can't help those in need, especially if you have the means to do so. Ask people what they need, rather than assuming you know, and then be creative and make it happen. Next, make it an E.P.I.C. habit.

ALTRUISM

Altruism is the principle of taking action for the betterment of others when you have nothing material to gain from that action. It's selflessness for the concern of others—sometimes at the expense of your personal welfare. The point here is self-lessness. Try to give of yourself without expecting anything in return. Rather, think of how your actions can be undertaken for the true benefit for others.

We often see amazing humanitarian efforts after natural disasters like a hurricane or earthquake, or an act of terrorism like 9/11 in New York City. These events reveal the altruistic aspect of our human nature. The rescue efforts of the fire and police personnel who raced into the Twin Towers to save the lives of others is a powerful example.

On September 11, 2001, Rick Rescorla became a hero who gave his life to save the lives of thousands. He was a decorated former Army officer who was working security at Morgan Stanley at the World Trade Center. After the first plane hit the first tower, he received a phone call from the Port Authority to not evacuate his employees. He vehemently disagreed, knowing that anyone on the floors above where the plane hit would die, as the floors were sure to collapse. He ordered the immediate evacuation of the more than 2,700 individuals in the second tower, successfully getting them out before the second plane hit and saving their lives. During the evacuation, Rescorla called his wife and told her, "I have to get these people out safely. If something should happen to me, I want you to know I've never been happier. You made my life." He was last seen heading upward in the South Tower. His body was never recovered.

These are unique circumstances, not daily occurrences. But if you look at your life now, I'm sure you can find areas where you can ignite some altruistic action. Consider what small act of kindness you could perform, and then take action.

BENEFITS OF CHARITY

- Giving to others increases your personal joy and happiness, especially when you have a meaningfully positive impact in another's life.
- Giving makes you feel a part of a greater good.
- Giving encourages others to give and creates a "pay it forward" effect.

EVERYDAY EXCELLENCE IN CHARITY

- Actively seek opportunities to volunteer in your community—find your local food bank by going to www.feedingamerica.org and entering your zip code; go to www.redcross.org and click on the volunteer tab, or look for opportunities at one of the 4,300 Boys & Girls Clubs across the United States (www.bgca.org) where perhaps you can volunteer to be a tutor or mentor.
- Lead by example with random acts of kindness. Consider paying for the food/coffee order for the car behind you at a drive-through restaurant; plan to double your dinner recipe so you drop off a fine home-cooked meal to your elderly neighbor; or make a book of coupons as a gift

for a new mom with offers like a "free night of babysitting" or "two hours of running errands" to help give her a well-deserved break. I like to keep gift cards to Starbucks or Target in my car or purse to give to the homeless when the chance arises.

- Care for others. Moving is often an overwhelming endeavor. Next time a family member or friend moves, if you are able, offer to pay their security deposit, first month's rent, or first mortgage payment. If offering financial help may not be something you can do, that's fine; set time aside to be there on move-in day and help lighten the physical load. Set up their furniture, unpack, and set up their kitchen, even consider making a few calls to set up their new accounts for cable/internet, electric, and so on.

- Grow in self-compassion. If you don't reach a goal like getting an "A" on an exam, or fall short of raising $1,000 for the necessary upgrade for the speaker system in the high school music department, don't be hard on yourself; rather, celebrate what you did accomplish so you are empowered to continue to pursue this goal again next time around.

- Share your "favorites" with others so they too can benefit the way you have. Maybe it's a new self-charging phone case or "the best" Mexican restaurant with authentic food that's off the beaten path. Share creative gift ideas for those hard-to-shop-for people, like personalized note pads or tote bags, a subscription to a wine club for the wine enthusiast, or a year of monthly flower deliveries to cheer up someone who lives alone.

CHAPTER ELEVEN
WISDOM

Wisdom is not a product of schooling but of the lifelong attempt to acquire it.

—Albert Einstein

What exactly is wisdom? If you're not clear on your answer, you're not alone. That's because there is no specific, unified definition of wisdom, and there never has been. Different definitions arise through the influences of religion, philosophy, culture, and science. However, there is one underlying theme: wisdom involves insight toward the greater good, often a moral good.

Traditional dictionary definitions of wisdom will range from a person's accumulated philosophical or scientific learning, to the ability to make good judgments based on what you've learned, to the teaching of philosophers from the past. It seems not even the dictionary can nail down a precise meaning.

A common theme, however, is that wisdom assists you in making good decisions with knowledge based on a life of experience, learning, discerning, and deep understanding—and true wisdom does not depend on your level of education or intelligence. Some practical characteristics of being wise include listening to, not just hearing, what others have to say, practicing active understanding, using knowledge and insight to make better decisions, accepting wisdom from others, problem-solving, and making ethical choices.

It's not uncommon to use words like "knowledge" and "intelligence" when discussing wisdom. Although these terms are similar in that they relate to our minds, they differ in their specific meanings and application to our lives. They are part of the process when growing in wisdom. Let's break this down and take a closer look to get a better understanding.

Knowledge is learned information—facts, data, and ideas from a variety of sources such as academic study, research, observation, and experiences. The more you know about any given topic or situation, the better you understand it. For example, in this book I've presented information about virtues and character from reading, studying, and researching this topic, which then enabled me to gain even more knowledge, especially after the practical application of E.P.I.C. living in my life. When information is learned, it becomes knowledge. The theoretical understanding of E.P.I.C. is also considered knowledge because the information is put together to formulate a broader understanding of what E.P.I.C. means. My goal is to share this knowledge (information) with the hope that you will be able to apply the E.P.I.C. theory in your lives.

Intelligence is the ability to learn or understand new things—the ability to perceive and process information by using logic, comprehension, reasoning, problem-solving, and creativity—and then apply this retained information to solving dilemmas and dealing with new situations. In other words, intelligence begins with the ability to learn and then recognize and solve problems using the knowledge you have stored. Intelligence is used to understand both simple and complex ideas from a knowledge base.

Intelligence is often associated with academic honors and career accomplishments. You're probably familiar with the concept of IQ (intelligence quotient), which is a numerical score based on several tests designed to measure an individual's reasoning ability. IQ levels don't correlate directly with career advancement or success, and therefore it's more useful to think of intelligence as a skill set that helps you to think critically in a variety of areas. Using the knowledge from this book, you will come up with creative ways in a variety of different settings in your personal life to apply E.P.I.C.—this is using your intelligence. While IQ is to a large degree something you're born with, you can learn and develop beneficial forms of intelligence.

Perhaps you have heard about EQ—emotional quotient—or a person's emotional intelligence. EQ refers to your ability to be conscious of your own emotional state and that of others, to differentiate emotions, and to act accordingly. Those who study EQ believe that if you can understand and manage your emotions, you will be more successful. A few examples of EQ include the ability to identify with any given emotion, like "I am excited" or "I am frustrated"; thinking before reacting; handling negative feedback with grace; developing empathy; and the ability to forgive. Emotional intelligence can be learned and understood, and then used to increase happiness and personal fulfillment.

The concept of moral intelligence (MI) is of great value, especially with regard to E.P.I.C. living. Moral intelligence is the capacity to understand right from wrong. People with high moral intelligence possess and act on their strong ethical convictions. Moral intelligence is ability-based. It can be taught and learned. Interestingly, today we see the practical application of MI in the worlds of business and leadership; however, living E.P.I.C. encourages the use of moral intelligence in your life.

There is also SI, social intelligence, sometimes referred to as tact or common sense in social settings. This is the ability to determine from your environment which behaviors work better than others, such as conversational skills that promote communication, good listening skills, and even the ability to manage the impression you're making on others. While standing on the sidelines of hundreds of lacrosse games, I have heard the phrase "lacrosse IQ," which describes a player who has the ability to make wise, strategic decisions that positively impact the team during active play. This same type of intelligence can be applied to any sport.

The common thread with all these variations of intelligence is how intelligence can give you an advantage in life. Intelligence gives you the ability to perceive and process information for positive practical purposes and outcomes.

To recap using this book as an example, the information in this book and the concept of E.P.I.C. living is knowledge. Intelligence is the ability to use this knowledge and apply it to your life. It's finding ways to build your personal character through virtues as those unique opportunities present themselves.

Now, let's add the power of wisdom. Wisdom is using knowledge and intelligence to make decisions solely for the purpose of a positive outcome and avoidance of a negative outcome. Wisdom develops over time. We use experiences and knowledge to make educated decisions that are for the greater good—a positive outcome. Choosing to apply E.P.I.C. to your life because it embraces a moral life that delivers happiness and personal fulfillment is wisdom.

HERE'S A CLEAR BREAKDOWN

Knowledge: Learning about the virtues (honesty, love, perseverance, etc.) and how they can be used positively in our daily lives and how the lack or improper use of these virtues can be a disadvantage.

Intelligence: Using virtues in unique ways in your life and discovering how to integrate more frequent use of these virtues.

Wisdom: Choosing to incorporate E.P.I.C. living into your life because a better character will increase moral values, which will lead to immediate and long-term happiness and personal fulfillment. Wisdom is being insightful and considering many possible outcomes before choosing the one that is most beneficial. It's understanding that what you do is contagious, deciding to choose actions that promote good, and avoiding actions that are dangerous and negative.

I often use the analogy of a toolbox with my children. I emphasize that they are already equipped with the "tools" (virtues) to get them through life with happiness and personal fulfillment. We gain knowledge as we grow up by learning which tools we have and how they can positively impact our lives. These tools are used to build character. When unexpected circumstances or problems arise, the tools can be used to rebuild and solve problems—that's intelligence. Over time, you will develop the power of wisdom. You will be able to look back at personal experiences that had positive outcomes when you used the tools properly and negative outcomes when you didn't. In other words, you need your toolbox to build your character and repair unexpected setbacks in life, and in doing so, you will become wiser.

WISDOM IN BUSINESS
Let's say you want to build a social media app. You must first take a class on computer coding to learn how to communicate

with a computer and program it to execute the tasks needed to accomplish your goal. This *knowledge* is learned in the classroom, online, and in books. Intelligence then uses the knowledge base from the learned language of computer coding to create the app and problem-solve a wide array of coding variations for the app. *Intelligence* helps you troubleshoot errors in lines of code that disrupt proper execution. You leverage your knowledge base to figure out how to make the necessary changes for your app to run the way you've envisioned it. *Wisdom* is setting out to create an app that is positive and for the greater good while being very cautious about avoiding negative use or abuse of the platform.

On a larger scale, let's look at Twitter. This global company built a media platform originally designed as an SMS (short message service) for people to update what they were doing within a small group. It was social and focused on keeping people connected—a positive vision. As Twitter evolved, it became more of an information and news platform and people began posting negative and sometimes completely untrue content.

In 2018, CEO Jack Dorsey met with the House Committee on Energy and Commerce as part of a hearing titled "Twitter: Transparency and Accountability" to discuss his priority in maintaining the integrity of Twitter by instituting initiatives to "increase the health of public conversation" so users would feel safe while using the platform.[47] Dorsey wanted to be sure abusive content and suspicious accounts would be removed. Since then, Twitter has raised its level of integrity, working diligently to create a healthy environment that embraces freedom of speech without harmful, negative content. The task is far from accomplished and requires ongoing oversight. But putting the

---

[47] E. Alvarez, "Twitter wants to 'increase the health of public conversation'," Engadget, September 5, 2018, https://www.engadget.com/2018-09-05-twitter-jack-dorsey-public-square-health.html.

new oversight in place reflects wisdom. Implementing corporate strategies (corporate policy changes, establishing new divisions to address negative content, and reengineering the coding to pick up on such content) to take a stance against negative content while working toward the positive, proper use of the platform was the correct response to the situation.

The phrase "knowledge is power" is straightforward, yet I believe the message is more about the underlying notion that what you do with that knowledge is where the real power lies. This is true wisdom. Use knowledge as the foundation to exercise intelligence so you can ultimately act with wisdom—with good intentions for good outcomes. My point here is that *you* have the knowledge, the intelligence, and the wisdom to live E.P.I.C.

There are many opportunities to grow in wisdom in our daily lives.

- You're likely using wisdom daily with your innate understanding that the more information you have (knowledge), the better insight you'll possess and the better decisions you can make. When unexpected problems arise, use information gathering as an integral part of finding a solution. Asking important questions to figure out the how and the why of a situation can lead you to a more successful outcome. Think of a time when you've been to the doctor with a medical issue—the number of questions you're asked can be remarkable. You may wonder what some of those questions have to do with your problem. The questions are asked because it's crucial for your doctor to uncover pertinent information in order to find the most successful outcome.
- Don't assume: This one is obvious. We can all relate to a time we misjudged a situation or a person. When Avery

was in first grade, the school put on a kickoff cocktail party for the parents to meet one another. On our way to the party, I decided to see if anyone I knew was attending. The electronic invitation offered an option where I could see guests who RSVP'd by last name and guest count. I noticed a couple and just assumed I would be meeting a traditional mother and father duo. Not the case—one of our parent couples were two wonderful women. I felt horrible making this assumption, especially since I am a supporter of the LGBTQ community, yet I appreciated this reminder to think more broadly and beware of assumptions. Looking back, this was also a form of unconscious bias (a learned stereotype that you're not even aware you have). We all have some level of unconscious bias that affects our view of the world. Unconscious biases are often discriminatory, especially related to race and religion, and they can exist toward any social group. The Black Lives Matter movement isn't just about the explicit bias against Black Americans, but also the underlying implicit bias (unconscious bias) that still exists. The important point here is that we all need to be honest with ourselves and think about the assumptions we make on a daily basis. Many are obvious, such as when you find yourself in a predicament or that moment you suddenly realize you made an assumption. Beware of those not-so-obvious assumptions, the unconscious biases. When we apply excellence to the virtue of wisdom, we can make the effort to uncover these biases in ourselves and work to remedy them.

• Trust your intuition. I have overcommitted myself many times in my life, spreading myself too thin to adequately handle my responsibilities. There were times I knew that

I should say "no" but said "yes" anyway. When the twins were in preschool, I was asked to be a classroom parent. I hesitated because I knew this would be a big time commitment (weekly blast emails with calendared events, managing parent concerns, planning parties, field trips, and other special events) which I didn't have. I knew if I did say "yes," it would be a strain on me and thus my family. I went against my intuition, agreeing to be a classroom parent. It all worked out and I had a fun year being intensely involved with my daughter's school, but my intuition was right. I was spread too thin with my time and responsibilities and wasn't able to make my children a priority, which I had promised myself I always would.

- Choose the harder right over the easier wrong. It may seem hard to keep a secret, or honor your commitment, or avoid temptation. But in the end, we know that less-than-desirable outcomes happen when the easier wrong choice is made.

- Prepare and set yourself up for success. No one likes the feeling or realization of being unprepared. Whether you haven't read all the materials for a business meeting or have worn unstable shoes for a full day of mountain hiking, we all know that lack of preparation can and often does leave you in a predicament you could have easily avoided.

EVERYDAY WISDOM

Take a moment and think about what your wisdom may be. Perhaps a person said something that had a tremendous impact on you and your life, or perhaps you learned something of great value from an event. We all have truths that we hold near and dear to us as personal lessons in wisdom. What are your "pearls of wisdom"?

We use wisdom in the hundreds of decisions we make throughout each day, and we innately factor in the outcomes and potential consequences of these decisions before we take action. If you focus closely on making wise decisions, you will see better results and more success, and thus happiness. That's living E.P.I.C.

Many years ago, I learned a valuable lesson that I use to this day. During my daughter's freshman year in high school, we attended the annual kickoff meeting for all parents and players before the start of the lacrosse season. This was our first meeting and we were both nervous and excited for this gathering. The room was filled with players from the freshman, junior varsity, and varsity teams. Tables with sign-up forms for volunteer duties and apparel orders lined the room. The meeting began with coaching staff introductions, the goals of the season, and some details about player placement during the decision-making process. We then transitioned to the topic of player expectations on and off the field. On-the-field expectations included proper sportsmanship, attendance, 100 percent effort, and cooperation while being coached; off-the-field expectations included academic priorities and social parameters. In an effort to enforce these expectations, each player was required to sign a code of conduct regarding proper behavior. If this contract was broken, the player would not be allowed to play in upcoming games and would be subject to removal from the team if the violation was extreme. The guidelines were black and white. It was wise of the coach to have this conversation while parents and players were present together under one roof to avoid any possible misinterpretation.

The final topic was directed to the parents: potential parent complaints. I was impressed that the coach was brave enough to address this topic publicly and in front of the players. She was poised and positive and gave excellent advice. She encouraged emails from parents as she wanted open communication, however, she said if parents were upset or concerned about something and chose to write her an email, they should use the "twenty-four-hour rule" before sending the email. She said that, based on her prior experience, emails sent in the heat of the moment regarding a frustration or concern were often full of anger. Furthermore, those negative emails could potentially be seen by other faculty and staff at the school. She wasn't preaching, she was teaching. I have embraced these words of wisdom in all areas of my life. Clearly, she was steering us away from a potential path of negativity and directing us toward a path of peace and happiness.

After this meeting, I took the coach's pearl of wisdom to heart and have learned to wait until negative emotions subside before launching into important discussions. A little cooling-off time makes it much easier to keep emotions in check and clarity at hand. I often say, "Let's talk when the dust settles." Everyone knows that I am referring to when emotions subside. I have also focused on beginning such discussions by outlining what I think others see as the problem. Then I try to just listen. What's shocking is that there was never a time when I wasn't surprised to learn a new, relevant piece of information. I try to be unbiased and allow each person to express their interpretation of the situation. Only then do I respectfully share my thoughts and feelings. I also use this method when mediating between my children. When everyone feels their voice can and will be heard, conflict resolution and applied wisdom can establish reasonable and respectful solutions. In the end, whatever the outcome of the conflict, there is a sense of happiness in knowing that your voice has not only been heard, but understood.

Here's another sports-related example of the powerful effects of using wisdom: Nick Saban has been a football coach for more than twenty-five years. The majority of his time has been spent at the college level, primarily the University of Alabama. He has an extremely impressive record as a football coach with a winning percentage of a whopping 79 percent. So how does Coach Saban maintain such a level of success? Outside of rigorous training and game strategy, he stresses the players' individual focus on the process, not the wins and losses. Coach Saban teaches his players to focus on striving for excellence in all areas of their lives, both on and off the field. He demands excellence in physical training during both the regular season and the off-season, excellence in studying all aspects of the game and the team's strategies, excellence in academics, and excellence in morals. Coach Saban believes that if emphasis is placed on the process, the winning will come. He has faith in the process. Based on the wisdom of applying excellence to every facet of his players' lives, he believes that the ultimate outcome will be success, and yes, happiness as a result of those victories.

Wisdom has one more bonus: It's a valuable asset that can be shared and taught. As you become more aware of how virtues constitute your character, you can easily impart this valuable insight to others so they too can live with greater happiness and personal fulfillment.

If you're a parent, you naturally take on the role of teacher. There are endless opportunities to share your wisdom with your children. It's like the old proverb, "Give a man a fish and he will eat for a day. Teach a man to fish and you will feed him for a lifetime." I often have teaching moments (what I call TMs)—opportunities for me to interject my "mom wisdom" into a situation. This can open the door for a general discussion where I can make a point or even, in some cases, present a potential problem. When I take advantage of TMs, it takes the onus off any one particular child. Typically, I begin with, "Wait, I need a teaching moment here, no one is at fault, but what if . . .? Or how do you think . . .?" Kids are smart. I simply offer them a different perspective, which is especially helpful as independent thinking grows.

We all possess wisdom and use it to varying degrees in our daily lives. It is developed and cultivated throughout our life span. Wisdom requires a willingness to learn from life's lessons and be transformed as a result. This is huge! Wisdom supports the E.P.I.C. journey and makes an even more compelling argument for applying excellence to our character. Without knowledge of the virtues that reside within you, you will not be able to impart the wisdom it takes to live E.P.I.C.

BENEFITS OF WISDOM

- Wisdom is thought-provoking and challenges you to think broadly with a thorough knowledge base so you can make decisions with good intentions that will benefit many with better outcomes.
- Wisdom enables you to be creative and open to new experiences, to problem-solve based on overarching goodness.
- Wisdom is a form of humility, in that it supports an eagerness to continually learn from experience and from others, while understanding that you will never know everything there is to know.

EVERYDAY EXCELLENCE IN WISDOM

- Develop a growth mindset by continuing to educate yourself.

- ♦ Read or listen to books on tape. The *New York Times* bestsellers list is a great place to get ideas on current trends and topics of interest. Download a copy of *Mindset* by Carol Dweck to gain a deeper understanding of the power of mindset. See if your local college or university offers continuing education classes. Make today the day you finally take that class you've always wanted to take, like Introduction to Basic Guitar, French, Coding, or iPhone Photography.
- ♦ Use technology. Download educational materials that are at your fingertips (pun intended). Whether it's podcasts, documentary series, movies, webinars, or TED Talks, the opportunities seem endless for us to expand our knowledge and wisdom from online resources.
- Learn from others:
  - ♦ Mentorship is an excellent way to learn on-the-job training, grow personal relationships, and seek guidance. Be brave and ask "the pro" for advice. If you are going to begin a series of watercolor painting classes, ask the program coordinator if they can recommend a mentor to teach and help you along the way. Join support groups where you can get help from those who have experienced what you may be going through, like AA for addiction or a grief support group for widows or widowers. Even consider working with a life coach or therapist if you're seeking direction and meaning in your life.
  - ♦ Online communities like Meetup and Clubhouse are growing in popularity as platforms to meet new people and learn new things on a wide variety of topics.

- Make wise decisions:
  - Critical thinking and the decision-making process are comprised of three key components. First, explore every angle and ask questions. When a child runs to their parent because one of their siblings has just hit them, although this is "wrong," more information is needed. Was it in self-defense? Who threw the first punch? Could this have possibly been an accident? These answers will shape how you handle this situation. Second, weigh and measure the pros/cons. If you have just received two job offers, chances are you'll have to carefully consider differences in salaries, earning potential, healthcare benefits, hours, and so on before making a final decision. Finally, understand the positive and negative impact your decisions will have on others. Will a new job affect the quality and quantity of time with my family? Will this be better or worse than before? Will this job interfere with the concept of life balance?

CHAPTER TWELVE
PRUDENCE

Prudence does not mean failing to accept responsibilities and post-poning decisions; it means being committed to making joint decisions after pondering responsibly the road to be taken, decisions aimed at strengthening that covenant between human beings and the environ-ment, which should mirror the creative love of God, from whom we came and towards whom we are journeying.

—Pope Benedict XVI

So, what exactly is prudence? Is it a historical fiction character's name or a seldom-used term from centuries ago? In either case, prudence seems outdated. It's time to dust off this perspective because the truth is you use prudence all day, every day. And as soon as you see prudence for what it is, you will leverage this virtue for a better quality of life.

The word prudence originates from the Latin term pru-dentia or "foresight." More specifically, it can be defined as "the ability to govern and discipline by the use of reason."[48] In other

---

[48] Paul F. Kisak, ed., *Human Virtues: "The Traits of Moral Excellence"* (CreateSpace, 2016), 97.

words, you're being prudent when you make an educated assessment based on information or knowledge that has practical and positive implications.

Dr. Edward Sri, Catholic theologian, speaker, and best-selling author, has excellent insight on prudence. "Prudence is the virtue that most immediately helps us live our lives on target."[49] When we regret a decision, find ourselves in a sticky situation that was easily avoidable, or just sense our lives are not heading in the right direction, it is often because we lack prudence.

Another way of looking at it is that, "Prudence helps us apply reason and practical wisdom to our everyday actions and decisions, big or small. Through counsel, judgment, and decisiveness, we come to make prudent decisions that help steer our lives in the right direction."[50] And this is where I like to think of prudence as a tool I use to set myself up for success, which hasn't always been the case for me.

I learned about prudence unexpectedly and the hard way. I will never forget the first time I took a flight with my daughter Marisa. She was about fifteen months old and we were on a flight from Chicago to New York. I carefully packed the diaper bag, calculating the exact number of bottles, jars of baby food, diapers, and crunchy snacks to carry us through our day trip. Up until this point in my life, I hadn't traveled by air more than a handful of times, so the idea of flight delays never occurred to me. I am sure you can see where this is going. Not only were we delayed, but worse, we were stuck on the plane sitting on the runway for three hours. Not only didn't I plan for this, I didn't plan for her to have an upset stomach. I used up all of her bottles, food, diapers, and her extra change of clothes before we even

---

[49] Edward Sri, "The First Step of Prudence," https://edwardsri.com/2018/06/14/the-first-step-of-prudence/.

[50] "Growing in Prudence," https://goodconfession.com/growing-in-prudence/.

took off. I was in a panic. She was unhappy and uncomfortable, and everyone around us knew it. We made it to New York, but the anxiety and fear I had to deal with could have been avoided had I been more prudent. I am now known to have everything under the sun when it comes time to pack. Picnic, vacation, hike, short car trip—no matter the outing, I am prepared.

This wasn't the only lesson learned on this flight. I also learned another lesson with deeper meaning—the importance of being at your best. This was the first time I traveled as a passenger responsible for someone else. I took the safety briefing a bit more seriously and listened more attentively. I was caught off guard when the protocol in event of cabin depressurization, when the oxygen masks drop, was to place the mask over yourself first and then assist children with the proper placement of their face masks. This is not a parent's first instinct, and I remember mentally challenging this advice. But it makes sense. I would need to be equipped first in order to help my child. This single example taught me to take time to prioritize and to think differently about how important it is for me to be at my best. That had not occurred to me until I had children. I have shared and used the "oxygen mask" analogy across other areas of my life. Most notably, when the twins were born, I began "coffee with Kristin"—a time I set aside for myself by setting my alarm for 5 am every morning, before the babies woke up, so that I could start my day organized, ready for the first cry. Beginning my days prepared was a game changer for me. Responding to them with warm bottles in hand rather than flying out of bed in crisis mode to answer the cries of two babies changed the rest of the day. Years later, I still wake up before the kids and enjoy a few moments to prepare for the day ahead.

In my home, the most common use of the virtue of prudence happens when I ask myself or my children if what they are doing or planning on doing is a wise decision. For example, when we lived in Connecticut, my kids would often leave for school on winter mornings with their hair wet from morning showers and wearing lightweight spring jackets. Was this wise? Probably not. Sometimes they would open up their backpacks to begin a weekend's worth of homework on Sunday night. Not wise.

I tend to think of scenarios that could backfire and try to avoid them at all costs. For example, I have learned from firsthand experience that postponing packing for vacation until the day before we leave will lead to disaster, such as missing favorite clothing items, suddenly realizing shoes no longer fit, or not having enough bags to pack for all seven of us. Over time, I have grown wiser, making checklists and packing several days in advance so we can avoid my previous crisis-management scenario.

Just as packing in advance shows prudence, we use this virtue when we practice good judgment, insight, discretion, foresight, and sensibility. We all apply prudence in one way or another throughout each day. Think about some recent decisions you made, from what to eat to which clothes you put on to when you went to sleep. Which decisions were wise? Which were not so wise? My guess is that when you think of the unwise decisions, you're thinking about the less-than-desirable outcomes that came from those decisions. If you give the outcomes more importance before you make the decision, you're using practical wisdom—prudence.

Prudence impacts us in two ways. First, as an intellectual virtue, you have either information or the ability to gather information, and you are able to evaluate that information. These are more day-to-day decisions based upon being prepared or contingency planning that will increase the odds of a favorable outcome. Second, when examined as a moral virtue, prudence reminds you that you should act correctly. This is where we see decisions that are based on morally right behaviors versus wrong behaviors. Prudence is seen in the actions you take, and in order to choose the correct action, you need the insight to make the best decision.

In other words, prudence is used to direct human behavior toward a good end, and it is used in the decision-making process. Prudence uses knowledge and life experiences to differentiate between right and wrong, whether this information is fact-based or morality-based. Using this information, prudence applies practical reasoning to make those decisions that will consistently lead to a good outcome and ultimately deliver success and happiness.

For example, let's look at driving while intoxicated. It's illegal and deadly, yet there are an estimated ten thousand deaths per year involving drunk drivers. The facts are relatively straightforward: alcohol impairs driving abilities, which can result in fatalities, injuries, and arrests. Knowing this, the prudent conclusion is that it is wrong to drive under the influence; choosing to avoid driving while intoxicated is the morally right decision.

DWI repeat offenders clearly have not grown in prudence and continue to live with the negative consequences of additional arrests and potential human injury to themselves and others. On the other hand, the one-time DWI offender who now abides by the law has grown in prudence. The virtue of prudence brings an immense benefit to the quality of your life and is sure to deliver the E.P.I.C. promise of happiness and personal fulfillment.

Have you ever had one of those days where everything seems to be going wrong and life feels like it's crumbling all around you? I often say to myself, *You can't make this stuff up* on days like that. Multiple events around you are out of your control and you're doing your best to make split-second decisions. For me, my ability to be prudent kicks into high gear on those days. I go into something like survival mode.

Many years ago, as a family, we experienced one of those days. We were living in Connecticut, and an unexpected mid-March storm ripped through our town. It left a tornado-like path of destruction. I was with one of my older daughters at a swim meet about an hour north, and the town we were in was completely unaffected by the storm. A babysitter was at home with my three younger children. My husband, Anthony, was with our eldest daughter at a lacrosse event. When the storm hit, everything went haywire. More than half of the trees in our yard fell down—one through the roof of our home. There was a widespread power outage in our town and several of the neighboring communities, and poor cellular signals made it difficult to get through to anyone. Communication was sporadic at best. I couldn't reach the sitter or Anthony.

Anthony managed to make it back to our house an hour after the storm began. He went into the attic to see the damage from the fallen tree, and as he approached the gaping hole in the roof, a gust of wind came through and sent him tumbling across the room. Just then more trees fell in our yard, this time crisscrossing the driveway and blocking in the cars. The path of destruction from the storm continued to escalate. It became apparent to Anthony that living in our home for the next week or two would be dangerous without power, heat, and running water. With this foresight, he acted prudently and booked the last room at a nearby hotel. He and our sitter quickly packed up the kids in the SUV so she could drive over the lawn to get onto the road. She drove down our street only to find more obstacles as she approached the intersection with the main road: police barricades, more downed trees, dangling electrical wires. What was normally a five-minute causal drive took her thirty minutes of detours and rerouting to get to the hotel safe and sound.

The nearby restaurants were all closed due to the storm and the sitter now had three hungry kids to feed. Anthony suggested she immediately go to Costco, which was nearby, and buy food and water to last for a few days. She got in and bought the basics just as the store was closing due to the storm. The key here was that Anthony was not only able to focus on safety from moment to moment, but he actively planned for the future, thinking about what we would need next. The sitter was in lockstep with Anthony, helping and making everything better all along the way. Yes, this is foresight, and yes, this is prudence.

Prudence is equally valuable when planning for the future. We use prudence as we navigate through life. Two months after college graduation, my eldest daughter, Marisa, began working full-time for a finance firm. She was eager, energized, and equipped with a degree in economics. On her first day of training, a session with the human resources department helped her sort out all of the necessary paperwork, from health insurance brochures describing which medical plan was best suited to meet her needs, to numerous government forms for wage reporting, to unique perks her company offered. She was able to make her way through most of these new-hire details until the income reporting forms were ready for the final sign-off. She was asked if she wanted to start a 401K—a retirement savings account. Being a new graduate and in some debt, Marisa was shocked to even hear the word "retirement," especially since she hadn't started working yet.

Her immediate thought was no. Why, when for the first time in her life she would finally have some money to spare, would she stash it away for a distant retirement in forty years? She wanted money and she wanted it now. If she were to invest her spare funds in retirement, her entire salary would just cover living expenses, including rent, utilities, food, and transportation. Then it occurred to her that there must be a good reason why the topic of retirement was coming up now, but what was that reason? Puzzled, she asked one of the human resource advisors, an older, father-like figure. He explained that if you put money aside in a 401K account, the company would match these funds, so you'd actually make money. He also pointed out that when a 401K is established at a young age, the investment has years and years to increase. He added that she would never regret this investment now, but if she waited, she would always regret it.

This gentleman was teaching her to be prudent at a young age and to invest wisely. Prudence was presented to her as a way to make a wise decision for her future benefit. Marisa was definitely a bit uneasy but gave it a shot and took his advice. A mere four years later, her 401K account boasted what was nearly equivalent to her first year's salary. Recently, she decided to make a total career change, and with her 401K account she had the financial confidence to do so.

Marisa learned firsthand the importance of being prudent. This one lesson has had an enormous impact on how she continues to plan as she navigates life as a young adult. She now actively seeks advice, researches, and weighs possible outcomes before she makes life-impacting decisions. She continues to rejoice and feel successful with her prudent decision regarding her future retirement.

You can get a good image of a person who acts prudently by thinking of a person who continuously and consistently makes responsible, wise decisions—the person who seems to always be prepared for the future, perhaps the person you go to for advice.

Every day I pause and ask myself if I am making a wise decision. I stop and take the time to consider the pros and cons of any given situation and gather as much information as possible. I give great weight to responsibility and accountability. There are also other, less obvious everyday scenarios where I find prudence to be helpful. The first is the concept of regret and my decision-making process. The second is one of my personal favorite survival skills, being prepared and using contingency planning skills.

Most of us have said, "I know I am going to regret this, but ..." or "I hope I don't regret this. . . ." Prudence heeds these intuitive warnings and shifts decisions that ensure better outcomes. Over the years, I have learned the hard way what happens when you take an action that you know you will later regret. Maybe it's an unnecessary comment that can hurt someone's feelings, an email or a text message that was then forwarded to others, creating a messy situation. I now know how to hold my breath on occasion and delete messages that I wouldn't want people outside the conversation thread to see. Being prudent has made me embrace accountability and increased my confidence. I've grown in the virtue of wisdom by learning from my mistakes and making changes for the better. Living E.P.I.C. doesn't mean you have to fight enormous battles all day long. It can be enacted tiny step by tiny step in making better decisions.

Regret is the feeling that we would be happier if we had done something differently in our past. The majority of us know of a time when we regretted our actions, or perhaps regretted that we didn't take action. What's interesting about regret is that for some people it can provide motivation for a positive change in their life and for others it can cause a negative outcome. Consider the example of a major corporation whose business is declining because of regrettable decisions. Some executives of this corporation could be inspired to correct the wrongs and commit to rebuilding the business. Others could become emotionally consumed with the negative impact and drive the company out of business. In either case, regret is a part of their lives. What they do with it is their choice.

Over time, I have learned to use my fear of regret as a motivational force. And I have used prudence to avoid regret as much as possible. Taking the time to act with prudence has opened my life up to opportunity, happiness, personal fulfillment, and a lot of peace. Placing an emphasis on outcome has been the key. I simply ask myself, *What have been some of my biggest regrets? If I could go back and change my actions, do something differently, what would that be and why?* What's better though, is to find ways to avoid regret altogether.

Contingency planning has been a huge part of my growth as a parent, especially as it relates to managing the complexity of my children's academic, athletic, and activity schedules and transportation. This hearkens back to my phrase, "You can't make this up. . . ." For example, I could be in the ER with one child while another missed the bus and was stuck at school without a ride home and the third was on the side of the road with a flat tire. At times like these, if someone were to ask how my day was, I would reply, "Well, I'm well past plan B and onto plan F." I joke, but it's very real. Having contingency plans has allowed me to multitask many needs in a given moment. In the above example with a kid at the ER, this is what we have in place:

- If any child is off to the ER, that's where you will find me.
- If a kid misses the bus home, follow this plan: Go to the office, stay there with the adults, and wait for me to pick you up, or get a ride home from someone you know. The goal is you are safe and with adults you can trust.
- Flat tire—all drivers have AAA insurance policies with roadside assistance in their names.

One could argue that part of the reason for all of this organization is that I parent many children. I agree to a certain extent. However, the elements of being prepared and flexible and having the ability to reduce widespread chaos in a split second gives me peace of mind and sets me and my family up for success. The simple things I list below help keep us out of potentially sticky situations. I try to always be prepared, which is directly tied to contingency planning. These are basic, but they show forward thinking and planning:

- Always have cases of water, batteries, and flashlights safely stored at home.
- Always keep cash and nonperishable foods in the house.
- Carry backup portable chargers, even in the car.
- Keep water and extra apparel in the car.

If you pay attention to your choices, you can and will reap the benefits of developing and growing prudence in your everyday life. By reading this chapter, you're already investing your time in learning how employing daily practical wisdom with foresight can guide you as you explore the virtues and how they impact your life on your E.P.I.C. journey.

BENEFITS OF PRUDENCE

- Prudence gives you the ability to use knowledge and wisdom every day for desirable and favorable outcomes.
- Prudence enables you to approach life with patience and reason instead of reacting impulsively and without reason.
- Prudence allows you to be deliberate and purposeful.
- Prudence helps you to plan appropriately for the future.

- Prudence allows you to manage and leverage your assets such as money, skills, and resources.
- Prudence focuses on positive goals and outcomes.
- Prudence prepares you for success and happiness in all aspects of your life.
- Prudence and foresight can help to reduce unnecessary stress.

EVERYDAY EXCELLENCE APPLIED TO PRUDENCE

- Be prepared:
  - Educating yourself is a priority. When you interview for a new job, be sure to wear proper attire, bring a notebook, calendar book, and something to write with. Have questions prepared for the interviewer. Do research on the company or organization and thoroughly educate yourself on its history, the current status, and future potential of the business, even the competitors.
  - Contingency planning: Prepare for plan "B"—potential foreseeable circumstances that may negatively impact you. When my children were younger, I never planned what to do in the event of a fire in our home. I just assumed everyone knew what to do. Then one day, my eldest daughter came home from kindergarten with a homework assignment. Practice a fire drill with your family. My husband and I had to discuss several options for an exit route until we came up with the most logical and safest for our family. Had we not had this assignment, there would have been a lot of confusion of where to go and what to do in the event of a fire. Thankfully we never needed to use this

contingency plan, and thankfully this exercise taught us a lot about the real value of being prepared. Create a variety of "family action plans" that describe what to do in the event of natural disasters like blizzards and earthquakes, or in-home emergencies like the fire example above or home flooding and power outages.

♦ Avoid impulsive actions that could present a challenge down the line. Buying an expensive car that is out of your price range because it was the deal of a lifetime will surely put a strain on your finances for years to come, or maybe while shopping at the local farmers market you see a young family with a crate of adorable "free puppies" and you decide to take one home with you. In the moment of spontaneity, you may not have realized the amount of time and money that will be needed to care for your new pup. Be wise, take a moment or two, and think before you act.

♦ Focus on life balance—create and customize a personal pie chart with slices reflecting general categories in your life like career, personal relationships (family/friends), mental wellness, physical wellness, personal growth, and leisure, to name a few. The idea here is to conceptualize important areas in your life that impact your overall health and wellness.

Part Three
Your E.P.I.C. Mindset at Work in the World

CHAPTER THIRTEEN
EMBRACING THE E.P.I.C. MINDSET

If my mind can conceive it and my heart can believe it, then I can achieve it.

—Muhammad Ali

Our mindset is a dominant influencer in our lives. It's the belief system we use to interpret situations, the way we think, our viewpoints. Think of mindset as our *mental inclination* or attitude. Mindset can purposely and inadvertently shape our perception of the world, which then affects the way we interact with the world. Mindset is a differentiator between success and failure, happiness and unhappiness.

Classic examples of opposite mindsets include the go-getter versus the naysayer, the optimist versus the pessimist, the risk-taker versus the risk-averse, and the rigid versus the flexible. Can you relate to any of these? Who do you know who fits one of these profiles? How would you describe their lives—are they thriving or mediocre, happy or unhappy?

I can tell you from firsthand experience, the naysayer mindset makes life mundane and boring. The go-getter mindset brings a life filled with excitement and adventure. From toddlerhood on, my children shared the same spirit of independence, fearlessness, curiosity, and creativity fueled with questions like, "Can we? Why? Why not?" All too often, I would answer with "No" and "Because you could get hurt or make a mess." They wanted to reach new heights on swings, bake concoctions without following recipes, ride their bikes to distant places, always driven by their go-getter mindset. The lens through which they saw life was focused on the excitement of exploring the unknown. My lens was fixed on maintaining a comfort zone, reining the kids in with my naysayer mindset. Then it occurred to me that the kids were always happy and eager to explore and grow, and I was not. I cautiously tried to shift from my naysayer mindset to their mindset. I quickly realized what my kids already knew. Taking risks, making mistakes, trial and error, was actually a lot of fun. Soon we were learning and growing together. And you know what else? The bonds between us became stronger. I shared in their happiness when I broke out of my comfort zone and embraced their growth mindset.

Several years ago, I witnessed something that brought home the power of mindset. I was part of the senior luncheon committee at our church. We planned and presented homemade buffet lunches for the seniors in our community throughout the year. For these lunches we set up the gymnasium like a banquet room. We used colorful linens, centerpieces, and balloons, and worked to gather enough raffle items so everyone left with a small gift. I looked forward to socializing and spending time with our seniors. As our friendships grew, it became more apparent that our guests were either complainers or complimenters. The complainers were set in their cranky ways—the food was too hot or too cold, too salty, too spicy, not sweet enough. No matter how hard we tried to remedy their concerns, they were never happy. On the other hand, the complimenters were always pleasant—it's perfect, thank you so much, don't worry, I would love to try something new. The difference was staggering. It was so endearing to see people in their eighties happy, smiling, and appreciative of a simple homemade meal as opposed to those who were unhappy, unappreciative, and critical. It occurred to me that this was the way they approached everything in their lives—it was their mindset and had little to do with the luncheon. Our complimenter guests were happy, joyful, and a pleasure to be around, and our complainers were unhappy, cranky, and people I politely avoided.

MINDSET INFLUENCERS

Thankfully, we can choose our mindset. This is spectacular news and key to this conversation. Embracing and creating a mindset for lasting happiness and personal fulfillment is up to you, and you can change it at any time. We all have the ability to support perspectives that will benefit us and avoid or resist perspectives that hold us back.

So how does this happen? It's as simple as being aware of what can influence your mindset, then embracing and executing a mindset that will put you on course for happiness and personal fulfillment.

Many things influence our lives (past and present) and play a part in influencing our viewpoint. The first and most influential impacts come from parents, guardians, and those who shaped our childhoods. Naturally, these individuals take on the role of teacher and provider. Built into their role is taking responsibility to share with and direct children according to their beliefs about best practices and perspectives for living a successful life.

My grandmother grew up during the Great Depression. Whenever we visited her, whether it was a holiday or just a fun visit, we grandchildren were taught to save, spare, reuse, and never, ever waste. I have a fond memory of waking up one morning at her house, walking into her kitchen, and seeing her lifting sand-filled, one-gallon plastic milk cartons over her head. Her homemade hand weights put a new spin on working out in a home gym! I remember thinking what a brilliant idea this was. Gram's mindset was shaped by growing up with strictly limited resources, and she was both creative and frugal. To this day, I see myself influenced by many of her thrifty ways when it comes to being resourceful.

Personal experiences can deeply influence our mindset. These can be emotionally inspiring or emotionally damaging. While growing up, my husband Anthony saw his mother, a single parent, struggle financially, working three jobs while raising three young boys. Seeing firsthand the hard work that went into earning money and the value of a dollar, he began saving every penny. As he saved to buy his first car, he even carved out the pages of a book that he kept on his bookshelf to hide his money inside. He wanted a car so he could drive it to a job, where he could work to earn money, which he knew would lead to more opportunities. He has always believed hard work pays off, just like his mother. He was emotionally inspired and shaped by his mother's work ethic and today he heads a company with the motto "Get your money right" so other people can benefit from the financial guidance his mother didn't have access to.

Another factor influencing your mindset can be your social circle. Are they positive and energetic? Caring and giving? Or are they (fill in the blank here)? The point is, the people you are around will influence your mindset.

Consider also the people that surround you, the community where you live. I noticed this when we moved to California. It never even occurred to me to consider what my new community would be like. Instead, I thought more narrowly, focusing on transitioning the kids into their schools and the basics of setting up a new life on the west coast. I was delightfully surprised to learn that we were immersed in a worldly and culturally diverse community. When I went to my first parent meeting at the twins' school, I met families from Sweden, Korea, Japan, India, Mexico, Poland, and other countries. My entire family was amazed and humbled to have the opportunity to feel part of the bigger world in our small community. As we were learning and experiencing, we were growing.

As you can see, many factors can influence your mindset. Good, bad, right, or wrong, begin thinking about your perspectives and the influence these have had on your life, your career, your relationships, and even your personal growth. Watch carefully for those negative people who can influence you in their unproductive and damaging direction. Focus instead on surrounding yourself with people who lift you up and make you better just by being near them.

Like many of us, I am not the person I was in my younger years. And for this I am grateful because with life experiences, I have grown wiser as I have grown older. I have learned and embraced the importance of a proper mindset, an E.P.I.C. mindset, for my happiness and personal fulfillment.

A PURPOSEFUL MINDSET

In 1952, Dr. Norman Vincent Peale, a Christian minister, published the revolutionary book *The Power of Positive Thinking*. He wrote about our ability to change our lives for the better with positive approaches. He discussed visualization, draining your mind of negativity and replacing it with positivity, letting go of the negative habit of worrying, and believing with faith and self-confidence that you can achieve your goals. All measures were driven by embracing a positive outlook on life. His message was so inspiring and impactful that his book landed on the *New York Times* bestseller list and remained there for more than three years. To date, fifteen million copies have been sold worldwide.

When I first read this book about thirty years ago, I was looking for a strategic advantage in my life. The answer came in the form of pursuing happiness and inspiration, a delightful surprise I wasn't expecting. It was apparent to me that I had to change my mindset for the better in order to change my life for the better. It didn't happen overnight, but it did happen. Even today, I am certainly not always positive and often have to remind myself to get back on track. But it's not all that hard to make the correction, especially since I know in my heart of hearts that it's the right thing to do.

GROWTH VERSUS FIXED MINDSET

As I began my journey to live E.P.I.C., I knew it would be much easier if I had an E.P.I.C. mindset. I knew my mind had to embrace the concept of building character before E.P.I.C. virtues could impact my life. I simply left it at that, until I read *Mindset* by Carol Dweck.

After twenty years of research, Carol Dweck, a Stanford-based psychologist, published her findings related to achievement. Her studies show that our personal success can be powerfully influenced by the way we think about our individual talents and abilities.

Dweck identified two major mindsets: the growth mindset and the fixed mindset. The growth mindset is based on the belief that your basic qualities are things you can cultivate through your efforts, your strategies, and help from others. Individuals who possess the growth mindset challenge themselves and put forth the effort necessary to fuel these challenges. The key with the growth mindset is effort. The growth mindset allows for error as an opportunity for learning. Success in the growth mindset is in stretching yourself without the fear of failure.

By contrast, believing that your qualities are carved in stone—the fixed mindset—creates an urgency to prove yourself over and over. People with the fixed mindset often feel intellectually superior and see applied effort as a weakness. They also see failure as a measurement of a person. In some cases, this can be catastrophic for the individual, especially if they actually applied effort, which was seen by them as a weakness to begin with.

To better understand the growth mindset versus the fixed mindset, let's look at an excerpt from *Mindset*.

"We offered four-year-olds a choice. They could redo an easy jigsaw puzzle or they could try a harder one. Even at this tender age, children with the fixed mindset—the ones who believed in fixed traits—stuck with the safe one. Kids who are born smart "don't do mistakes," they told us. Children with the growth mindset—the ones who believed you could get smarter—thought it was a strange choice."[51]

The children with the fixed mindset focused on the high likelihood of achieving success, and the children with the growth mindset wanted to keep pushing their abilities without the emphasis on guaranteed success. They were not afraid of failure.

---

[51] Carol S. Dweck, *Mindset: The New Psychology of Success* (Balantine Books, 2007) .

Below are some quick facts I have gathered to help encourage you to consider the benefits of a growth mindset.

CHARACTERISTICS OF A GROWTH MINDSET:

- Loves to learn; believes that intelligence is developed
- Embraces challenges
- Learns from failures and setbacks
- Happily asks for help
- Puts forth effort and hard work
- Embraces success of others as inspiration
- Learns from constructive criticism

CHARACTERISTICS OF A FIXED MINDSET:

- Avoids challenges
- Believes intelligence and talent are fixed
- Gives up easily
- Finds failures humiliating
- Views asking for help as a sign of weakness
- Employs negative thinking, such as "I always fail, I can't, it's too hard"
- Feels threatened by success of others, experiences feelings of jealousy

BENEFITS OF A GROWTH MINDSET:

- Fulfillment
- Resilience
- Inspiration
- Striving to reach goals
- Higher motivation

- Lower stress, anxiety, and depression
- Better personal relationships
- Better performance

As I was reading Dweck's book, it was apparent that a growth mindset was precisely what I needed to become a better person. Then it occurred to me that the success and happiness I had been experiencing was not just because I was trying to be E.P.I.C., but because I had dabbled with the growth mindset. It was a win–win combination.

THE BENEFIT MINDSET DEFINITELY SUPPORTS THE E.P.I.C. MINDSET

The benefit mindset evolved from the impactful work of Carol Dweck and the growth mindset she studied. It is based on the motivation to have a positive and meaningful impact in the world by developing personal strengths. The benefit mindset is when people feel that there is "real value in being of value—to themselves, to others, to nature, and to the future."[52] There is a shared benefit. If I am working toward becoming the best version of myself, this will positively impact the world around me.

"Bringing together two areas of research—a 'being well' perspective from positive psychology and a socially and ecologically oriented 'doing good' perspective—the Benefit Mindset is presented as a mutually supportive model for promoting wellbeing on both an individual and a collective level."[53]

---

[52] Ashley Buchanan, "Benefit Mindset Schools Guide," Cohere, November 6, 2016, http://www.benefitmindset.com/wp-content/uploads/2016/11/Benefit-Mindset-Schools-Guide.pdf.

[53] Ashley Buchanan and Margaret L. Kern, "The benefit mindset: The psychology of contribution and everyday leadership," *International Journal of Wellbeing* 7, no. 1 (2017), https://doi.org/10.5502/ijw.v7i1.538.

The benefit mindset aligns with the E.P.I.C. journey. Although the E.P.I.C. journey focuses on you as an individual growing in character by growing in virtue, little by little, for increased happiness and personal fulfillment, there is a benefit to everyone around you. The reality is we live interrelated lives. You are directly and indirectly impacting everyone around you. Developing a fresh perspective of learning, growing, and challenging ourselves throughout our lives will be a key factor in our success and happiness.

Have an E.P.I.C. mindset!

CHAPTER FOURTEEN
VIRTUE CONTAGION

Emotion goes inside-out. Emotional contagion, though, suggests that the opposite is also true. If I can make you smile, I can make you happy. If I can make you frown, I can make you sad. Emotion, in this sense, goes outside-in.

—Malcolm Gladwell

Whether you're aware of it or not, and whether you like it or not, your emotions are contagious. If I am in a happy and joyous mood, this emotion transfers to those around me. If I am irritable and unhappy, this too transfers to those around me. This fact directly relates to E.P.I.C. living. If you live as a person of excellent character, not only will everyone around you witness the positive emotions of happiness and personal fulfillment that you experience, they too will feel this positivity and even perhaps begin to take similar E.P.I.C. actions by means of virtue contagion.

Living E.P.I.C. is win-win-win. The first win is the personal benefit of excellent character. The second win is that those around you benefit from your genuine, positive presence and persona. When you focus on the virtue of charity, they will feel more love; when you focus on gratitude, they will feel more appreciated. The third win comes from emotional contagion: the people you impact will begin integrating E.P.I.C. into their personal lives.

HOW DO WE KNOW EMOTIONAL CONTAGION IS REAL?

In the early 1990s, psychotherapist Dr. Elaine Hatfield of the University of Hawaii at Manoa realized that she seemed to be catching what her patients felt in each session. This sparked such an interest that she began to research the phenomenon of emotional contagion. Specifically, she focused on the synchronization of facial expressions and other body responses that result in the mimicking of emotion. *Emotional Contagion,* written by Dr. Hatfield, John T. Cacioppo, and Richard L. Rapson, is an extensive book that delves into the intricacies of emotional contagion with supporting evidence that looks at relationships between animals; relationships with family members (especially newborns and parents); clinical research by legends such as Sigmund Freud, Carl Jung, and Wilhelm Reich; social-psychological research; and historical research.

Psychologists coined the term "emotional contagion" to describe this phenomenon, which makes us consciously and unconsciously mimic the emotions of others around us. In essence, the feelings and emotions that you experience in any given moment can trigger the same feelings and emotions in someone else. Emotions actually become synchronized between people. As Seth Godin said, "Emotions are far more contagious than any disease. A smile or panic will spread through a group of people far faster than any virus ever could."[54]

---

[54] www.seths.blog/2014/05/emotional-handwashing

Emotional contagion begins the moment you make eye contact with another person. You receive a subtle, emotional cue and begin to mimic the emotion that you've interpreted. This is known as a neurological response of mimicry. Body language—such as a person's stance, hand gestures, even facial mannerisms—can also be unconsciously imitated. This transfer of emotion from one person to another occurs in milliseconds, with the mimicking of physical reads such as posture, facial expressions, and some aspects of speech. Typically, we are unaware that this is happening, which is known as nonconscious mimicry.

Think back to a time when someone came running to find you to share some exciting, good news. They were smiling, giddy, bouncing off their toes. You anticipated the shared excitement and even began to crack a smile. You were emotionally connected and eager before you were aware of the good news. As the news broke, your excitement increased and now you were both smiling, giddy, and happy. The emotion was contagious. This happened every time one of my children lost a tooth. Screeching with delight, they would run into the kitchen with a tooth nestled in the palm of their little hand, eager to show me the evidence, while smiling ear to ear to show me the new space among the remaining teeth. Within seconds, the other kids would come running to the kitchen with joy in anticipation of good news. Soon everyone in our home became filled with excitement, high-fiving and congratulating. A front tooth brought a whole other level of thrill. The excitement didn't end in the kitchen. As the news spread like wildfire to grandparents and friends, the excitement was contagious.

My mother has always had a special way of making anyone who comes into her home feel incredibly welcomed. She eagerly greets everyone with the same level of enthusiasm, whether they're a stranger or an immediate family member. Her genuine, upbeat welcome is contagious. When I was growing up, I could see this transfer of emotion to our visitors as she made them feel as if they were guests of honor. I have fond memories from my high school years of returning home late in the evening after a long day at school followed by either rowing practice or work, exhausted and often cranky. My mother always greeted me with such excitement and joy—almost as if I hadn't seen her in weeks. I looked forward to her genuine, happy welcome because I needed it. My spirits were instantly lifted by the transference of her positive emotion.

Behaviors can be contagious as well. Many years ago, I worked at a daycare's infant room, which had eight babies aged six weeks to nine months. The room wasn't large, and space was limited with eight cribs, two rocking chairs, a few swings, and a section of floor space for tummy time. In other words, we had tight quarters. It was a well-known fact that as soon as one baby began to cry, they all began to cry. It was contagious. So, at the first peep of a cry, not only did we answer their call for help with a warm bottle, fresh diaper change, or rocking to help them fall asleep, but we also acted with an underlying urgency to prevent an outbreak of crying. We knew the babies' personalities and preferences, and with a few tricks of the trade (pacifiers, favorite toys, and blankets), we kept the outbreaks to a minimum.

We've talked about emotional contagion as both a positive and a negative. What about the neutral scenario? When I was studying psychology in nursing school, we were taught that it was imperative to keep calm and nonbiased when working with patients or clients as it related to their challenge at hand. We were instructed to keep our emotions neutral and never show panic, shock, or worry on our faces. I used this purposely neutral emotion in my home life whenever the kids would get injured or there would be some sort of emotional crisis. I knew if they saw me panic, they too would panic, cry harder, and make it difficult for me to help them. Add to the mix a few worried siblings (contagion) and I would be in for a landslide of household chaos. Luckily, I had enough of a medical background that I could distinguish a real emergency from a nonemergency. I told the kids, "When you see me worry, then you worry," which also told them, "If I am not worried, you shouldn't be worried." I was actually telling them to mimic my behaviors and emotions.

While this approach has worked well with taking care of others and their personal crises, it hasn't done much to manage my personal stress. I have always had a vision of creating euphoric holiday memories for my family. I wanted those times to be incredibly meaningful, joyful, and relaxing. Well, I hope they were at least meaningful and joyful, because relaxing they were not. Why? Because I was not relaxed! I was stressed, and that's the emotion my kids caught. They could see it and feel it. I was always overwhelmed with the ins and outs of the holiday season, even as I tried to consciously keep a positive, upbeat mood so the kids would feel this same emotion. Year after year, I approached the holidays with the same vision of those euphoric holiday memories and year after year, the holiday stress returned.

Buying presents was one thing, but keeping track of and hiding them was another. My bright idea of taking screen shots of the gifts backfired one year when I handed my iPhone to six-year-old Ellie to play with, and she proceeded to scroll through the photos. After a few moments, she tipped the phone toward me, pointed at one of the pictures, and asked, "What are these?" I panicked that she would put two and two together and realize Santa and his presents had some help from me. But calmly I replied, "Oh, I was just organizing them." Ellie accepted my answer and I returned my phone to her with the game page open and ready to play. Five holiday concerts had me scrambling at the last minute, running from closet to closet in the kids' rooms trying to piece together the proper concert attire, which ranged from black bottoms and white tops to reindeer antlers and Santa hats. Every year brought a new twist that I wasn't properly prepared for. Panic around the sign-up for build-your-own gingerbread houses based on a first-come, first-served basis created a whole new level of stress—I needed five houses! The trip to the fire department parking lot to pick the perfect tree created some memories, all right—mostly that it's hard to get seven people to agree on anything. And let's not forget the Elf on a Shelf tradition. It was my job to move the elf each night, hiding it somewhere new for the kids to find in the morning. Every year, I would occasionally forget to move the elf, thus creating a totally contagious meltdown the next morning—if the elf hadn't moved, had he actually reported to Santa about how well-behaved the kids had been that day? You can imagine the uproar.

With much trial and error, I finally found a technique that helped me stay upbeat and positive. You guessed it: emotional contagion. Instead of focusing on my output, I thought about catching the positive emotions associated with the holidays. Where did I find the source of the spirit of the holiday season? My children. I opened myself up to receive their holiday excitement. Instead of trying to create the happy holiday spirit and send it to them, I realized it already existed in the hearts and souls of my children.

Emotional contagion doesn't always need face-to-face interaction. Many years ago, a dear friend received the tragic news that her father-in-law was diagnosed with stage 4 liver cancer and given the prognosis of three to four months to live. The diagnosis was an utter shock to everyone. I wasn't close with him—we saw one another a few times a year during the holidays and in passing when we were at her home at the same time. He was a carefree person, beloved by all, and always smiling and happy. When my friend called to tell me the news, I heard a trembling in her voice and knew immediately that something bad had happened. My heart sank. Then she told me about his diagnosis. I felt the heaviness of her emotional pain and anguish, even though we were not physically near each other. The emotion was transferred. He passed away a few months later. At the funeral mass, I glanced over, saw her weeping, and began crying myself. While I was sad for the entire family, I was crying mostly because I saw her wiping away her tears. The emotions, and in this case the behavior as well, were contagious.

Social media is an incredibly powerful platform for transferring emotional contagion along with news and personal opinions. This contagion can occur without direct interaction or cues. Just think about the platforms where you're given the option to click the thumbs up or thumbs down icon to deliver your feelings. A simple emoji can transfer your emotional feelings. The ability to send a message to an unlimited number of people with the tap of a button is incredibly impactful and far-reaching. Even the phenomenon of news and trends going viral—becoming contagious—is an everyday occurrence.

Shortly after creating a Facebook account, I realized that the original purpose of connecting people was spot on. I had a visual glimpse into the lives and interests of family and friends with whom I had lost touch. I connected emotionally with their photographs and commentary on a wide variety of topics. I soon realized that I was catching the mood of the people I followed. For example, I began following an old friend from high school who was publicly sharing the details of his bitter divorce. Every time I opened up Facebook, I saw his most recent update, which was negative and filled with anger. It became clear he was using Facebook to let the world know how horrible a person his ex-wife was. I immediately felt his negativity and resentment. Then within about five seconds, a few short scrolls away, I'd see friends who were sharing photos of them coddling their newborn babies in a hospital bed surrounded by family and friends. Immediately, I felt their joy and excitement. Every time I logged into Facebook, I experienced a roller coaster of mixed emotions.

When Instagram was introduced, it seemed a much happier place to spend my online social time—perhaps because at that time it was more photograph-based and less comment-based. As I added people to follow, I found I was more selective, consciously choosing to follow people who were fun and happy. I then took it one step further. I began to search for accounts that made me feel better, like "positive thoughts and more," "power of positivity," and "mindset of excellence." I set up my feed to bring me upbeat and inspiring messages in an attempt to purposely promote my own happiness.

CONTROLLING CONTAGION: SENDER/RECEIVER

When I first learned about the phenomenon of emotional contagion, it made me uncomfortable. The term "contagion" in and of itself made me feel as if I were somehow an innocent victim. What was I catching? Add to that the personal nature of emotions, and I felt vulnerable. It had never occurred to me that people in my surroundings influenced me throughout the day. However, once I began to better understand emotional contagion and its role in human interaction, my concerns eased and I began to wonder, *How can I have a say in this contagion?*

If I am catching emotions from someone, then someone must be catching emotions from me. I wondered, *What am I transferring? How am I influencing my family and friends? And is this something I like, or do I need to make a change?* I immediately realized that I have the ability to control what I send with emotional contagion, and therefore logically, I have the ability to control what I receive from others.

In the most basic sense, if today I were to choose to be super positive and happy all day long—both while alone and with everyone I came in contact with—then I am sending this positivity. The same applies to negativity. Not that I would ever choose this, but I could be angry and irritable to everyone I come in contact with, inadvertently treating them poorly by sending them my negativity. This realization made me feel more responsible and accountable for the emotions that I was sending.

I can also decide what emotions I receive from those around me. Naturally, the majority of us would rather be in the midst of positive, upbeat people than miserable, angry people. With an understanding of emotional contagion, we can learn to ward off or even avoid the transmission of negativity, just like we can search for and capture the transmission of positivity.

A few years ago, I attended an "Unleash the Power Within" event by life coach and business teacher Tony Robbins. I had read a few of his books, which I found inspiring. I had listened to some of his podcasts, as well, but I needed something more to really capture his energy. I thought if I were to see him live, I could receive or catch his energy, enthusiasm, and emotion. I was right: the impact of experiencing a motivational speaker live and in action was extremely powerful and contagious.

On the other hand, I avoid at all costs those toxic people that we all come across from time to time. They're not hard to find because they are manipulative and judgmental. They blame everything on others, criticize people freely, and simply lack good character. Over the years, I have encountered a few people that I steer clear of for this exact reason. They have actually tried to persuade me to take on their angry and vengeful viewpoints. I am so uncomfortable in their presence that I do one of two things: If I can, I physically remove myself, and if I can't, I employ a defense system of sorts, like an emotional shield that keeps me from meeting them at their negative level. I make a deal with myself to not fall into their trap of trying to persuade me to ascribe to their viewpoint. I use the analogy with my kids of how Wonder Woman uses the hardware on her wrists and her shield to deflect anything negative. You don't aim that negativity back to anyone; you protect yourself by aiming it into the ground and getting rid of it.

Emotional contagion is a positive byproduct of E.P.I.C. As you experience happiness and personal fulfillment, you naturally send this positive sentiment to those around you; you set an example of living E.P.I.C. for others to see; you have the wisdom to be conscious of what you choose to receive and what you choose to deflect—again a benefit for you and for others.

EMOTIONAL CONTAGION—KEY POINTS

- Emotional contagion is the subtle spread of emotions.
- It occurs whether you're aware of it or not, and flows both to you and from you.
- Take responsibility for your influence, negative or positive, by keeping track of what emotions you're sending out into the world.
- Make a habit of sending positive emotion and protecting yourself from receiving negative emotion.
- An incredible impact of living E.P.I.C. is that, through emotional contagion, you influence others' emotions and behaviors through your own emotions and behaviors.

As I have become more aware of emotional contagion, I now more easily recognize my strengths and weaknesses. I'm aware of days when my emotional contagion is good for my family and friends and days when it isn't. I have found the advantage of learning how to manage emotional contagion. When I keep in mind the simple fact that happiness spreads happiness and misery spreads misery, I do my best to avoid the latter.

Living E.P.I.C. begins small with subtle changes within your daily life. Your immediate family and friends are not only the first to be impacted by your emotional contagion, but they will also be the most influenced. Ralph Waldo Emerson is credited with saying, "What you do speaks so loudly that I can't hear what you say." When you choose to live E.P.I.C., you send out the benefits of excellence in your character and positively impact the lives of those around you. As you emulate E.P.I.C., everyone benefits.

CHAPTER FIFTEEN

FEED YOUR SUBCONSCIOUS: CREATING E.P.I.C. HABITS

Summing it all up, friends, I'd say you'll do best by filling your minds and meditating on things true, noble, reputable, authentic, compelling, gracious—the best, not the worst; the beautiful, not the ugly; things to praise, not things to curse.

—Philippians 4:8

We have the absolute ability to shape and influence our mind by using our thoughts and feelings. Indeed, learning how to rein in and access the power of our conscious and subconscious minds can change our lives dramatically. It's a powerful, rewarding path to personal growth.

The concept of the subconscious mind can sometimes feel a bit uncomfortable. This happened to me in college when I took a class on Freudian Theory. I was open to the concept that the subconscious existed, but I felt uneasy when I thought about it.

It seemed like a place of unknown, suppressed emotions—some happy, some angry. I remember being terrified that my college professor might ask me a trick question that would reveal something embarrassing from my subconscious. Good news: I made it through the class without embarrassment. Even better news: I learned that our subconscious is not necessarily a scary place, but rather a space from which we can supercharge our efforts to change our lives.

With a basic understanding of the subconscious and the role it plays in our daily lives, I am confident you too will be pleasantly surprised by the positive influence your subconscious mind can have in your life.

You've undoubtedly heard the phrase, "You are what you eat." When I was in elementary school, I saw the same poster every day while I stood in line at lunchtime. It showed two children sitting at a cafeteria table. One was happily eating healthy food and the other was looking a bit ill, eating junk food. The caption? "You are what you eat." The message was loud and clear that how your physical body functions depends on how well you nourish it.

This same concept holds true with your thoughts. There is wisdom and warning in the phrase, "You are what you think." Quite simply, at the end of the day, your life is shaped by your thoughts. We have thousands of thoughts throughout the day in our conscious mind. Whether you're aware of this or not, what you think—your perspectives or viewpoints—feeds your mind. As you think these thoughts again and again in your conscious mind, they become impressed upon your subconscious mind. Eventually, these thoughts that are now in both your conscious and subconscious minds will grow so pervasive that they take on a power of their own. They begin to impact other areas of your life. Pessimistic, self-defeating thoughts like, *I'll never be able to . . .*

or *I'm not good enough to* . . . can and do impact your outer life, thereby decreasing your success and happiness. At the opposite end of the spectrum, optimistic, self-enhancing thoughts like, *I'll get it done, I just need to figure out how* support a growth mindset, taking on a power of their own, and helping you achieve your goal. Your conscious and subconscious minds work in tandem with one another.

CONSCIOUS MINDS VERSUS SUBCONSCIOUS—A BASIC UNDERSTANDING

Throughout the history of literature, philosophy, and religion there are references to and evidence surrounding the discussion of the power of the mind. This is not new information. Thousands of years ago, it was understood that what we think can shape who we are and how our lives unfold.

Ongoing research and study have shown that a tremendous amount of influence stems from the conscious and subconscious activity of our minds. Let's look at what science currently believes.

What exactly are the conscious mind and subconscious mind? Your conscious mind is that which you are *aware* of— your thoughts, memories, feelings, sensations, and environment in the here and now. It's what you perceive from your thoughts and from actions.

At this very moment, you're *aware* of what you're doing. As you are reading this book, you're *aware* of your physical location, perhaps sitting on a beach or in your family room; you can tell how you're feeling emotionally and physically—hopefully this book is inspiring you; you're interpreting and analyzing the facts, and gaining an understanding of the learning process from fact to wisdom; you're putting together the information and thinking through what E.P.I.C. means and how it can make sense in your life; you're evaluating the real-life examples with reason and logic, maybe even asking yourself, *Does E.P.I.C. make sense? Will living E.P.I.C. really make a difference in my life?*; you're intentionally making the decision to continue to read the next page in this book (or maybe not) and to execute voluntary actions, perhaps sipping some water as you read or answering texts every so often. This is your conscious mind at work.

The subconscious mind stores your beliefs and long-term memories. It serves as a data bank of all that you've experienced—what you've seen, done, thought, and felt—good and bad. When we need to recall something we are using our subconscious mind. It is home to our learned behaviors, habits, emotions, and intuition. And it serves to keep our human body functioning on autopilot (breathing, heartbeat, etc.).

Your subconscious is also busy at work as you read this book. The information (knowledge) you've read in the previous chapters has been stored in your subconscious mind. Without knowing it, the emotion you are feeling as it relates to this book, good or bad, is leaving an impression on your subconscious mind while the information is being stored. We know this because when you actively recall what E.P.I.C. is about, you will not just be able to discuss the content, you will also experience an emotion associated with how the book made you feel as you read it. If you like it, you may enthusiastically recommend it to your friends. If you don't, you may just as enthusiastically tell your friends not to read this book. Or you may feel neutral about it and encourage your friends to make their own assessment if they decide to pick it up.

So how do our conscious and subconscious minds work together? The most obvious example is as you read (conscious), you are storing the knowledge (subconscious). And as you interpret the material (conscious), emotions are created and attached to E.P.I.C. and stored (subconscious). Perhaps you're voluntarily taking notes or annotating as you read, a skill you were taught in high school that has become a habit. The *conscious* mind is voluntarily writing, but it's acting on the influence of the habit and learned behavior of annotating, which is stored in your *subconscious* mind.

There are two key points to keep in mind about our subconscious mind. One, it doesn't differentiate between good and bad, or positive and negative emotions. It's driven by the intensity of any given emotion. Second, the subconscious mind uses emotions to awaken the conscious mind and guide behaviors. The stronger your emotion, the more impact it will have on your subconscious mind. Your subconscious mind will work on its own to send your conscious mind messages, often without you even being aware.

Occasionally, I feel anxious and antsy for no specific reason. Maybe I've woken up anxious and it takes me a minute to remember that it's because I have an important meeting or event that day. A heavy feeling in my chest often accompanies my anxiety. I've literally said out loud, many times, "I am anxious, and I don't know why. I can't think of why." The answer is my subconscious busy at work, sending me a message about a worry or fear that I can't recall in my conscious mind, perhaps a warning of sorts.

It's frustrating because I tend to be a fixer, and not knowing what's bothering me makes this need to fix things even more of a challenge. Typically, a few days after feeling anxious, I'm able to clear my head and come up with a reason for my anxiety that nine times out of ten circles back to a concern for my children. When they were younger, I was often worried about their physical safety—their first time sledding alone down a hill, maybe, or that time I caught one of them walking along the top of the six-foot stone wall at the base of our driveway. As they've grown older, I worry more about their emotional well-being. When Avery landed the lead female role in her class's production of the musical *Spamalot*, I was a wreck. She had never sung outside of the school choral program, and I was so nervous and afraid for her. Over the years, I've gotten better at identifying my anxieties. I usually know the source of my worries, and I can remedy them with some deep breathing, a sigh of relief, and faith in my children's ability to stand on their own.

Fear responses are not the only things hard-wired into us. Repeated encounters with material that makes us happy, calm, or grateful can also make a strong impression on our minds and our reactions. Have you ever tried to make yourself feel better when you needed a lift of your spirits? My daughter Marisa would watch some of her favorite Disney movies to capture the many positive messages they are known to deliver. As a family, we've all connected to another Disney production, the movie *Miracle* about the 1980 US hockey team winning the Olympic gold medal. We get emotionally charged with inspiration whenever we recall the movie. Why? Because of our emotional connection and personal agreement with the messages throughout the movie. The benefits of dedication and hard work don't come easily, but the discipline involved pays off through the virtue of fortitude and the power of teamwork. To paraphrase one line in the movie, "The power of teamwork means playing for the name on the front of your jersey, not the name on the back." In other words, think of your team, your group, your family—not just yourself. Whenever this movie comes up in conversation, our subconscious minds relay our positive emotional connections as we recall what the movie is about and the memories of our favorite scenes. We become inspired and reminded to believe dreams, hopes, and aspirations can and do come true with hard work and dedication.

Many people love to reminisce. I have boxes of old photographs from before the digital era that tap into all sorts of family memories—some happy, some endearing, some sad, and some that instantly spark an outbreak of laughter. Seeing the physical picture takes place in our *conscious* mind, and it's our *subconscious* that reminds us of the emotions and memories associated with those photographs.

Although there are distinct differences between the roles of the conscious mind and the subconscious mind, it is important to know there is a constant, two-way flow of communication between them, working to direct our daily functioning. And this is why soon you will see the power we have to use our minds with purposeful thought to our benefit.

As I think back to the beginning of my E.P.I.C. journey, it all began with a single thought. I had to find a way to change for the better. I consciously asked myself how I would do this, as I didn't really understand the process at that time. And then I would circle back to those original words, "to find a way to change for the better"—a positive and empowering thought. This didn't exactly come naturally to me; it took effort. I had many flaws and still do. However, through this process, I experienced firsthand the impact my thoughts had on my life. The nicer I was and the more selfless my decisions, the happier I was. And when I would stumble backwards, holding onto anger and negativities, the worse I felt. It became apparent to me that it took effort to stay positive and upbeat. The benefits were and still are so immense that it's a path I choose to walk on a daily basis.

As I eased into this journey, I figured I would just make subtle changes here and there, and I would have a better individual character. I set an achievable bar. But before long, I was challenging myself to grow better in all areas of my life—be it a better wife, mother, daughter, sister, friend, volunteer, or family cook. I learned that as my thoughts began to transform my conscious and subconscious minds, the effects permeated other parts of my life and everything improved.

At the beginning of my E.P.I.C. journey, my biggest challenge was to overcome the thought that I was a victim, which was based on a negative sentiment. I knew I had to change my perspective, thought process, and mindset to be positive and hopeful. My intentions were spot on; I just had to execute. Little by little, my actions began to restore peace for all of us.

I had to change my thoughts to be positive. I began to think more prudently, more glass half full instead of half empty. I *purposely* tried to find the positive light in everyone and every situation. I *purposely* planned family events where everyone felt included instead of continuing to have separate birthday parties and holidays for each side of the family. I knew that, initially, it would make everyone feel uneasy, but these events were those ice breakers that had to happen for a change for the better. It did, but it was a slow process. I *purposely* persevered when setbacks occurred, and there were many. These ranged from hearing what I took as an unappreciative comment after days spent cooking a holiday meal ("Oh, I don't eat any of the foods you've made anymore") to tension-filled phone calls complaining about one another. I reminded myself that, in these calls, I too was a complainer. I *purposely* remained calm and peaceful, promoting a loving family atmosphere. I *purposely* stayed on course, and we all moved in a positive direction.

We can all learn to be more active, accountable, and purposeful as we shape ourselves into people of character, and thereby achieve our goals and aspirations. We can *purposely and consciously* choose our thoughts, and therefore harness the immense power of our subconscious mind, to guide us to be E.P.I.C. in all areas of our lives.

USING YOUR CONSCIOUS AND SUBCONSCIOUS MIND TO YOUR ADVANTAGE

We have the ability to harness the power of our subconscious mind. How? We have to program it with the positive outcomes we seek. Think of the concept of making an impression. If we purposely repeat in our mind a specific message, our subconscious mind will accept this message as an impression and begin to take actions to see that our desire be fulfilled.

Auto-suggestion

In 1937 Napoleon Hill published a book, *Think and Grow Rich,* in which he compiled what he felt were key principles for personal achievement and success. One of these was auto-suggestion. Hill believed, "You may VOLUNTARILY plant in your subconscious mind any plan, thought, or purpose which you desire to translate into its physical or monetary equivalent. The subconscious acts first on the dominating desires which have been mixed with emotional feeling, such as faith." In other words, the more we feed our minds with our desires, the more likely they will come to fruition.

Anything we set our minds to begins with a simple thought or an idea from our *conscious* mind. Think about dreams and aspirations. They all begin with a single thought. The more we feed that thought with emotion, the more it becomes embedded in our *subconscious* mind. Knowing this, we have the ability to decide what to impress on our subconscious mind. And when we do this with passion and emotion, our suggestion or desire will take firmer root in our subconscious, increasing the likelihood of making our thoughts become realities. This is how auto-suggestion works. Remember this applies to both negative and positive emotion. Your subconscious mind doesn't differentiate. Earlier when I mentioned the positive impact of your subconscious mind, I was referring to your ability to choose positive content for positive outcomes and reduce negative content to reduce negative outcomes. You can also use auto-suggestion to change negative thoughts into positive thoughts, thereby shifting negative outcomes in your life to more positive outcomes.

Years ago, I had an idea. Why don't I write a book that I can give my children as a blueprint for a happy and successful life? This idea stuck with me for years, but I never acted upon it. Then one day, I decided to get started. I took charge, got excited, and became passionate about the content and the final product. I would close my eyes and embrace my vision with conviction all the way through to publication and widescale distribution. I used auto-suggestion. I used my conscious mind to impress upon my subconscious what I intended to do and my subconscious listened. And now you're reading the book I wrote.

Certain types of prayer can be very similar to auto-suggestion. We are emotionally charged with passion and belief as we mediate, visualize, and repeat our desires over and over. The main difference is that in prayer we ask for divine intervention; in auto-suggestion we do not.

There are many books on the topic of auto-suggestion. One of my personal favorites, *The Power of Your Subconscious Mind* by Dr. Joseph Murphy, suggests that the subconscious mind is programmable. In programming your mind, you will reap what you've sown, good or bad. You have the power to choose how you want to approach situations in life, how you want to be seen, what you will achieve. The subconscious mind is literal and listens to whatever your conscious mind tells it, so be sure to focus on the positive and avoid the negative. We can use our conscious mind to program our subconscious mind to be E.P.I.C.

Self-educate: fill your subconscious mind and build your data bank

During my college years, when I was struggling to find my way, I turned to my faith. Occasionally, I would open up the Bible and whatever page I randomly landed on was where I began to read, hoping to find a clue or a hint to happiness. There were a few times when I was shocked at how appropriate a random verse was to me at that specific point in time, but the majority of the time this didn't seem to happen. I would try to make it happen which didn't work out so well—Bible verses taken out of context are not especially enlightening—so I tried a more organized approach. Knowing the Book of Proverbs was supposed to be filled with wisdom, I decided to read this section to get some answers. It worked. Occasionally there was relatively straightforward advice on success and happiness; sometimes I had to decipher the proverb. In either case, I always felt a sense of hope and happiness as I read the passages. In hindsight, that makes sense because the Book of Proverbs is actually filled with words of wisdom as they relate to virtuous living. Without even being aware of this, I was filling my data bank with the knowledge of the value of virtues and personal character.

Today, there are hundreds of books, TED Talks, podcasts, and apps to help you learn more about personal character, virtues, and excellence. We have to take the time to self-educate and not simply take the concepts for granted. You'll be surprised how you're using virtues all day, every day. Any topic that you consciously seek information on and study has substantial sticking and staying power. Whenever I consciously seek new information and self-educate, it's because I am looking to fulfill a need or desire, which makes me emotionally invested. This helps me to better store and integrate what I have learned into my daily life. Embrace learning and grow in knowledge and wisdom.

Feed your subconscious: Create E.P.I.C. habits

I was shocked to learn that up to 40 percent of our day is built around habits. Yet it makes sense, because if I look at a typical day in my life, there is definitely a lot of routine, especially the first hour I'm awake. From the moment my feet hit the ground, I begin going through the motions. I am barely awake, and I have already taken my shower. I wear the same outfit—jeans (denim or white) and a t-shirt—make our bed, go straight to the laundry room, start my first load of the day, feed the dog, turn on the hot water for my tea . . .you get the idea. As soon as the kids begin their school day, my day will vary in tasks, but I can tell you this, whenever I have to go to the grocery store, I drive on the same road, park in the same row, grab a cart, and walk my same path around the store before I drive that same road back home. There are about four grocery stores within a five-mile radius, but do I switch it up? Not all that often. I don't even have to think about what I'm doing, I just execute this routine, and it's my subconscious working for me.

Charles Duhigg, author of *The Power of Habit: Why We Do What We Do in Life and Business,* talks about the cycle of a habit in the form of a loop: cue-routine-reward. There's a *cue* that leads to some action or behavior, then the *routine,* which delivers a *reward.* This loop is repeated again and again, creating a habit. When we want to change a habit, we need to change the routine while keeping the cue and reward the same.

When I am at home, every morning, I drink hot tea with two tea bags (one matcha and one traditional green tea) and a splash of vanilla coconut creamer. If I travel, I drink hot coffee with milk and sugar. I have the same morning cue, starting my day with a warm beverage that has a kick of energy, but I change my routine (habit) when I substitute the coffee for tea when I'm not at home. Both deliver the same reward of a tasty, satisfying burst of caffeine. I am equally happy in either scenario. I have different habits based on where I am, a different method to get the same reward.

Create the habit of growing in virtue bit by bit when opportunities arise, and your subconscious will surely adapt to their execution throughout your day. Years ago, I had a terrible habit of avoiding conversations with strangers whenever I was out and about in our community. I was typically rushing and distracted, keeping my eye on the kids, but in all honesty, I was more comfortable avoiding small talk. As I moved around, whether it was in the grocery store or a restaurant, a simple "hello" was about all I would commit to. The reality was my behavior was not very E.P.I.C. I wasn't approachable or sociable to those who wanted to help me, especially when I was clothes shopping. Whenever a sales associate would check in with me to see if I was looking for anything in particular or wanted to share with me current offers and new trends, I would clam up. Although it wasn't my intention, I am sure I came off as being cold and even inconsiderate. I decided to be kinder and more compassionate, warming up to strangers in my everyday life. Regardless of where I was or what I was doing, something as simple as a warm, genuine, eye-to-eye smile created a shared happiness. Interestingly, the *cue* was the same—strangers or sales associates approaching me. The *habit* changed when I changed my behavior to be more E.P.I.C., and you guessed it, my *reward* was win-win-win. I had a new positive habit, I was happier being more E.P.I.C., and hopefully those around me felt the warmth of a conversation instead of the chill of a curt "hello."

The power of your mind can and should never be underestimated. Simply knowing how your conscious and subconscious minds work is a great advantage. Be strategic, recognize and avoid negativity, and be creative to actively grow in positivity. I have definitely benefited from this knowledge throughout my life. It has helped me to be more cognizant of how negative thoughts can wreak havoc in my life and how positive thoughts can propel me toward success and happiness.

Aspire to be E.P.I.C. Have faith in E.P.I.C. Think of creative ways to live E.P.I.C. Educate yourself on various virtues and grow your knowledge "data" bank. See the value of how virtues work to your benefit in your own life and how misuse or lack of virtue does not. Take actions to be E.P.I.C., little by little, throughout your day. Use the power of auto-suggestion to grow in character and positively change your life. Make it a habit to be E.P.I.C.

CHAPTER SIXTEEN

E.P.I.C. VISUALIZATION: SEE IT, BELIEVE IT, RECEIVE IT

The secret of achievement is to hold a picture of a successful outcome in mind.

—Henry David Thoreau

Visualization is a relatively simple tool that, when used correctly and with intention, can be incredibly powerful. To put this tool to work, you create a mental picture—in other words, you see a physical object, action, or outcome in your mind—and concentrate on that specific picture for a well-defined purpose. The most successful visualization occurs when you envision *exactly* what you want to achieve, how you will achieve it, and what it feels like to have achieved it. You can use visualization in all aspects of your life, not just on the journey of becoming E.P.I.C.

By striving to fulfill what you visualize, you grow as a person. You will become more creative as you personalize and enhance your visions with detail and emotion. You will increase your self-confidence as you experience little successes along the way to fulfilling your image. And you will increase your positive mindset as you fulfill your visions with an "I can" attitude.

After wrapping up a lecture on visualization, one of my professors held up a copy of *In the Mind's Eye,* by Arnold Lazarus. He began nodding his head up and down in a "yes" motion as he gave his overview of the book and spoke with passion as if he, himself, had experienced a personal benefit. I found this intriguing and somewhat convincing, so I bought the book to see for myself what visualization was all about.

When I transferred to Marist College to complete my BA degree, I was excited to have a fresh start and seek new opportunities, but I experienced new challenges as well. I had to take a heavier course load to make up for lost credits and work multiple jobs to support myself and get out of debt. I thought perhaps visualization could help me reach my personal goals of academic honors and financial stability.

Before falling asleep, I would visualize myself earning mostly As—not perfection, but high grades—and experiencing the comfort of having ample money to support myself, to save a little and spend a little. I pictured myself looking at the top left corner of returned exams and papers, acing them with grades that put me at the top of my class and feeling that sense of accomplishment. Then I used that image and applied it to all of my courses. I envisioned myself working one job with the earning power to grow past base level. Maybe it would take place over time, maybe through tips or commissions, but I had to have the opportunity to earn more. I saw myself sitting at my dining room table at the end of the month, crunching numbers, discovering new ways to save money and be more efficient with expenses. I colored these visions with emotion and the amazing feeling of happiness. I visualized myself hitting new thresholds of success little by little, day by day, all the while being sure not to lose sight of my ultimate goal: academic honors and financial stability.

Immediately I had a new-found sense of empowerment as I embraced the responsibility for the outcomes in my life. My visions began to actualize. With each small success, my confidence grew and life seemed to turn around. My first semester junior year, I had all As and one B. At the beginning of my second semester, I landed the best job I'd had up until that point, working at a popular department store selling cosmetics. I had a base hourly rate which was higher than any other hourly position I'd ever held, a 4 percent commission on all of my sales, and the opportunity to earn overtime during the holiday season. To top it off, as an employee I received a 40 percent discount on my in-store purchases.

In June of my senior year, I graduated with high honors, on time, and debt-free. I also was promoted to a management position, earning even more money. Visualization worked! Not only did I achieve what I set out to accomplish, but also the journey was fun and I was thriving. I created happiness from the inside out. I owned it. My slump had ended. I fulfilled the picture I had painted for myself.

I also used a form of visualization during nursing school. The coursework included a tremendous amount of memorization, ranging from the diverse array of cells in microbiology, to chemical exchanges in chemistry, to knowing human anatomy inside and out. Fortunately, I am a visual learner and there was an endless supply of pictures to help me along. Our exams always included pictures from the textbook, with lines extending to the margins of the paper with simple instructions to "Label the part." As I studied, I would close my eyes and visualize the textbook picture over and over again until that image was secure in my mind. This visualization process was relatively straightforward and quite successful, judging by my test scores.

Before conceptualizing E.P.I.C., I aspired to be a good person and to have a positive impact on the world—just as so many of us do. It was a general, basic, undefined goal, but one I believed in and held myself to. My approach was to simply "flaw" less often and learn from past mistakes, being careful not to repeat them. The problem was that I then waited for opportunities to come to me. I had a vague, fixed mindset. Without a vision, I didn't have clarity on what being a "good person" looked like. I couldn't grow toward my goals as much as I wanted to—at least, not until I created E.P.I.C. as my vision.

I knew I needed to begin my E.P.I.C. journey with a clear, concise vision. Based on my transformation and positive experience with visualization in college, I knew that this was the most valuable technique I could use to keep laser-focused and achieve my goals. Now I had to get more specific with what excellent character would look like as it applied to me, and only me, building little by little, with all of the opportunities in my daily life to make virtue-based decisions.

One of the books that has influenced me the most in terms of making positive changes in my life is the aforementioned *In the Mind's Eye* by Arnold Lazarus. It provides a comprehensive overview of the power of visualization across all aspects of life, from healing physical and mental illnesses to improving relationships to achieving personal goals. Lazarus believed, "If you repeatedly and consciously picture yourself achieving a goal, your chance of actual success will be greatly enhanced."[55] Lazarus also discusses goal rehearsal, which is a process of using active visualization to achieve real success in a variety of areas,

---

[55] Arnold Lazarus, *In the Mind's Eye* (The Guilford Press, 1984), 61.

including athletics and peak performance, social settings where certain behaviors are encouraged or discouraged, reducing fears and anxieties, breaking habits, and overcoming sadness and psychosomatic conditions.

Creative Visualization by Shakti Gawain is another great book. It discusses four basic steps for creative visualization: set your goal, create a clear idea or picture, focus on it often, and give it positive energy. I like Gawain's point about giving your visualization positive energy, which helps keep the image alive and inspiring. In *The Art of Mental Training: A Guide to Performance Excellence,* author DC Gonzales uses the term "imagineering," which he attributes to Walt Disney. Gonzales writes ". . . the key with Imagineering is that you not only see and watch, but that you actually *feel* yourself succeeding, over and over again."[56] What a great image to help reinforce the concept of visualization. These and other resources are as close as your e-reader, library, or bookstore.

REAL-LIFE VISUALIZATION

Visualization is a common strategy used by many successful individuals across all walks of life. It's also highly personal, not just because you've created it and no else can actually see what you're seeing, but because you have the added piece of personal investment and passion that is important to bring life to your vision.

Brian Scudamore, founder of 1–800-GOT-JUNK, credits the success of his business to "painting a picture" of what he wanted

---

[56] DC Gonzales, *The Art of Mental Training: A Guide to Performance Excellence* GonzoLane Media 2014. p. 45.

his company to look like—in other words, he envisioned how he wanted it to look, feel, and act.[57]

In 1997, eight years after growing his company to $1 million in revenue, 1-800-GOT-JUNK? hit a plateau. The company wasn't growing the way it had been. Scudamore needed to make a change, so he shifted his perspective from what wasn't happening to what could happen. "I closed my eyes and envisioned how I wanted 1-800-GOT-JUNK? to look, feel, and act by the end of 2002. . . . For the first time, I went into extreme detail. I turned this 'painted picture' into a one-page document, blew it up, and then framed it in our headquarters for everyone to see. It contained not only tangible business achievements, like the number of franchises we would have and the quality of our trucks, but also more sensory details, like how our employees would describe our company to their family members and what our customers would say they loved best about working with us. In the five years that followed, roughly 96% of what I'd written down had come to fruition--even my wildest dream of appearing on the Oprah Winfrey Show. I've shared this simple technique with thousands of others; many who have gone on to build large companies. And we still use it religiously."[58]

Inventor Nikola Tesla is well-known for having developed the AC (alternate current) system of supplying electricity. When you plug in your morning coffee maker and see that green light come on, you have Tesla to thank. Tesla was also a master at visualization. As a young boy he would imagine himself traveling to faraway cities and countries. In these imaginary trips, he would stretch himself as far as he could into the

---

[57] Brian Scudamore, "This Visualization Technique Helped Me Build a $100M Business," Inc., October 21, 2015, https://www.inc.com/empact/this-visualization-technique-helped-me-build-a-100m-business.html.

[58] Scudamore, "Visualization."

actual experiences, like making friendships that were as real as if they were those of his actual life. He was acutely aware of his unique ability to bring life to what he saw in his mind, and he used this skill as an inventor, saying, "I needed no models, drawings or experiments. I could picture them all as real in my mind." What is even more intriguing is how he used visualization to create his inventions. "My method is different. I do not rush into actual work. When I get an idea I start at once building it up in my imagination. I change the construction, make improvements, and operate the device in my mind. It is absolutely immaterial to me whether I run my turbine in thought or test it in my shop. *I even note if it is out of balance.* There is no difference whatever, the results are the same. In this way I am able to rapidly develop and perfect a conception without touching anything."[59]

For decades, many successful athletes have used visualization to help them reach peak performance. Sports psychologists have become a crucial part of coaching teams, with a large component of their work dedicated to mental imagery and the actualization of those images. Boxing legend Mohammad Ali trained his mind by visualizing himself at the end of a bout with one arm raised by the referee and him holding the other up, declaring himself a champion; gymnast and Olympic gold medalist Mary Lou Retton practiced her routines mentally and repetitively every night; professional golfer Jack Nicklaus said, "I never hit a shot, not even in practice, without having a very sharp, in-focus picture of it in my head."[60]

---

[59] Nikola Tesla, *My Inventions: The Autobiography of Nikola Tesla*, Martino Fine Books: 2018. 5-6.

[60] Mental Toughness Trainer, https://www.mentaltoughnesstrainer.com/sports-visualization-the-shortcut-to-great-performances/.

I enjoy learning new sports, and just recently picked up golf. I set a short-term goal to go to the local driving range two to three times each week. The first time out didn't go so well. The ball went to the left, to the right, even two feet in front of me. I knew exactly why: I didn't know how to properly swing the club because I couldn't visualize it. The backswing—how far back should my arms extend? Should my hands be high above my shoulders or level with the ground? The downswing—fast or slow? The weight shift—when and how?

That night, I began searching online for the motion of the proper golf swing. I watched slow-motion videos of professional golfers and teaching tutorials. I mentally rehearsed the image of a proper golf swing and then envisioned myself following the same exact motions. On my second visit to the driving range, I felt more confident as I held a mental picture of what to do. Although I still had a lot of room for improvement, I hit a few great shots that inspired me to keep practicing and visualizing. Today, I continue to replicate the swing I see in my mind on and off the range. I am improving little by little.

AN INTERESTING STUDY INTO THE POWER OF VISUALIZATION

Several references point to the power of visualization when attempting basketball free-throw shots. While the details vary, this is the spirit of what they found: A group of students were asked to take a series of shots which were tallied (successful versus unsuccessful). After doing so, they were divided into three groups. The first group was asked to practice free-throws for a set number of minutes a day for thirty days; the second group was asked to exercise at the gym every day for thirty days and then spend thirty minutes with their eyes closed visualizing hitting the free-throw; the third group was instructed to do nothing.

At the end of the thirty-day period, all three groups were asked to return to the gym and take the same number of free-throws they had at the beginning of the study. The results showed two groups—the group that practiced the free throws, and the group that did not practice physically but simply visualized the free throws—*both* had almost a 25 percent improvement rate. The group that did nothing at all had no improvement. The mental reps in the group that visualized reinforced the incredible positive power of visualization.[61]

The use of visualization is also commonplace in theatre and film. Actors mentally picture the character they have to portray. They embrace that character's personality, mannerisms, and even their mindset. In a specific type of acting, method acting, the actor inhabits the character emotionally. The added element of emotion makes a powerful difference in their performances.

Jim Carrey, comedian and actor, is a passionate advocate of visualization and intention. In a 1997 interview with Oprah Winfrey, he discussed his personal experience with visualization when he was just beginning his acting career. He would drive to Mulholland Drive every night, park his car, and visualize himself "having directors interested in me and people that I respected say, 'I like your work' and visualize things coming to me that I wanted."[62] Actor Will Smith, also passionate about visualization, said, "If we dream something, if we picture something, if we commit ourselves to it, that is physical thrust toward realization that we can put into the universe." Arnold Schwarzenegger, body builder, actor, and former governor of California, attributes much of his success to

---

61 Phil Cicio, "Power of Visualization," Success thINC, https://www.philcicio.com/power-of-visualization/.

62 Jim Carey, "Visualization Empowerment," interview by Oprah Winfrey, 1997, https://www.youtube.com/watch?v=RwTS0uh2faE&feature=youtu.be.

visualization. "When I was very young, I visualized myself being and having what it was I wanted. Mentally I never had any doubts about it."[63]

POWER TO HEAL

Visualization delivers success that is not just performance-based; many people believe it can help us heal emotionally and physically. Since ancient times, cultures and religions around the globe have used prayer and meditation to bolster the healing process. For all of recorded time, the power of our mind and the mind/body connection have been used in the healing process.

Techniques such as meditation and guided imagery are used in the process of visualization for healing purposes. Encouraging and positive results have been shown in the reduction of pain and depression for patients suffering from fibromyalgia[64] and in the reduction of tremors in patients with Parkinson's disease.[65]

In *Fighting Cancer from Within*, Martin L. Rossman suggests the use of guided imagery as a useful adjunct in the treatment of cancer. He writes, "It has been shown to increase both the numbers and aggressiveness of natural killer cells when practiced over time, and has been shown to reduce complications from surgery, relieve pain, and reduce adverse side effects of chemotherapy.

---

[63] "The Secret of Tiger Woods, Arnold Schwarzenegger and Jack Nicklaus' Success," Stand.Out.And.Reign!, June 29, 2012, https://standoutandreign.wordpress.com/2012/06/29/the-secret-of-tiger-wood-arnold-schwarzenegar-and-jack-niclaus-success/.

[64] Belleruth Naparstek, "Guided Imagery Lowers Pain, Depression in Fibromyalgia Sufferers," Health Journeys, June 18, 2015, https://www.healthjourneys.com/blog/guided-imagery-lowers-pain-in-fibromyalgia-sufferers.

[65] Annie Stuart, "Parkinson's Disease and Guided Imagery," WebMD, December 12, 2020, https://www.webmd.com/parkinsons-disease/guide/parkinsons-guided-imagery#1.

Imagery is a psychological and medical intervention likely to increase your odds of recovery."[66]

There have even been cases of spontaneous recoveries and spontaneous remission after patients practiced guided imagery or visualization. In 2011, David Seidler, Oscar-winning screenwriter of *The King's Speech*, credited his spontaneous remission from bladder cancer to supplements and visualization. In the two weeks prior to his cancer evaluation, he said, "I spent hours visualizing a nice, cream-colored, unblemished bladder lining." To his surprise and that of his physician, he was cancer-free. He also mentioned that while he was visualizing, he shifted his thinking and stopped feeling sorry for himself. Sure sounds like a mindset change to me![67]

Visualization can promote emotional wellness and be used to decrease anxiety, worry, fear, and depression.[68] This type of usage can increase confidence, self-image, and motivation, and create bolstered faith and spiritual connectedness.

I encourage you to use visualization as a technique in achieving whatever it is you have your sights set on.

VISUALIZATION TECHNIQUES

Use visualization to your advantage and actively create a mental picture of exactly what you want to see happen in all parts of your life. Begin with a general vision of what you want to achieve. Then narrow it down with specificity. Personalize and embellish it with color and emotion. Bring that image to life.

---

[66] Martin L. Rossman, *Fighting Cancer from Within* (Holt Paperbacks, 2003).

[67] Elizabeth Cohen, "Can you imagine cancer away?," CNN, March 3, 2011, http://www.cnn.com/2011/HEALTH/03/03/ep.seidler.cancer.mind.body/index.html.

[68] João Luís Alves Apóstolo and Katharine Kolcaba, "The Effects of Guided Imagery on Comfort, Depression, Anxiety, and Stress of Psychiatric Inpatients with Depressive Disorders," *Archives of Psychiatric Nursing* 23, no. 6, (December 2009): 403–411, https://doi.org/10.1016/j.apnu.2008.12.003.

Live it and experience the feeling you associate with that image being fulfilled. Feel the feeling now, in present time. Use meditation and guided imagery for extra help in visualizing your goals and aspirations.

This is an opportunity to examine any thoughts or visions that you may see as factors holding you back from living a happy, fulfilling, and successful life. No matter what your aspirations and goals may be, taking the time to self-check any negative imagery is extremely important and beneficial. Use creative visualization to replace negative imagery with positive imagery.

Once you've created your image, replay that vision over and over. Rehearse it. Feel it. See it. Think of visualization as a two-fold process. The first step is the creation of an actual vision (vivid color, details, and emotion) of what you want to achieve. The second step is repeatedly mentally rehearsing, seeing, feeling, and achieving your image.

STEP BY STEP

- The image: Have a clear, concise picture of exactly what you wish to achieve. Make sure to build a positive image. Work through a few versions and then embrace this image with your mind, body, and soul. Believe it is happening or has already happened so you can feel it as if it were already real.

- Carve out time: Make time each day to relax and visualize your goal. Find a quiet, peaceful place where you can close your eyes for five to ten minutes without being interrupted and meditate on your visualization. See this as a time to create a silent mental space that you can fill with your mental image. It can be first thing in the morning before you get out of bed, or perhaps shortly thereafter with a cup of tea or coffee, or as you fall asleep in the evening. Sometimes when I know I will be in my car waiting a little while for my children, I jump on the opportunity to close my eyes for five minutes to visualize.

- Relaxation: Find a place where you know you can relax. It might be a comfortable chair or sofa, a favorite part of your home, outside under a tree, or at your workplace in an unused conference room. Think "de-stress" and position your body to be receptive to this. Begin by clearing out and releasing all tension. Unfold your arms and legs, loosen up your neck and shoulders by dropping them downward, unclench your hands, and consciously let your hips sink into wherever you are seated or lying down. Close your eyes and take a slow, deep inhale, then slowly and completely exhale that breath. Repeat five times. Begin visualizing.

- When you visualize, be sure to create a positive feeling around your image. Allow yourself to feel the outcome of the image with excitement and empowerment, both physically and mentally.

- Take ownership of your vision with positive affirmations.

- Remember, you must live and feel your image as if it were happening right now.

Create a visual picture of yourself being E.P.I.C. Conceptualize virtuous behaviors, going above and beyond in your daily life. Color these images with passion, inspiration, and the positive emotion of happiness and joy as you experience the rewards of living E.P.I.C.

BENEFITS OF VISUALIZATION

- Significantly increases the ability to achieve a desired outcome.

- Keeps you focused on fulfilling your mental image.
- Activates a mental course of action to fulfill the desired mental image.
- Increases motivation and ability to fulfill the mental image.
- Optimizes performance.
- Increases self-confidence and self-discipline.

THE LAW OF ATTRACTION

The person who sends out positive thoughts activates the world around him positively and draws back to him positive results.

—Norman Vincent Peale

The Law of Attraction says whatever you think often about will grow rich in your mind, which will in turn become a reality. The emotions, thoughts, and feelings that you emit will attract similar emotions, thoughts, and feelings back into your life. The Law of Attraction uses energy or vibrations from the universe to fulfill the motion of attraction back to you.

This law is happening in your life right now. Take a moment to seriously consider this. What could you be thinking or feeling that is being reflected in your life? Be warned, the Law of Attraction doesn't differentiate between negative and positive thoughts. If you're struggling or life isn't going the way you wish, is there a chance the Law of Attraction is fulfilling something inside of you? "You become what you think about most, but you also attract what you think about most."[69] The law is in

---

[69] John Assarat, quoted in Rhonda Byrne, *The Secret* (Atria Books, 2006).

constant motion, always working to support *you* in creating *your* own reality.

The Law of Attraction is nothing new and has deep roots in history. Hinduism teaches the concept of Karma, a cycle of cause and effect that says what happens to a person is a result of their actions. Christianity teaches ". . . for whatsoever a man soweth, that shall he also reap" (Galatians 6:7-9; King James Bible) and "If you believe, you will receive whatever you ask for in prayer" (Matthew 21:22). In Buddhism, it is believed that Buddha wanted his followers to know "what you have become is what you have thought."[70]

Jack Canfield, motivational speaker, corporate trainer, entrepreneur, and coauthor of the *Chicken Soup for the Soul* series is also the coauthor of *Key to Living the Law of Attraction: A Simple Guide to Creating the Life of Your Dreams*. In this book he gives an excellent description of the Law of Attraction. "Like attracts like. If you are feeling excited, enthusiastic, passionate, happy, joyful, appreciative, or abundant, then you are sending out *positive* energy. On the other hand, if you are feeling bored, anxious, stressed out, angry, resentful, or sad, you are sending out *negative* energy. The universe, through the Law of Attraction, will respond enthusiastically to both of these vibrations. It doesn't decide which one is better for you, it just responds to *whatever* energy you are creating, and it gives you more of the same."[71]

In 2006, Rhonda Byrne published the worldwide blockbuster *The Secret*. This book can be credited with the renewal and massive popularity of the concept of the Law of Attraction.

---

[70] "What Is The Law Of Attraction? Open Your Eyes To A World Of Endless Possibilities," https://www.thelawofattraction.com/what-is-the-law-of-attraction/.

[71] Jack Canfield and D.D. Watkins, *Key to Living the Law of Attraction* (Florida: Health Communications, 2007), 8.

Byrne had been struggling personally and emotionally for quite some time until her daughter gave her a copy of *The Science of Getting Rich*. The title of Wallace D. Wattles's book may be misleading. The message was not entirely about money and wealth, but about how your mind is an active participant in getting what you want from life and how it pulls toward you what you are thinking and feeling. This book had such a profound impact on Byrne that she wanted to share the secret—the Law of Attraction—with the world.

There is no doubt in my mind that the Law of Attraction has impacted my life. During my first two years of college, I began to lose faith in myself and my abilities. I fell into a cycle of a failure mentality that became self-fulfilling. During my junior year, when I began to visualize my goals and aspirations, I broke that negative cycle and embraced life with an "I can" positive outlook. I would have never imagined in a million years something as simple as holding a vision and a positive outlook could deliver such results.

Use the Law of Attraction to manifest your personal goals and aspirations. If your goal is to be the next Olympic great and this is something you've set out to achieve, your life will actually surround you with opportunities and circumstances to achieve your Olympic dream. If it is providing your family with an environment of love, happiness, and everlasting bonds, then you will be attracting this into your life. Using this powerful law to help you achieve your goals and aspirations is similar to visualization. The difference is that visualization uses a mental picture and the Law of Attraction uses your thoughts and emotions.

Understanding that, ultimately, you have created your own life, good or bad, is profound. I knew I had to embrace visualization and the Law of Attraction to live my E.P.I.C. journey. When

I decided to write this book, I had a specific vision of what I wanted to share. I saw this book in three sections: the first would explain the concept and benefits of E.P.I.C.; the second would help paint the picture of how virtues that you are familiar with and are already using can help you to live E.P.I.C.; and the third would contain how-to suggestions on integrating being E.P.I.C. into your life. I even kept a binder on my desk as if it were a book, with the title "Live E.P.I.C." so I could be inspired by the feeling of having written a book that could potentially have a positive impact on others.

BENEFITS OF THE LAW OF ATTRACTION

- Increases your awareness of how impactful your thoughts and beliefs are in shaping your life.
- Serves as a source of momentum and energy to help achieve goals and aspirations.
- Inspires us to live with intention and to focus on what we want in our lives—from goals and dreams to happiness and personal fulfillment.
- Enables us to use our thoughts and mindset as tools to create and fulfill goals and aspirations.
- Uses the power of visualization and meditation to help achieve goals and aspirations.

CHAPTER SEVENTEEN
A NEW UNDERSTANDING OF FORGIVENESS

Forgive not because they deserve forgiveness, but because you deserve peace.

—Author unknown

I am not an expert on forgiveness, but I do want to share with you my life-changing experience with it. As you know, my E.P.I.C. journey began that day in church where I sat emotionally drained, desperate for relief from the persistent negative onslaught that my personal relationships brought me. I sought an instant miracle: happiness. I received no miracles, only messages that I had to change and grow into a person of character.

And I had to forgive.

I had mixed feelings about the concept of forgiveness. Raised Roman Catholic, I found forgiveness to be both familiar ground and a long stretch. I simply couldn't grasp the concept that forgiving myself or others would give me happiness. I decided to put the issue on the back burner and focus on something I could benefit from for sure: growing in character. In essence, I separated character growth and forgiveness as I set about changing my life.

Much to my surprise, I found time and again that forgiveness is absolutely a part of character development. Here is the breakdown.

Virtue of Faith: I had to fight the counterintuitive nature of forgiveness and have faith that this was part of the solution to restore peace and happiness in my family. I had to have faith to offset my grip on anger. Thankfully, I already had faith in God knowing that if I did what He asked, my prayers would be answered.

Virtue of Charity: I had to continue to strive for that robust feeling of mutual love we once shared. I had to grow in compassion to be more understanding, which helped with the process of forgiveness.

Virtue of Honesty: I had to take a hard, honest, unbiased look at my flaws and how they led to conflict. If forgiveness was going to help restore our loving relationship, I needed to work toward a solid foundation built on trust through honesty.

Virtue of Wisdom: I learned from my mistakes. I knew I had made unwise decisions driven by negative emotion, and I had to avoid repeating this behavior at all cost. I also learned that in many scenarios there is usually an explanation (not an excuse) for hurtful behaviors or mistakes. Understanding this differentiation enabled me to more readily forgive.

Virtue of Prudence: I knew the decisions I made to promote peace and happiness were an essential part of forgiveness, and I had to make some decisions that left me feeling uneasy inside, because they were the "harder right over the easier wrong." I had to work toward forgiveness to prevent the possibility of strife permeating to our extended family as well. And finally, I knew how deeply detrimental unforgiveness would be for my children if they were to grow up in a home of anger instead of love and forgiveness.

Virtue of Perseverance: I knew the process of forgiveness was going to be an enormous task. I knew there would be countless setbacks and that it would take a long time, likely years. However, the virtue of perseverance fueled my every thought and every action. I was emotionally invested to fight for a peaceful and loving family life. I knew I had to make the commitment and I knew I would never quit.

Virtue of Gratitude: I grew in humility when I mustered up the courage to ask for forgiveness. I felt tremendously grateful when I received forgiveness. As I grew in gratitude, I grew in forgiveness.

I was also mistaken to think that I was not the *beneficiary* of forgiveness. As I gradually let go of my anger and frustration, I began to fill with peace, love, and happiness. The relief and liberation from anger is hard to describe. Once you experience it, however, you realize that forgiveness is 100 percent about *your* happiness, not the offender's.

This is why we forgive. Yes, it's the right thing to do, but perhaps it's more accurate to say, "It's the right thing to do FOR YOU." Forgiveness releases harbored anger that only *you* feel and allows peace and happiness to fill *your* heart, setting *you* emotionally free. Remember, as humans we are all driven toward happiness. Our decisions are made with this intention. Whether those decisions are good or bad, we make them believing they will deliver a happy outcome. Forgiveness is another way in which we can fulfill our human instinct to seek happiness.

E.P.I.C. AND FORGIVENESS

When I began researching virtues, I deepened my understanding of vices, as well. Virtues are morally good and lead to happiness; vices are not morally good and tend to lead to unhappiness. Vices exist where virtues lack. For example, vices of charity are hate and greed; vices of perseverance are laziness and easily giving up; vices of honesty are lying, cheating, and deceitfulness. Do you recall the number line analogy in the beginning of this book? You can use this same image where vices fall to the left of center, sending you on a negative path, and virtues are on the right of center, sending you on a positive path. Understanding vices sheds light on personal areas where I was lacking, but I didn't spend much time focusing on them because of their negative nature. Instead, I chose to put my energy and efforts toward positive things and focused on growing in virtue.

The virtue of charity seemed like a good place to begin since loving, peaceful relationships were what I so desperately wanted. What did I find? The vice of anger. I thought to myself, *Yes, this seems to make sense. Hatred opposes love, and hatred and anger seem to go hand in hand.* Because my journey was about self-improvement, I had to ask myself if I harbored anger. Unequivocally, yes, I did. I was angry. I'd lost the fun-loving relationship with my mother-in-law that I once had and so desperately wanted again, and I was angry with myself for making decisions that lacked character.

I felt overwhelmed by the enormity of this challenge. So I started with baby steps and a tremendous amount of faith, trusting that over time this forgiveness piece would work. Little by little, I began practicing forgiveness. Often during phone calls or visits, I felt hurt by comments or insinuations, and I am sure Roseanne often felt the same with my comments or insinuations. I promised myself I would stop replaying them in my mind, growing in anger, or sharing them with my family and friends to gain their angry support. This took practice and it was hard. There were moments when body language would speak volumes, like when I would open my front door, welcoming Roseanne. No hugs or smiles were exchanged, and she wasn't happy, but she did her part and made the effort to try to combat her emotions at our house. I would try to crack a joke or start conversations about the kids to break the ice. I continued my pursuit of happiness by working to keep everyone feeling loved and respected. I never regretted those baby steps. I thought to myself, *How can there be a downside in trying to create peace? There's only upside.*

TO RECONCILIATION AND ROBUST LOVE

Over the course of many years, Roseanne and I slowly worked together to reconcile. I think we held onto the memories and feelings of the amazing, heartfelt, and fun friendship we had when Anthony and I were dating. There was no specific moment when suddenly everyone was happy and all was forgiven. Our path of forgiveness was gradual. Everyone had to be receptive to forgiveness to be authentic, and that receptivity happens at different times for different people. Eventually, love replaced anger; faith replaced hopelessness; wisdom replaced negative acts of instant gratification; gratefulness and humility replaced pride until we were completely liberated from all negative sentiment. We did it! We achieved an E.P.I.C. experience—healing emotionally through forgiveness.

In the fall of 2011, Roseanne called me with devastating news. I was driving home from the grocery store when I picked up her call. Her voice trembled as she said, "Kris, I have very bad news." I knew I needed to concentrate on this call, so I pulled over into a gas station. I had some of the kids in the car and didn't want them to hear my conversation, so I left the car, phone in hand. Roseanne told me she had been diagnosed with stage 3 lung cancer and there was no cure. I remember leaning over the slate blue hood of my car, crying with her. I vowed we would get through this together.

From that day on, our relationship grew to a whole new level. Although she was living in South Carolina and I was in Connecticut, I was driven to do as much as I possibly could to take care of her from afar. We spoke almost every day about everything from the complexity of her medical care with her many physicians to the grandchildren's latest and greatest news. I found the most joy in simply listening. The last years of Roseanne's life were incredibly special for us. She and I continued to grow in love until the day she left for Heaven. I am forever grateful for my journey with Roseanne. Had it not been for what was initially a nightmare of an experience, I would have never embarked on my E.P.I.C. journey or understood the power of forgiveness.

Trying to describe the life-changing, positive experience of forgiveness is like trying to describe falling in love. You need to feel it to really appreciate what it is. I became a much more peaceful and happy person. I lost my skeptical viewpoint and replaced it with a positive one. I became more compassionate and understanding. I would never in a million years have imagined this to be the result of forgiveness. Forgiveness is truly E.P.I.C.

FORGIVENESS: THE CHALLENGE

I had to overcome two hurdles before I tried forgiveness. The first was to accept the counterintuitive belief that letting something go would give me something in return, especially happiness. The second was understanding what forgiveness is really all about. Many myths and misconceptions can deter us from even considering forgiveness as part of our character growth.

COUNTERINTUITIVE AND CORRECT

In *The Path to Forgiveness,* Dr. Preston VanLoon uses the term "counterintuitive" to capture the unique nature of forgiveness. He says, "Few people tend at first to take the high road and forgive, because it is counterintuitive to their natural instinct. Practicing forgiveness enables you to rise above your impulses to take a higher moral ground and be a peacemaker."[72]

For this reason, forgiveness has been one of the most difficult concepts for me to grasp. It simply didn't make sense. Here's how I understood it: I, the victim, had to let a perpetrator get away with an injustice in order for me (the victim, remember?) to become happier. That is completely illogical and unfair and ridiculous!

Part of the difficulty with this concept are the many common misconceptions and myths related to what forgiveness is and what it is not. Also, it's difficult to convince someone that they are gaining something when they let go of something, which is where the virtue of faith steps in. This was certainly the case with me. Prior to my E.P.I.C. experience with forgiveness, if I had been treated unfairly, I gripped anger tightly and held it close to my heart. Replaying the offense (basically self-inflicting

---

[72] Dr. Preston VanLoon, *The Path to Forgiveness,* Blue Mountain Arts: 2018. 70.

emotional pain) to keep it alive helped me justify my anger and hold my offender accountable for their behavior. It felt like a way of keeping my offender a prisoner, as I felt they should be.

Here's the counterintuitive part. I was the real prisoner in this situation. I was shackled by the negative and destructive grip of anger, unhappy and unable to move forward in a positive direction toward happiness. My offenders were off living their lives, having a good time, whether they were remorseful or not. The key that unlocked the prison door, setting *me* free to be happy, was forgiveness.

Many great leaders, including Buddha, St. Augustine, and Nelson Mandela, have been attributed with this great quote: "Resentment is like drinking poison and then hoping it will kill your enemies." This image has helped me better understand the problem with holding onto anger and how I am actually the one suffering.

A NEW UNDERSTANDING OF FORGIVENESS: MYTHS AND MISCONCEPTIONS
What forgiveness is NOT. . .

Forgiveness is not a pardon, nor is it forgetting the offense or trusting the offender.
Once I understood that forgiveness didn't mean that I had to agree to an offense (which felt like saying, "It's okay," instead of saying, "It is *not* okay"), I became more self-assured and self-confident. I was able to stand up for what I believed, yet at the same moment, I knew I needed to let it go and move on.

I am one of the lucky ones. I have forgotten the majority of incidents that angered me and those that I did to anger others, in the case of Roseanne. She and I were able to rebuild trust. This is not always the case. Forgetting an offense is not part of the equation for most people. It's nearly impossible to forget many injustices, especially in extreme situations of physical and emotional violence. And trust? Forgiveness doesn't mean you can trust that there won't be another offense. In fact, you should proceed with caution when it comes time to trust and tap into the virtue of wisdom.

In *Unshackled and Free: True Stories of Forgiveness*, Chris Tian shares chilling memories of being molested by a Catholic priest as a young boy. The emotional and physical pain of the abuse coupled with threats of hurting Chris's mother if he told her about the abuse cannot be pardoned or forgotten, nor can this priest be trusted. However, Chris was able to turn his life around with forgiveness. "The alcohol, drugs, self-harm incidents, my trust issues and other relational injuries nearly cost me my life. I found life anew through Christ Jesus and by walking through some long and painful inner healing. I can never forget, yet I can forgive and while yes, I would give him a second chance, yet I wouldn't let him be tempted or tested by giving him complete access to another little boy."[73] Chris found healing with the power of forgiveness.

Forgiveness is not a sign of weakness.
I feel like this misconception comes from the image of someone on their knees, crying and begging to be forgiven. It seems to imply that tears of sincerity are a sign of weakness. Perhaps the association of weakness involves allowing ourselves to be vulnerable. I agree with the vulnerability piece, but isn't the first step of bravery and courage acknowledging that there is risk and facing that risk head on? Forgiveness takes a lot of courage, which in turn requires character growth.

---

[73] Chris Tian, *Unshackled and Free: True Stories of Forgiveness,* Body and Soul Publishing: 2012. p. 43.

THE REWARDS OF FORGIVENESS
What forgiveness IS. . .

Forgiveness is liberating. It opens the door for personal happiness and love.
Just saying, "You're forgiven" is not enough. You will know true
forgiveness when you feel liberated and free of anger.

Sarah Montana is an accomplished screenwriter and actress.
She's written scripts for the Hallmark Channel, a play, and the
movies *Love to the Rescue* and *Two Turtle Doves*. In 2008, her world
was forever changed when her mother and brother were murdered
in their home during a burglary. For the next seven years, Sarah
thought she had forgiven the man who murdered her family. She
said she made him a nonperson rather than the face of all evil, and
that nonperson was whom she could forgive. He was almost like
an act of nature, a tornado or flood, that she could forgive. At the
time, she thought this was enough, that this was "forgiving."

When she began to write a play about her family's murder,
she needed to research her villain, the man who had murdered
her mother and brother. Much to her surprise, she learned that as
a prisoner, he was spending twenty-three hours a day in solitary
confinement, experiencing terrible violations of human rights.
Suddenly, this nonperson became a person to her. In reference
to the pain she felt seeing her mother and brother dead in their
coffins, she said, "When I pictured him [their murderer] beaten,
starving, crying out in a dark cell, that was just as painful." She realized she was still connected to him in their shared trauma. In order
to get rid of this traumatic connection that was destroying them
both, she had to truly forgive him. But *how* do you forgive some-
body who's murdered your brother and mother? She couldn't find
the answer anywhere; no self-help book, psychology journal, or
online search had the answer. At that point she realized she needed
to understand something first: before you can learn *how* to forgive,

you must learn *why* to forgive. The answer, in Sarah's words: "To set you free. When you're saying 'I forgive you,' what you're really saying is, 'I know what you did, it's not okay, but I recognize that you are more than that. I don't want to hold us captive to this thing anymore. I can heal myself, and I don't need anything from you.' After you say that and you mean it, then it's just you."[74]

Eventually, Sarah wrote the man a letter, telling him she had forgiven him. Without thinking, she dropped that letter into a mailbox. She describes that moment as: "For the first ten steps, there was this lightness of being, and then the lightness started to feel like a lurch in your stomach, when you hit the spiritual tripwire."[75] Sarah's experience was not unlike that described by many people who experience the liberation of letting go of the emotions attached to offenses. She's passionate about her personal transformation with forgiveness, giving it a "ten out of ten" ranking in the world of life experiences.[76]

Forgiveness is possible even if reconciliation isn't.
Although Roseanne and I experienced reconciliation, this may not always be the case for everyone. You can and should walk away from some perpetrators, like unhealthy situations where physical and emotional abuse continue or other scenarios where repeat offenses aren't ending. Sometimes the offender has passed away or can't be found, making reconciliation impossible. There may be another natural course of evolution where you choose not to reconcile. There may even be circumstances where someone chooses not to forgive you, in which case that's out of your control. If you

---

[74] Sarah Montana, "Why forgiveness is worth it," filmed March 2018 at TEDxLincolnSquare, New York, NY, video, https://www.ted.com/talks/sarah_montana_why_forgiveness_is_worth_it.

[75] Montana, "Forgiveness."

[76] Montana, "Forgiveness."

focus on what you can control, you can strive to learn, grow, and make a meaningful change for the better.

Forgiveness is a process.
Forgiveness takes time and practice. Even though Sarah Montana experienced a moment when she could pinpoint that feeling of liberation, it took many years for her to get there. It's easy to let go of small offenses, like getting dangerously cut off by an exiting car on the highway, or driving two hours to a hockey game to find out that your name was the only name mistakenly left off the blast email list with the cancellation notification. If we use these little offenses to practice letting go of anger, we will better equip ourselves for those bigger offenses. Good news: we can get in a lot of reps in our daily lives.

Forgiveness mimics the epic journey we see in literature. It's long, there are challenges, but in the end, after much perseverance and fortitude, the hero emerges with victory. This journey requires choosing to travel on either the path of forgiving or the path of not forgiving after experiencing an offense. Neither path is easy when you're struggling with hurt and anger, but the pain you experience while growing into forgiveness will be forgotten as the burden of anger is lifted.

The path of not forgiving is actually harder, albeit easier to understand. Living with anger and resentment is more difficult and more painful than working toward forgiveness. Unknowingly, you're actually growing in anger. Every day you continue to do this, you're taking a day of happiness away from yourself. It's a hard path with no reward.

Forgiveness is empowering and will have a profound impact on your life. You have the ability to regain personal power and restore yourself from hurt. On February 12, 1993, Mary Johnson answered a phone call that no parent wants to receive. Her son, twenty-year-old Laramiun Byrd, had been shot and killed. Ms. Johnson talked about her hatred, saying, "Hatred began when I found out who had taken Laramiun's life." She said her hatred grew and grew, extending to everyone, even her family.

After the trial ended, Ms. Johnson received a poem from someone about two mothers in heaven with the message that mothers of murdered children should come together and heal. She said, "I kept hearing over and over in my mind, 'This is what you should do, this is what you should do.'"[77] She decided that, before she met with other mothers of murdered children, she needed to go to prison and see Oshea Israel, the convicted murderer, to see if she had forgiven him. She knew this was part of her process to heal from the death of her son. When they met, she approached him with an open mind, saying, "I don't know you and you don't know me, you didn't know my son and my son didn't know you, but we need to lay a foundation and we need to get to know one another." After their conversation, Israel agreed to meet Ms. Johnson again. They shook hands and then Israel asked Ms. Johnson if they could hug. She agreed. When they embraced, she began to cry and started to collapse. Israel held her up. She said when she felt him holding her up, she believed that was the moment where some bonding began. She talks about feeling something in her move from her feet up and release out of her. "And I instantly knew that all that anger and the animosity, all the stuff I had in my heart for twelve years for you — I knew it was over, I had totally forgiven you."[78] Mary Johnson shared that her relation-

---

[77] "The Forgiveness Project | Mary Johnson and Oshea Israel," YouTube, https://www.youtube.com/watch?v=JJDqceiwR2U.

[78] YouTube, "Forgiveness Project."

ship with Israel ". . . is beyond belief," and she now treats him as she would her own son.[79]

Today, Ms. Johnson's passion for the power of forgiveness is evident in her work with the organization she founded, From Death to Life, dedicated to ending violence through healing and reconciliation.[80]

THE PROBLEM OF ANGER

In the Bible, Ephesians 4:26-27 says, "In your anger do not sin: Don't let the sun go down while you are still angry, and do not give the devil a foothold." This is a firm warning about the stronghold of anger. It also makes me think about the workings of our subconscious mind and its ability to grasp the power of emotion—negative or positive—while we sleep at night. There is much wisdom in this verse, and we should heed its warning.

A personal perspective

Anger is arguably one of the most toxic of negative emotions. I think of anger like fire. It spreads a path of destruction. It comes in all sizes, from a little candle to a volcanic eruption. It can start quickly and fiercely and be all-consuming, or it can smolder over time while gaining momentum, then burst into flames. Or it can simply die out.

Years ago, when the twins were about five years old, I found two melted solo cups along with a burnt candle hidden behind one of their beds. In a split second, I experienced a rush of emotion: shock and terror knowing what could have happened to my children, to our family, and our house had a fire erupted.

---

[79] "Mary Johnson and Oshea Israel," StoryCorps, https://storycorps.org/stories/mary-johnson-and-oshea-israel/.

[80] https://www.theforgivenessproject.com/stories-library/mary-johnson-oshea-israel/

And I experienced extreme anger because they knew they shouldn't be playing with fire and yet they were. Plus, I experienced immense gratitude, thanking God that nothing bad had happened.

I lost my cool and was completely furious. I yelled throughout the house for the twins to come up to their bedroom. When they arrived, I yelled some more about how dangerous their behavior was, knowing full well I wasn't having the impact necessary to convey how serious this situation was. But honestly, how could they have understood? They had primarily been taught fire safety, not the dangers of fire. I decided they needed to see it to believe it. We went downstairs where I had them sit at the kitchen counter with an iPad in front of them, and I had them watch an age-appropriate video on the hazards and dangers of fire. Finally, they got the message, loud and clear.

If only there were a way to communicate the danger of holding onto anger that matched the seriousness we use to communicate the danger of fire. We should treat it like fire: work to find the source of anger and extinguish it, make changes to see that it doesn't happen again, repair any damage, and learn and grow from the experience.

It's okay to get angry. Anger is a natural emotion which can provide important information, especially as it relates to being treated wrongly. But harboring anger only serves to feed this emotion, because anything we feed will grow. Growing anger is much like a growing fire—it spreads and destroys everything in its path. Anger is destructive emotionally and at times physically, when it generates outbursts from throwing something to actual violence such as rape. The emotional pain manifests in you being miserable and unhappy. Anger causes stress and unresolved anger can cause health-related issues. And anger can spiral out of control, the way a fire can, causing destruction in all directions.

THE E.P.I.C. PARALLEL

The power of forgiveness parallels perfectly with the E.P.I.C. journey. Similar to the importance of character development across all cultures, the concept of forgiveness has been highly valued for centuries. Many religions have fundamental beliefs based on forgiving your enemy as a means to seeking peace and love. Without forgiveness, anger and resentment stifle the inner peace and personal growth our human nature craves.

Forgiveness, like E.P.I.C., is a journey in and of itself. It is a process. It takes time and can't be rushed. And if you're anything like me, it may take some convincing for you to even consider trying to forgive. You will have good days and bad days, but little by little you will grow as you progress. You have the opportunity to practice forgiveness daily and when you do, you will feel how much happier you can be.

Forgiveness also embraces the positive nature of self-improvement. As you invest in yourself and grow in forgiveness, you experience greater happiness and personal fulfillment.

Finally, forgiveness, like all virtues, is designed for our benefit. When we authentically practice forgiveness, we benefit, as do those around us. When we lack forgiveness, we experience the negative effects of anger and its related emotions.

On my E.P.I.C. journey, I have used virtues as tools to build and grow my personal character. Forgiveness is another tool to help build character. I encourage you to think about people and situations in your life where there may be strife and consider taking action to forgive. Remember, forgive for *you* and *your* happiness.

BENEFITS OF FORGIVENESS

- Forgiveness releases anger and fills you with overwhelming peace and happiness.
- Forgiveness is a catalyst for emotional healing.
- Forgiveness grows other virtues such as charity and faith.
- Forgiveness helps you to become more merciful, compassionate, and loving.
- Forgiveness embraces or reclaims a growth mindset.
- Forgiveness fosters overall healthier personal relationships.
- Forgiveness can improve mental health—less stress and hostility; fewer symptoms of depression; improved self-esteem.
- Forgiveness can improve physical health—lower blood pressure; a stronger immune system.

EXCELLENCE APPLIED TO FORGIVENESS

- Make a commitment *to* yourself, *for* yourself, to forgive with the goal of feeling truly liberated from anger and negativity.
- View forgiveness as a means to rid yourself of the toxicity of anger.
- Actively educate yourself on how to forgive with books, podcasts, support from others, and counseling.
- Make a list of who you have anger toward and why. Work to forgive everyone in your life whom you feel might have a negative grip on your happiness.
- Know you are not perfect and you err. Practice forgiveness daily by letting go of small day-to-day grievances.

CHAPTER EIGHTEEN

BECOME THE CEO OF YOUR LIFE: E.P.I.C. LIFE BLUEPRINTS

Have you ever considered the fact that you are the CEO of your life? It's true. You are the highest-ranking person in your life responsible for many of the decisions and the outcomes in your life.

A chief executive officer (CEO) can be defined as "the highest-ranking executive in a company whose primary responsibilities include making major corporate decisions, managing the overall operations and resources of a company, acting as the main point of communication between the board of directors (the board) and the corporate operations, and being the public face of the company."[81]

---

[81] Adam Hayes, "Chief Executive Officer (CEO)," Investopedia, February 9, 2022, https://www.investopedia.com/terms/c/ceo.asp.

Now, let's see how this translates into you being the CEO of your life.

A chief executive officer (CEO) is the highest-ranking executive in a company (you are the main person in your life), whose primary responsibility includes making major corporate decisions (you are responsible for the decisions you make in your life), managing the overall operations (you manage the moving parts of your life, career, education, family, health so these are working harmoniously) and resources of a company (you manage the assets in your life that help support the operations like money, education, and people), acting as the main point of communication (you are the center of interpersonal communication, relationships—both personal and professional) between the board of directors (your family, friends, and those around you) and corporate operations (day to day living), and being the public face of the company (*you* are the person everyone sees and knows).

The analogy here is not to imply or suggest you should apply a business model to manage your life; rather, it's to help you create a vision where you can be an e.p.i.c CEO of your life.

BLUEPRINT

We've discussed *Live E.P.I.C.* in the context of self-improvement—growing in personal character by growing in virtue. Now I'd like you to consider E.P.I.C. as a blueprint for your entire life. You can easily apply it to any area of your life at any given moment to reduce negative outcomes and increase positive outcomes.

I've found that the e.p.i.c blueprint can positively impact your life in three major areas: Whomever you are in your personal life—spouse, parent, friend—you can be E.P.I.C. Whatever you do as a professional (where you invest your time, energy, and talents), you can be E.P.I.C. And finally, the way in which you handle situations or circumstances in your life can be E.P.I.C.

Simply ask yourself, *How can I be E.P.I.C. in _____?* Your answer can be sparked by the blueprint concept. Consider the application of excellence to virtues under these different scenarios by reflecting back on the virtues we've discussed and thinking of ways you can grow in them. Let's look at a few examples.

Example of a profession or what you do:
"HOW CAN I BE E.P.I.C. AS A STUDENT?"
Faith
Excellence in Faith

- Students who knowingly challenge themselves academically believing they will be able to achieve their goals earning certifications, diplomas, and degrees.
- Those students who believe in themselves and actively pursue their passions, talents, and desires.

Lack of Faith

- Students who have a negative outlook on their academic abilities.
- Students who avoid an academic challenge because they believe they aren't qualified or capable when in fact they are.

Charity
Excellence in Charity

- Students who proactively extend their resources and friendly tips to help their peers advance in their studies.

- Students who are compassionate and understanding with peers who struggle academically, knowing they may simply need more assistance with learning.

Lack of Charity

- Students who frown upon or complain about academic accommodations their fellow students may receive because of learning differences.
- Students who knowingly withhold valuable information from their peers which would help them, like changes in test dates or extra-credit opportunities.

Honesty

Excellence in Honesty

- Students who are completely honest with their assignments and exams.
- Students who tell a professor if their grade is wrong when it's too high and the earned grade is actually lower in the same way they would if the grade was too low and they had earned a higher grade.

Lack of Honesty

- Students who cheat or plagiarize on their schoolwork and/or lie to their instructors.
- Students who see group projects as an opportunity to slack off and rely too much on their peers.

Wisdom
Excellence in Wisdom

- Students who embrace an academic mindset to learn as much as they can, including reading or researching above and beyond the required course material.
- Students who understand that they are responsible for their success in the classroom and that this success will open doors of opportunity in the future.

Lack of Wisdom

- Students who do the coursework just to get by instead of understanding that the coursework is the foundation upon which new material will be built.
- Students who gravitate toward easy classes instead of challenging themselves with more difficult classes for greater opportunities that would benefit them in the long run.

Prudence
Excellence in Prudence

- Students who set themselves up for academic success by attending the majority, if not all, of their classes prepared with the proper materials and completed assignments.
- Students who may need academic support actively seeking this assistance with resources like tutors or supplemental learning tools supplied by their learning institution.

Lack of Prudence

- Students who put forth a poor effort in their assignments and studies.
- Students who frequently skip class.
- Students who rely on and in some cases expect their peers to give them their notes or other important classroom materials they missed.

Perseverance
Excellence in Perseverance

- Students who put forth the time and dedication to achieve their academic goals and potential.
- Students who work to overcome academic challenges and struggles.
- Students who set a high academic standard for themselves. If they are not pleased with their grade, they look for ways to improve it.

Lack of Perseverance

- Students who fall behind academically in any given class or academic program due to lack of effort.
- Students who willingly accept poor grades that may limit future opportunities for advancement and growth.

Gratitude
Excellence in Gratitude

- Students who actively show respect for their instructors with punctuality, proper classroom etiquette, and positivity.

- Students who show appreciation toward their instructors with a simple "thank you" as they exit the classroom.

Lack of Gratitude

- Students who are disrespectful to their instructors by interrupting or being disruptive in the classroom.
- Students who constantly complain about their instructors' teaching style or personality.

Students who lack character attend class with a pessimistic outlook. Their presence is disruptive, and they are sometimes rude and disrespectful toward their instructor and classmates. They are consistently unprepared for class with the wrong materials or uncompleted assignments. Their attendance is poor. They are less interested in learning and more interested in getting through the class or socializing. They do the bare minimum to pass the class. They are eager to take valuable information from others that could benefit them, like classroom notes, and are not willing to share valuable information that they may have. They cheat on exams and assignments as a means to bolster their grades. They are unreliable and the "weak link" in group projects.

The students who have character are upbeat and optimistic, respectful, kind, and courteous to their instructor and classmates. They absolutely believe they will do well in the class regardless of the difficulty of the subject matter. They actively persevere and put forth the extra effort when necessary. They are diligent and conscientious students learning the classroom material to the best of their ability (knowledge/wisdom). They are prudent with class preparation, with completed assignments, and the proper materials necessary on any given day. Their attendance is consistently strong. They take the time to help peers understand classroom material. They are honest and trustworthy and would never consider cheating. They are accountable for their work. They are likely the students who would take the lead on group projects.

Examples of a life situation: hurricane, tornado, flooding, fire, pandemic
(For this example, I will use a hurricane.)
"How can I be E.P.I.C. during a hurricane?"

Excellence in Faith

- Never stop believing that you can and will get through the impending storm.
- Consider potential challenges temporary with the understanding that you can and will successfully overcome storm damage and inconveniences.
- Embrace the power of unity with others (family, neighbors, friends, and strangers). Know you can trust and rely on one another.
- Believe the proactive measures you've taken to prepare for the storm will be beneficial.

Lack of Faith

- Catastrophic mindset that you won't survive the storm.
- Failing to believe preparation will be extremely helpful for you and/or someone else.
- Thinking that you won't receive assistance from neighbors, friends, even frontline workers in the event of a dire situation.
- Succumbing to irrational fears that can impair your ability to prepare and/or make wise decisions during the storm to forge through any potential crisis at hand.

Excellence in Charity

- Give, give, give—your time, supplies, even money to those in need.
- Be more compassionate and emotionally supportive toward others. Understand how devastating loss can be (homes, loved ones, jobs) and seek ways to help relieve their burden.
- Actively find ways to help others, especially those who were not able to take care of themselves prior to the storm.
- Check in with neighbors, friends, even strangers to see if they're okay and if you can help in some way.

Lack of Charity

- Hoarding critical supplies like food, water, shelter, even electricity while others are suffering without these items.
- Turning a blind eye to those in need.
- Allowing ill will toward someone in need to interfere with your ability to help them.

Excellence in Honesty

- Actively share survival tips and critical supplies that can positively impact others.
- Take the initiative to spread relevant news and updates (good and bad) with others to help keep them informed leading up to, during, and after the storm.
- Don't be afraid to ask for help if you are the one in need.

Lack of Honesty

- Lying to others about any supplies that you have which would be beneficial to them, or worse, that they may be in desperate need of.
- Purposely withholding pertinent rescue information from others.

Excellence in Wisdom

- Seriously heed the warnings from the experts and take necessary action for your personal safety and the safety of others. If you are told to evacuate, don't wait, evacuate.
- Proactively prepare for an impending storm in advance by taking the necessary precautions like boarding up windows or securing outdoor items that could become flying debris with strong gusts of wind.
- Educate yourself on the most essential items to have on hand during hurricanes—items like water, canned goods, blankets, batteries, and flashlights.
- Ask others what they have done to prepare for storms. Which measures have been helpful? Which were not?

Lack of Wisdom

- Failing to actively track the storm and keep up to date on storm-related information in your community.
- Being prideful in thinking you can handle whatever comes your way without sufficient preparation.
- Relying on and/or expecting others to take care of you.

Excellence in Prudence

- Take action as far in advance as you can to prepare for the storm before there are shortages of supplies in your community.
- Educate yourself and your family on the dangers associated with storms like live electrical wires or unstable debris and footings.
- Plan escape routes or places to go for safety and shelter prior to the storm, and be sure everyone you're with understands these procedures and plans.
- Prepare for plans B and C in the event of extreme situations.

Lack of Prudence

- Failing to stock up on crucial items for survival by waiting until the last minute, or worse, failing to prepare all together.
- Regardless of the strength of the storm, choosing not to heed to the warnings.
- Taking unnecessary risks that could be dangerous like leaving a safe location to venture out to a store for needed supplies during the storm.

Excellence in Perseverance

- Find new, creative ways to handle unexpected situations or solve problems at hand. For example, rerouting water flow away from your home to reduce the chance of flooding or perhaps rationing food and water.

- Be brave and courageous. Work through inconveniences and challenges to help your situation or to help others in difficult situations.

Lack of Perseverance

- Allowing fear to impair your ability to make wise decisions that would promote your safety and well-being.
- Failing to take actions that may be uncomfortable, yet necessary for survival due to fear.
- Giving up and giving in to the notion that you will deal with the ramifications of the storm once it passes.

Excellence in Gratitude

- Being grateful for the shelter and supplies you have, whatever they may be.
- Being sure to thank those who have helped you, from family and friends to frontline workers and even strangers.
- Take on a "pay it forward" mindset, helping others the way you have been helped.

Lack of Gratitude

- Being rude or unappreciative toward those who have helped you.
- Falsely expecting that others should share their supplies with you or take care of you.
- Being judgmental toward others and the decisions they are making in the way they choose to survive the storm. You likely don't know all of the facts.

Those who embrace E.P.I.C. during any natural disaster will rise to the occasion. They willingly share basic necessities, especially with those who don't have the means to purchase and gather necessary supplies. This simple action communicates care, compassion, and the understanding that we are in this together. They actively seek the most recent information (knowledge) to be sure they are updated and educated. They're wise and think broadly as they adapt to the changing world instead of resisting change. They're willing and driven to face the many challenges to overcome and survive this disaster. Finally, they appreciate and reflect upon all that they have to be grateful for, encouraging others to do the same.

For those that haven't been working on their virtues, the hurricane or other natural disaster may affect them much more negatively. They might be less likely to take the advice of experts and therefore be less prepared. This lack of preparedness can also endanger the lives of others who may be nearby or trying to help them. If goods or supplies are in shortage they may be less inclined to share and help out others.

Example of a personal role:
"How can I be E.P.I.C. as a friend?"

Excellence in Faith

- Friends who share their uplifting, positive viewpoint and mindset.
- Friends who remind you of your strengths and abilities, providing motivation and emotional encouragement.
- Friends who truly believe in you and support you with your goals and aspirations.
- Friends who are there in good times and in bad.

Lack of Faith

- Friends who try to dissuade or discourage you from pursuing your dreams and aspirations.
- Friends who try to negatively influence you with their pessimistic outlook.
- Friends who may act in a way that makes you second-guess yourself, making you feel insecure.

Excellence in Charity

- Friends who accept, embrace, and love you for your unique self. They are nonjudgmental.
- Friends who value, respect, and work to keep your relationship authentic, genuine, and intact.
- Friends who are generous and support you, especially during those times when you need it most.

Lack of Charity

- Friends who can act like a bully, pushing you around to behave the way they want you to.
- Friends who take advantage of you, what you have, or who you know.
- Friends who tend to be argumentative or confrontational.
- Friends who lack understanding and compassion during times when you need this emotional support.

Excellence in Honesty

- Friends who you can always rely on and trust with your deepest concerns or even secrets.

- Friends who are honest with you no matter what, even if they have to share difficult news or information.
- Friends who are true to their word and follow through on their commitments.

Lack of Honesty

- Friends who manipulate you or situations you're involved in for their personal benefit.
- Friends who inappropriately share your personal/private information, especially when you've asked them not to.
- Friends who partake in behaviors that are questionable, unethical, or even illegal.
- Friends who lie to you.

Excellence in Wisdom

- Friends who take action to preserve your friendship and avoid actions that would hurt your friendship.
- Friends who prioritize you and your friendship with respect.
- Friends who work to be E.P.I.C.

Lack of Wisdom

- Friends who frequently put their interests before yours.
- Friends who do all of the talking, especially about themselves, rather than investing their time asking about important things in your life.
- Friends who act in a way that appears to show lack of respect for you and your friendship.

Excellence in Prudence

- Friends who protect the integrity of your friendship.
- Friends who are respectful and reliable.
- Friends who work to keep in contact with you during busy times in life or when physical distance can be a barrier.

Lack of Prudence

- Friends who overly rely on you and are codependent.
- Friendships that are one-sided.
- Friends who comment or act in a way that makes you second-guess yourself, making you feel insecure.

Excellence in Perseverance

- Friendships that last a lifetime.
- Friends who share their qualities of perseverance and encourage you to work through personal challenges.
- Friends who work to overcome disagreement and seek peaceful solutions.
- Friends who are there to encourage you to be courageous and brave during difficult times because they want the best for you.

Lack of Perseverance

- Friends who frequently cancel their plans with you.
- Friends who lack the initiative to remedy a misunderstanding.
- Friends who avoid helping in times of need.

Excellence in Gratitude

- Friends who are happy to simply be in your company.
- Friends who appreciate you.
- Friends who are forgiving.
- Friends who in their own unique way make you feel appreciated.

Lack of Gratitude

- Friends who are "takers" or selfish.
- Friends who take you and your friendship for granted.
- Friends who hold grudges.
- Friends who "use" you for some personal benefit.

The description of an E.P.I.C. friend and a not so E.P.I.C. friend is straightforward and can be easily deduced from the discussion above, which is why this exercise can be so valuable.

THE TEMPLATE

To help spark this thought process, I have included a few bullet points for your reference.

Living with EXCELLENCE in Virtues
Excellence in Faith:

- Having a positive, upbeat, can-do attitude.
- Believing you can achieve your goals, aspirations, and dreams.
- Transforming ideas into realities.

- Inspiring and motivating those around you.
- Building a sense of community and strengthening personal relationships.
- Having a spiritual path.

Excellence in Charity:

- Being consistently happy and optimistic.
- Having unconditional loving relationships.
- Authentically concerned for the well-being of others.
- Proactively generous with resources, talents, and time to help others in need and/or thrive.
- Working to forgive, repair, and restore relationships.
- Giving without expecting something in return.

Excellence in Honesty:

- Embodying honesty and truthfulness.
- Taking responsibility for your actions.
- Established as trustworthy and reliable.
- Increased responsibilities and opportunities.

Excellence in Wisdom:

- Broad, reflective thinking that takes into consideration future outcomes and implications.
- Excellent level of knowledge, judgment, and advice to promote goodness.
- Actively seeking out knowledge. Being and staying informed.
- Living ethically and with virtue.
- Creative problem-solving with good intentions.

Excellence in Prudence:

- Seeks counsel before making important, impactful decisions.
- Decisive, well-thought-through decisions with good intentions.
- Avoids unnecessary risk or foreseeable potential problems.
- Being prepared in the present and future.
- Setting yourself up for good outcomes.
- Conscientiousness.

Excellence in Perseverance:

- Recognizing and accepting setbacks and/or obstacles as detours on a path to achieve goals and aspirations while staying on that path.
- Finding creative ways to overcome obstacles and seeing these as experiences to learn from.
- Persistence and staying focused on your goals.
- Greater self-confidence and resilience.
- Inspirational to others.

Excellence in Gratitude:

- Being humble.
- Admitting mistakes or misunderstandings; eager to learn and grow.
- Frequent reflection and greater respect/appreciation for what you have and/or the opportunities you've been given.
- Heartfelt kindness and expressions of thankfulness to others.

Living with lack of virtue
Lack of Faith:

- Negative, pessimistic outlook or viewpoint on many topics.
- Inhibited to take on difficult or seemingly unattainable tasks.
- Failure to believe in yourself or others and the ability to pursue goals and aspirations.
- Having a fixed mindset instead of a growth mindset.
- Less spiritual.

Lack of Charity:

- Unkind, disrespectful, rude behavior.
- Harboring anger, ill will toward others.
- Negative mindset.
- Unwilling to give of yourself and/or your resources to help those in need.
- Lack of compassion, or disregard for those who are struggling or suffering.

Lack of Honesty:

- All forms of deceit: lying, cheating, stealing.
- Bending the rules; manipulative behavior.
- Over embellishing or under representing facts.
- Untrustworthy.

Lack of Wisdom:

- Failure to self-educate and keep up to date with data, facts, and knowledge that will impact you or those around you.

- Poor effort in planning and preparedness for present and future.
- Lack of concern about the impact of your decisions on yourself and others.

Lack of Prudence:

- Taking unnecessary risks or willingly making poor decisions.
- Lack of due diligence; improper or lack of planning.
- Short-sightedness; failure to consider the broad picture.
- Ignorance.

Lack of Perseverance:

- Quitting on yourself or others; settling for less than your best.
- Allowing obstacles to become excuses to quit.
- Succumbing to challenges or difficulties.
- Lack of self-confidence and patience.
- Impaired by fear; lack of courage.
- Laziness.

Lack of Gratitude:

- Selfish, taker mindset.
- Expecting much in return as if you're owed something.
- Complaining.
- Being picky.
- Pride-filled.
- Taking privileges for granted.

The worksheet:

First determine the role or scenario in which you would like to become E.P.I.C. Then list a few sentences or bullet points to fill in the blanks below with examples, general or specific, of what/ how these virtues would look like to you when they are lacking and when they are excellent. Refer to the spark thoughts above.

EXCELLENCE of Virtue	VIRTUE	LACK of Virtue
	Faith	
	Charity	
	Honesty	
	Wisdom	
	Perseverance	
	Prudence	
	Gratitude	

CONCLUSION

Each day, we're given opportunities to choose to go beyond average and become excellent. Whether we're performing a random task or undergoing the personal growth and development discussed in *Live E.P.I.C.,* our mindful choices can help us experience personal fulfillment and happiness.

When we choose to live an e.p.i.c life, we are choosing to apply excellence to the development of the virtues that make up our character. We are choosing to be the best version of ourselves. It's like the wise advice a college coach gave my daughter her senior year in high school. "Get more As than Bs." You don't have to be perfect, just aim in that direction. We, too, can take on this mindset when we live an e.p.i.c life; we're not perfect, but when we shoot for excellence in virtue, we will grow. And as we grow in virtue, little by little, our lives become greatly enhanced. Positive results will begin immediately, and we gain a better understanding why misuse, or lack of virtue, can lead to trying situations and challenges.

I have found that the more I grow in virtue, the more my unvirtuous moments stand out. There are still days and times where I lack virtue—times where I catch myself, or better yet, when my children or husband catch me with a comment or viewpoint that isn't very E.P.I.C. It becomes painfully obvious to me that something just feels off. I know my behavior is less than my best. I don't see this as being bad or experience it as failure. Instead, I see it as an opportunity to grow.

The perfect example for me is when I become frustrated with technology. We all rely on technology, and any upgrade or change in an app, software, or connectivity can find me struggling my way through. If I am not careful, this frustration impacts those around me and they end up on the receiving end of a not-so-e.p.i.c version of Kristin. However, when I *believe* (virtue of faith) I can resolve the technological issue at hand, I can use the virtue of perseverance and work to gain some missing piece of information (knowledge) to help resolve the technological issue at hand. If I am successful, guess what? I have achieved personal fulfillment and am happy. If I am not successful, the virtue of wisdom tells me to walk away for a bit so that my frustration subsides and doesn't spill over to others. Regardless of what is challenging me, when I recalibrate and focus on growing in virtue, I find my way through, which leads me to personal fulfillment and happiness.

I encourage you to use the blueprint and worksheet to excel and grow toward your ultimate goal: happiness and personal fulfillment. For instance, if you are struggling in areas such as career growth or personal relationships, try mapping out attainable "reach" goals to grow in virtue and "far reach" goals that will push you to persevere for further growth in virtue.

It's never too late to live with excellence, to be the best version of yourself, to enjoy the journey of life. We are surrounded by opportunities all day, every day to be excellent. Give it a try, pick a virtue or two that are particularly meaningful for you and practice growing in these. Living E.P.I.C., growing in virtue little by little, will deliver on the promise of a life of personal fulfillment and happiness.

Live E.P.I.C.!

APPENDIX A:

E.P.I.C. LIVING WORKSHEETS

THE E.P.I.C STUDENT

EXCELLENCE in Virtue	VIRTUE	LACK in Virtue
• Students who knowingly challenge themselves academically, believing they will be able to achieve their goals, earning certifications, diplomas, and degrees. • Students who believe in themselves and actively pursue their passions, talents, and desires.	FAITH	• Students who have a negative outlook on their academic abilities. • Students who avoid an academic challenge because they believe they aren't qualified or capable when in fact they are.

EXCELLENCE in Virtue	VIRTUE	LACK in Virtue
• Students who proactively extend their resources and friendly tips to help their peers advance in their studies. • Students who are compassionate and understanding with peers who struggle academically, knowing they may simply need more assistance with learning.	CHARITY	• Students who frown upon or complain about academic accommodations fellow students may receive because of learning differences. • Students who knowingly withhold valuable information from their peers which would help them like changes in test dates or extra credit opportunities.
• Students who are completely honest with their assignments and exams. • Students who tell a professor if their grade is wrong when it's too high and the earned grade is actually lower in the same way they would if the grade was too low and they had earned a higher grade.	HONESTY	• Students who cheat or plagiarize on their schoolwork and/or lie to their instructors. • Students who see group projects as an opportunity to slack off and rely too much on their peers.
• Students who embrace an academic mindset to learn as much as they can, including reading or researching above and beyond the required course material.	WISDOM	• Students who do the course work just to get by instead of understanding that this material is the foundation upon which new material will be built.

EXCELLENCE in Virtue	VIRTUE	LACK in Virtue
• Students who understand that they are responsible for their success in the classroom and that this success will open doors of opportunity in the future.		• Students who gravitate toward easy classes instead of challenging themselves with more difficult classes, limiting themselves for greater opportunities that would benefit them in the long run.
• Students who set themselves up for academic success by attending the majority, if not all, of their classes prepared with the proper materials and completed assignments. • Students who may need academic support actively seek this assistance with resources like tutors or supplemental learning tools supplied by their learning institution.	PRUDENCE	• Students who put forth a poor effort in their assignments and studies. • Students who frequently skip class. • Students who rely on and in some cases expect their peers to give them their notes or other important classroom materials they missed.
• Students who put forth the time and dedication to achieving their goals and potential.	PERSEVER-ANCE	• Students who fall behind academically in any given class or academic program due to lack of effort.

EXCELLENCE in Virtue	VIRTUE	LACK in Virtue
• Students who work to overcome academic challenges and struggles. • Students who set a high academic standard for themselves. If they are not pleased with their grade, they look for ways to improve it.		• Students who willingly accept poor grades that may limit future opportunities for advancement and growth.
• Students who actively show respect for their instructors with punctuality, proper classroom etiquette, and positivity. • Students who show appreciation toward their instructors with a simple "thank you" as they exit the classroom.	GRATITUDE	• Students who are disrespectful to their instructors by interrupting or being disruptive in the classroom. • Students who constantly complain about their instructors' teaching style or personality.

THE E.P.I.C FRIEND

EXCELLENCE of Virtue	VIRTUE	LACK of Virtue
• Friends who share their uplifting, positive viewpoint and mindset. • Friends who remind you of your strengths and abilities, providing motivation and emotional encouragement. • Friends who truly believe in you and support you with your goals and aspirations. • Friends who are there in good times and in bad.	FAITH	• Friends who discourage you or try to dissuade you from pursuing your dreams and aspirations. • Friends who try to negatively influence you with their pessimistic outlook. • Friends that may act in a way that makes you second-guess yourself, making you feel insecure.
• Friends who accept, embrace, and love you for your unique self. They are nonjudgmental. • Friends who value, respect, and work to keep your relationship authentic, genuine, and intact.	CHARITY	• Friends who can act like a bully, pushing you around to behave the way they want you to. • Friends who take advantage of you, what you have, or who you know. • Friends who tend to be argumentative or confrontational.

EXCELLENCE of Virtue	VIRTUE	LACK of Virtue
• Friends who are generous and support you during those times when you need it most.		• Friends who lack understanding or compassion during times when you need this emotional support.
• Friends who you can always rely on and trust with your deepest concerns or even secrets. • Friends who are honest with you no matter what, even if they have to share difficult news or information. • Friends who are true to their word, following through on their commitments.	HONESTY	• Friends who manipulate you or situations you're involved in for their personal benefit. • Friends who inappropriately share your personal/private information, especially when you've asked them not to. • Friends who partake in behaviors that are questionable, unethical, or even illegal. • Friends who lie to you.
• Friends who take action to preserve your friendship and avoid actions that would hurt your friendship. • Friends who prioritize you and your friendship with respect.	WISDOM	• Friends who frequently put their interests before yours. • Friends who do all of the talking, especially about themselves, rather than investing their time asking you about important things in your life.

EXCELLENCE of Virtue	VIRTUE	LACK of Virtue
• Friends who strive to be an e.p.i.c friend.		• Friends who act in a way that appears to show a lack of respect for you and your friendship.
• Friends who protect the integrity of your friendship. • Friends who are respectful and reliable. • Friends who work to keep in contact with you during busy times in life or when physical distance can be a barrier.	PRUDENCE	• Friends who overly rely on you or are codependent on you. • Friendships that are one-sided to the other person's benefit. • Friends who may have offended you or hurt you and brush off their behavior, avoiding any conversation to remedy the situation.
• Friendships that last a lifetime. • Friends who share their qualities of perseverance and encourage you to work through personal challenges. • Friends who work to overcome disagreements in an effort to seek a peaceful resolution.	PERSEVER-ANCE	• Friends who frequently cancel their plans with you. • Friends who lack the initiative to remedy a misunderstanding.

EXCELLENCE of Virtue	VIRTUE	LACK of Virtue
• Friends who are there encouraging you to be courageous and brave during difficult times because they want the best for you.		• Friends who avoid helping you in times of need.
• Friends who are happy to simply be in your company. • Friends who appreciate you. • Friends who are forgiving. • Friends who in their own unique way make you feel appreciated.	GRATITUDE	• Friends who are "takers" or selfish. • Friends who take you and your relationship for granted. • Friends who hold grudges. • Friends who "use" you for some personal benefit.

THE E.P.I.C SITUATION:
AN IMPENDING HURRICANE

EXCELLENCE of Virtue	VIRTUE	LACK of Virtue
• Never stop believing that you can and will get through the impending storm. • Consider potential challenges temporary with the understanding that you can and will successfully overcome storm damage and inconveniences. • Embrace the power of unity with others (family, friends, strangers). Know you can trust and rely on one another. • Believe the proactive measures you've taken to prepare for the storm will be beneficial.	FAITH	• Catastrophic mindset that you won't survive the storm. • Failing to believe preparation will be extremely helpful for you and/or someone else. • Thinking that you won't receive assistance from neighbors, friends, even frontline workers in the event of a dire situation. • Succumbing to irrational fears that can impair your ability to prepare and/or make wise decisions during the storm to forge though any potential crisis at hand.
• Give, give, give—your time, supplies, even money to those in need.	CHARITY	• Hoarding critical supplies like food, water, shelter, even electricity while others are struggling without these items.

EXCELLENCE of Virtue	VIRTUE	LACK of Virtue
• Be more compassionate and emotionally supportive toward others. Understand how devastating loss can be (homes, lives, jobs) and search for ways to help relieve them during this time. • Actively find ways to help others, especially those who were not living independently prior to the storm. • Check in with neighbors, friends, even strangers to see if they're okay and if you can help in some way.		• Turning a blind eye to those in need. • Allowing ill will toward someone in need to interfere with your ability to help them.
• Actively share survival tips and critical supplies that can positively impact others. • Taking the initiative to spread relevant news and updates (good and bad), with others to help keep them informed leading up to, during, and after the storm. • Don't be afraid to ask for help if you are the one in need.	HONESTY	• Lying to others about any supplies that you may have which would be beneficial to them, or worse, that they may be in desperate need of. • Purposely withholding pertinent rescue information from others.

EXCELLENCE of Virtue	VIRTUE	LACK of Virtue
• Seriously heed the warnings from the experts and take necessary action for your personal safety and the safety of others. If you are told to evacuate, don't wait, evacuate. • Proactively prepare for an impending storm in advance by taking the necessary precautions like boarding up windows or securing outdoor items that could become flying debris with strong gusts of wind. • Educate yourself on the most essential items to have on hand during hurricanes—items like water, canned goods, blankets, batteries, and flashlights. • Ask others what they have done to prepare for storms. Which measures have been helpful? Which were not?	WISDOM	• Failing to actively track the storm and keep up to date on storm-related information in your community. • Being prideful, thinking you can handle whatever comes your way without sufficient preparation. • Relying on and/or expecting others to take care of you.

EXCELLENCE of Virtue	VIRTUE	LACK of Virtue
• Take action as far in advance as you can to prepare for the storm before there are shortages of supplies in your community. • Educate yourself and your family on the dangers associated with storms like live electrical wires or unstable debris and footings. • Plan escape routes or places to go for safety and shelter prior to the storm, and be sure everyone you're with understands these procedures and plans. • Prepare for plans B and C in the event of extreme situations.	PRUDENCE	• Failing to stock up on crucial items for survival by waiting until the last minute, or worse, failing to prepare all together. • Regardless of the strength of the storm, choosing not to heed to the warnings. • Taking unnecessary risks that could be dangerous like leaving a safe location to venture out to a store for supplies during the storm.
• Find new, creative ways to handle unexpected situations or solve problems at hand. For example, rerouting water flow away from your home to reduce the chance of flooding or perhaps rationing food and water.	PERSEVER-ANCE	• Allowing fear to impair your ability to make wise decisions that would promote your safety and well-being.

EXCELLENCE of Virtue	VIRTUE	LACK of Virtue
• Be brave and courageous. Work through inconveniences and challenges to help your situation or to help others in difficult situations.		• Failing to take actions that may be uncomfortable, yet necessary for survival due to fear. • Giving up and giving in to the notion that you will sort through the ramifications of the storm once it passes.
• Being grateful for the shelter and supplies you have, whatever they may be. • Being sure to thank those who have helped you, from family and friends to frontline workers and even strangers. • Take on a "pay it forward" mindset, helping others the way you have been helped.	GRATITUDE	• Being rude or unappreciative toward those who have helped you. • Falsely expecting that others should share their supplies with you or take care of you. • Being judgmental toward others and the decisions they are making in the way they choose to survive the storm. You likely don't know all of the facts.

The Worksheet

EXCELLENCE of Virtue	VIRTUE	LACK of Virtue
	FAITH	
	CHARITY	
	HONESTY	
	WISDOM	
	PRUDENCE	
	PERSEVERANCE	
	GRATITUDE	

APPENDIX B:

AN E.P.I.C. READING LIST

Bennett, William J. *The Book of Virtues*. New York: Simon and Schuster, 1993.

Brooks, David. *The Road to Character*. New York: Random House, 2015.

Canfield, Jack, and D.D. Watkins. *The Key to Living the Law of Attraction: A Simple Guide to Creating the Life of Your Dreams*. Florida: Health Communications, 2007.

Chapman, Gary. *The 5 Love Languages*. Chicago, IL: Northfield Publishing, 1992.

Cloud, Henry. *Integrity: The Courage to Meet the Demands of Reality*. New York: HarperCollins, 2006.

Duckworth, Angela. *Grit: The Power of Passion and Perseverance*. New York: Scribner, 2016.

Dweck, Carol S. *Mindset: The New Psychology of Success*. New York: Penguin Random House, 2006.

Emmons, Robert A. *Thanks! How Practicing Gratitude Can Make You Happier*. New York: Houghton Mifflin Harcourt, 2007.

Fuecht, Sean, Andy Byrd, Che' Ahn, Heidi Baker, Stacey Campbell, Darlene Cunningham, Dick Eastman, et al. *Integrity: Character of the Kingdom*. Pennsylvania: Whitaker House, 2016.

Gawain, Shakti. *Creative Visualization: Use the Power of Your Imagination to Create What You Want in Your Life*. California: Nataraj Publishing, 2002.

Gunaratana, Bhante. *Mindfulness in Plain English*. Massachussets: Wisdom Publications, 2015.

Huntsman, Jon M. *Winners Never Cheat Even in Difficult Times*. New Jersey: Wharton Publishing, 2009.

Isaacs, David. *A Guide for Parents and Teachers: Character Building*: Oregon: Four Courts Press, 2006.

Kehoe, John. *Mind Power into the 21st Century*. Canada: Zoetic, Inc, 1996.

Kilpatrick, William, Gregory Wolfe, and Suzanne M. Wolfe. *Books That Build Character*. New York: Simon and Schuster, 1994.

Kreeft, Peter. *Back to Virtue*. San Francisco: Ignatius Press, 1992.

Lazarus, Arnold, PhD. *In the Mind's Eye: The Power of Imagery for Personal Enrichment*. The Guilford Press, 1984.

Maxwell, John C. *Ethics 101: What Every Leader Needs to Know*. New York: Time Warner Book Group, 2003.

Murphy, Joseph. *The Power of Your Subconscious Mind*. New Jersey: Prentice Hall, 1963.

Nakken, Craig. *Finding your Moral Compass: Transforming Principles to Guide You in Recovery and Life*. Minnesota: Hazelden, 2011.

Niemiec, Ryan M. and Robert E. McGrath. *The Power of Character Strengths: Appreciate and Ignite Your Positive Personality*. USA: VIA Institute on Character, 2019.

Nolte, Dorothy Law and Rachel Harris. *Children Learn What They Live*. New York, Workman Publishing, 1998.

Peale, Norman Vincent. *The Power of Positive Thinking.* New York: Random House, Prentice-Hall, 1956.

Polly, Shannon and Kathryn Britton. *Character Strengths Matter: How to Live a Full Life.* Positive Psychology News, 2015.

Traeger, Randy. *Building Character One Virtue at a Time.* Oregon: Deep River Books, 2014.

Wade, Joel F. *The Virtue of Happiness.* Utah: Vervante, 2017.

White, Jerry. *Honesty, Morality, & Conscience: Making Wise Choices in the Gray Areas of Life.* Colorado: NavPress, 1979.

Williams, Pat and Jim Denney. *Humility: The Secret Ingredient of Success.* Ohio: Shiloh Run Press, 2016.

APPENDIX C:
SCIENTIFIC RESEARCH

GRATITUDE

Kleiman, Evan M., Leah M. Adams, Todd Barrett Kashdan, and John Riskind. "Grateful individuals are not suicidal: Buffering risks associated with hopeless and depressive symptoms." *Personality and Individual Differences* 55, no. 5 (September 2013): 595–599. https://doi.org/10.1016/j.paid.2013.05.002.

King, Ronnel and Jesus Alfonso D. Datu. "Grateful students are motivated, engaged, and successful in school: Cross-sectional, longitudinal, and experimental evidence." *Journal of School Psychology* 70 (October 2018): 105–122. https://doi.org/10.1016/j.jsp.2018.08.001.

Ou, Amy Y., Anne S. Tsui, Angelo J. Kinicki, David A. Waldman, Zhixing Xiao, and Lynda Jiwen Song. "Humble Chief Executive Officers' Connections to Top Management Team Integration and Middle Managers' Responses." *Administrative Science Quarterly.* 59, no. 1 (March 2014): 34–72. https://doi.org/10.1177/0001839213520131.

Renshaw, Tyler L. and Dana K. Rock. "Effects of a brief grateful thinking intervention on college students' mental health." *Mental Health & Prevention* 9 (March 2018): 19–24. https://doi.org/10.1016/j.mph.2017.11.003.

BELIEF/HOPE/FAITH

Cecilia C. Schiavon, Eduarda Marchetti, Léia G. Gurgel, Fernanda M. Busnello, and Caroline T. Reppold. "Optimism and Hope in Chronic Disease: A Systematic Review." *Frontiers in Psychology* 7, no. 2022 (January 2017): 1–10. https://doi.org/10.3389/fpsyg.2016.02022.

Long, Katelyn N.G., Eric S. Kim, Ying Chen, Matthew F. Wilson, Everett L. Worthington Jr., and Tyler J. VanderWeele. "The role of Hope in subsequent health and well-being for older adults: An outcome-wide longitudinal approach." *Global Epidemiology* 2 (November 2020): https://doi.org/10.1016/j.gloepi.2020.100018.

Mueller, Paul S. MD, David J. Plevak, MD, and Teresa A. Rummans, MD. "Religious Involvement, Spirituality, and Medicine: Implications for Clinical Practice." *Mayo Clinic Proceedings* 76, no.12 (December 2001): 1225–1235. https://doi.org/10.4065/76.12.1225.

Sharma, Vanshdeep, Deborah B. Marin, Harold K. Koenig, Adriana Feder, Brian M. Iacoviello, Steven M. Southwick, and Robert H. Pietrzak. "Religion, spirituality, and mental health of U.S. military veterans: Results from the National Health and Resilience in Veterans Study." *Journal of Affective Disorders* 217 (April 2017): 197–204. https://doi.org/10.1016/j.jad.2017.03.071.

Van Tongeren, Daryl R., Jamie D. Aten, Stacey McElroy, Don E. Davis, Laura Shannonhouse, Edward B. Davis, and Joshua

N. Hook. "Development and validation of a measure of spiritual fortitude." *Psychological Trauma: Theory, Research, Practice and Policy* 11, no. 6 (2019): 588–596. https://doi.org/10.1037/tra0000449.

Wang, Song, Xin Xu, Ming Zhou, Taolin Chen, Xun Yang, Guangxiang Chen and Qiyong Gong. "Hope and the brain: Trait hope mediates the protective role of medial orbitofrontal cortex spontaneous activity against anxiety." *NeuroImage* 157, no. 15 (August 2017): 439–447. http://doi.org/10.1016/j.neuroimage.2017.05.056.

HONESTY

Kelly, Anita E. and Lijuan Wang, PhD. "Lying Less Linked to Better Health, New Research Finds." *American Psychological Association* (2012), https://www.apa.org/news/press/releases/2012/08/lying-less.

CHARITY

Akin, Lara B., Christopher P. Barrington-Leigh, Elizabeth W. Dunn, John F. Helliwell, Justine Burns, Robert Biswas-Diener, Imelda Kemeza et al. "Prosocial spending and well-being: Cross-cultural evidence for a psychological universal." *Journal of Personality and Social Psychology* 104, no. 4 (April 2013): 635–652. https://doi.org/10.1037/a0031578.

Hofman, Stefan G., Paul Grossman, and Devon E. Hinton. "Loving-kindness and compassion meditation: Potential for psychological interventions." *Clinical Psychology Review* 31, no. 7 (November 2011): 1126–1132. https://doi.org/10.1016/j.cpr.2011.07.003.

Nelson, S. Katherine, Kristin Layous, Steven W. Cole and Sonja Lyubomirsky. "Do unto others or treat yourself? The effects of prosocial and self-focused behavior on psychological flourishing." *Emotion* 16, no. 6 (2016): 850–861. https://doi.org/10.1037/emo0000178.

WISDOM

Ardelt, Monika and Dilip V Jeste. "Wisdom and Hard Times: The Ameliorating Effect of Wisdom on the Negative Association Between Adverse Life Events and Well-Being." *The Journals of Gerontology: Series B* 73, no. 8 (October 2016): 1374–1383. https://doi.org/10.1093/geronb/gbw137.

Etezadi, Sarah and Dolores Pushkar. "Why are Wise People Happier? An Explanatory Model of Wisdom and Emotional Well-Being in Older Adults." *Journal of Happiness Studies* 14, no. 3 (June 2013): 929–950. https://doi.org/10.1007/s10902-012-9362-2.

Grossmann, Igor, Jinkyung Na, Michael E. W. Varnum, Shinobu Kitayama, and Richard E. Nisbett. "A route to well-being: Intelligence versus wise reasoning." *Journal of Experimental Psychology: General* 142, no. 3 (August 2013): 944–953. https://doi.org/10.1037/a0029560.

VISUALIZATION

Beizaee, Yaser, Nahid Rejeh, Majideh Heravi-Karimooi, Seyed Davood Tadrisi, Pauline Griffiths, and Mojtaba Vaismoradi. "The effect of guided imagery on anxiety, depression and vital signs in patients on hemodialysis." *Complementary Therapies in Clinical Practice* 33 (November 2018): 184–190. https://doi.org/10.1016/j.ctcp.2018.10.008.

Renner, Fritz, Fionnuala C. Murphy, Julie L. Ji, Tom Manly, and Emily A. Holmes. "Mental imagery as a 'motivational amplifier' to promote activities." *Behaviour Research and Therapy* 114 (March 2019): 51–59. https://doi.org/10.1016/j.brat.2019.02.002.

MINDSET

Ng, Betsy. "The Neuroscience of Growth Mindset and Intrinsic Motivation." *Brain Sciences* 8, no. 2 (January 2018): 20. https: //doi.org/10.3390/brainsci8020020.

Schleider, Jessica and John Weisz. "A single-session growth mindset intervention for adolescent anxiety and depression: 9-month outcomes of a randomized trial." *Journal of Child Psychology and Psychiatry* 59 (September 2017): 160–170. https://doi.org/10.1111/jcpp.12811.

FORGIVENESS

Bono, Giacomo, Michael E. McCullough, and Lindsey M. Root. "Forgiveness, Feeling Connected to Others, and Well-Being: Two Longitudinal Studies." *Personality and Social Psychology Bulletin* 34, no. 2 (February 2008): 182–195. https://doi .org/10.1177/0146167207310025.

Harris, Alex H.S., Frederic Luskin, Sonya B. Norman, Sam Standard, Jennifer Bruning, Stephanie Evans, and Carl E. Thoresen. "Effects of a group forgiveness intervention on forgiveness, perceived stress, and trait-anger." *Journal of Clinical Psychology* 62, no. 6 (March 2006): 715–733. https://doi .org/10.1002/jclp.20264.

Reed, Gayle L. and Robert D. Enright. "The effects of forgiveness therapy on depression, anxiety, and posttraumatic stress for women after spousal emotional abuse." *Journal of Consulting and Clinical Psychology* 74, no. 5 (2006): 920–929. https://doi.org/10.1037/0022-006X.74.5.920.

Waltman, Martina A., Douglas C. Russell, Catherine T. Coyle, Robert D. Enright, Anthony C. Holter, and Christopher M. Swoboda. "The effects of forgiveness intervention on patients with coronary artery disease." *Psychology &*

Health 24, no. 1 (February 2009): 11–27. https://doi.org/10.1080/08870440801975127.

EMOTIONAL CONTAGION

Fowler, James H. and Nicholas A. Christakis. "Dynamic spread of happiness in a large social network: longitudinal analysis over 20 years in the Framingham Heart Study." *The BMJ* 337 (December 2008): 23–27. https://doi.org/10.1136/bjm.a2338.

Totterdell, Peter. "Catching moods and hitting runs: Mood linkage and subjective performance in professional sport teams." *Journal of Applied Psychology* 85, no. 6 (2000): 848–859. https://doi.org/10.1037/0021-9010.85.6.848.

Kramer, Adam D. I., Jamie E. Guillory, and Jeffrey T. Hancock. "Experimental evidence of massive-scale emotional contagion through social networks." *Proceedings of the National Academy of Sciences of the United States of America* 111, no. 24 (June 2014): 8788–8790. https://doi.org/10.1073/pnas.13200400111.